Irene Young

Ann Jones is the author of seven books, including *Women Who Kill, Next Time She'll Be Dead,* and *Looking for Lovedu.* An authority on women and violence, her work has appeared in numerous publications, including *The New York Times* and *The Nation.*

ALSO BY ANN JONES

Uncle Tom's Campus

Everyday Death: The Case of Bernadette Powell

When Love Goes Wrong: What to Do When You Can't Do Anything Right (with Susan Schechter)

Next Time She'll Be Dead: Battering and How to Stop It

Looking for Lovedu: A Woman's Journey Through Africa

Women Who Kill

KABUL IN WINTER

KABUL IN WINTER

Life Without Peace in Afghanistan

ANN JONES

Picador

A Metropolitan Book
Henry Holt and Company
New York

www.picadorusa.com

Picador® is a U.S. registered trademark and is used by
Henry Holt and Company under license from Pan Books Limited.

For information on Picador Reading Group Guides, as well as ordering, please contact Picador.
Phone: 646-307-5629
Fax: 212-253-9627
E-mail: readinggroupguides@picadorusa.com

Designed by Kelly S. Too

Library of Congress Cataloging-in-Publication Data

Jones, Ann, date.
    Kabul in winter : life without peace in Afghanistan / Ann Jones.
        p.   cm.
    Includes index.
    ISBN-13: 978-0-312-42659-0
    ISBN-10: 0-312-42659-3
    1. Kåbol (Afghanistan)—Description and travel. 2. Afghanistan—
Description and travel. 3. Afghanistan—Social life and customs.
4. Afghanistan—History. I. Title.

DS375.K2J66 2006
958.104—dc22

                                                        2005052070

First published in the United States by Henry Holt and Company

10 9 8 7 6 5 4

For my friend Joan Silber

Agricola was aware of the temper of the provincials, and took to heart the lesson which the experience of others suggested, that little was accomplished by force if injustice followed.

He decided therefore to eliminate the causes for war.

He began with himself and his own people: he put in order his own house.

—TACITUS

CONTENTS

PART I

IN THE STREETS

I went to Afghanistan after the bombing stopped. Somehow I felt obliged to try to help pick up the pieces. I was a New Yorker who had always lived downtown, and for a long time after the towers fell I experienced moments when I couldn't get my bearings. I'd turn a corner and draw a blank. I'd have to stop to look around and think for a minute—which way is home?—as if all these years I'd relied on some subliminal sense of the mass of the towers behind me, or perhaps a shadow over my shoulder, so that I knew which way was which. I'd seen George W. Bush come to town to strut and bluster among the ruins, and as I watched him lug the stunned country into violence, my sorrow turned to anger and a bone-deep disappointment that hasn't left me yet. Surely America was capable of some act more creative than bombing a small, defenseless, pre-destroyed country on the other side of the world, or so I believed. Four thousand collateral civilian deaths in Kabul brought no consolation for the death of thousands, from around the world, in the fallen towers of the city that had so long been my home.[1] I thought America had lost its bearing too. So I left.

I came to Kabul by air, as most international travelers do,

because roadways in Afghanistan discourage overland travel. That was in December 2002, just about a year after the United States gave up on bombing the countryside to flush al-Qaeda out of the mountains where they'd holed up. In retrospect, high altitude heavy bombing was clearly not the best way to attack specific small bearded men on the ground—a practice Colin Powell called "bomb and hope"—but it shattered the country and made a mess of the roads.[2] They were already a shambles after twenty-three years of war—the Afghans fighting the Soviets, and then fighting each other. The Americans complained that by the time they got there, a month after September 11, 2001, in search of Osama bin Laden, there were no good targets left to bomb, but they bombed anyway. A year after they stopped, some of the main roads were still impassable while others were shell-pocked and worn down to the bare rocks of the roadbed. Rusting carcasses of Soviet tanks and upended armored personnel carriers lay along the track like fallen dinosaurs. Bridges had been blown up, and some of them had been replaced by makeshift structures that spread across the water like rafts. There were land mines everywhere, more per square mile than any place else on earth. Truck drivers stepped from the road to piss and lifted off in clouds of dust. So the way to travel was by plane.

In 2002, Ariana Afghan Airlines was the only international commercial carrier that could deliver me to Kabul, but it conducted business with a kind of blithe spontaneity unknown to airlines that sell you tickets in advance for scheduled flights. Unless you had influential friends or money for "gifts," you caught an Ariana flight by showing up in Dubai or Islamabad and asking around. They were doing the best they could, I supposed, considering that only months before American bombsights had locked on the Ariana fleet parked at Kabul Airport. I flew into Dubai in the middle of the night and snooped around the terminal, looking for an Ariana counter or an office. Nothing. A cleaner in the women's toilets,

a small, dark woman from Sri Lanka named Gloria, led me to a
café table in the lobby of terminal 2 and sat down to chat about
the good working conditions in Dubai. The rich rulers of the Emi-
rates, she said, respect the working class and take care of them.
She'd been working in the women's toilet for nine years. (It was
very clean.) The work was not too hard. The salary was good and
she got fifteen sick days yearly besides her paid vacation. She'd
earned enough to buy a house near the beach, and she invited me
to stay with her if the flight didn't materialize. I was on the verge
of changing my plans when she pointed to a young man hurrying
toward the café, lugging a big black briefcase. He was dressed in
black trousers and white shirt like any waiter in the West. "That's
him," Gloria said. "That's the ticket man."

He opened the briefcase at a nearby table and began to write
out tickets by hand. Business was cash only, as if even then with a
plane on the runway and tickets passing into passengers' pockets,
the company might still have to skip town. "Kabul," I said and put
down $185. "Kabul," the man said, writing out the ticket. When
he finished with me and a crowd of men wearing *perahan-o
tomban*—the long tunic and baggy pants of the Afghan man's
national outfit—he shoved the money into his briefcase and hurried away. For another couple of hours we waited, joined by
other passengers sufficiently well-connected to warrant tickets in
advance. Then someone at a gate called out "Kabul," and we
rushed forward in a mighty wedge, afraid of being left behind.
The men shouldered the women aside and jostled one another
through the door. I followed with two or three other Western
women, and we found ourselves on a bus where the men already
occupied all the seats. When the bus reached the airplane, the
men jumped up, plowed through the women, and charged up the
gangway. "It's the culture," said a young British woman who'd been
standing next to me, reading the look on my face. "Men first." She
was returning from leave to her job with a United Nations aid

program in Afghanistan. "Wait 'til you see the Afghan airports," she said. "They shut the women in a little room and don't let us out until the men are nicely comfortable on the plane."

The plane was old—a gift from India—bare bones and not crowded. There were no movie screens, no glossy magazines, no duty-free sales. The flight attendants were men, except for one young woman who carried a tin teapot up and down the aisle. She clutched a pale pink scarf over her face and politely averted her eyes as she addressed the passengers: "Tea?" The plane climbed out of Dubai and crossed the Gulf. Then we were over Iran where dark mountains rose in clumps like fortresses. The pilot announced that we had passed into Afghan air space. The passengers applauded. The wave-washed desert below was dark and dun-colored and forbidding, with no sign of village or road. Desolate. Then a river appeared, and fields and enclosures—signs of life after all—as the terrain began to gather itself in ridges rising toward a horizon white with snow and ice. The Hindu Kush. Then we were flying over mountains—treeless, featureless mountains—not the discrete picturesque peaks of Swiss postcards but a random snarl of jagged rocks, as if a great swath of the earth's surface had been thrust up from beneath. Men in caves perhaps, striking back. At last the plane topped the mountains and swung into a broad deep bowl that opened out before us, pale in the bright sun and thin air. Above the center of the bowl, trapped by a hedge of mountains, lay a mass of black smog, dense and opaque: a tangle of twisted strands of oily soot and smoke, like a great pot-blackened Brillo pad. Here and there it thinned to reveal aspects of the city beneath: flat roofs, dirt roads, a ruined fort. Then the plane descended into that soup and the light dimmed.

I GOT SICK RIGHT AWAY. EVERYONE DOES. IT'S NOT JUST THE ALTI-tude. It's a kind of initiation for new arrivals from more fortunate lands that enjoy such luxuries as unleaded gasoline and pollution control. The airport stinks of petrochemicals. Outside the odor is the same, and on the drive into town, my nose closes, stuffed with dust. Breathing becomes an effort and then a struggle. Within days my chest feels bruised and aching from the job of staying alive, and my head hurts through and through. I envy the Afghans their impressive and practical high-bridged noses, the natural air filters of people in arid lands everywhere. It's depressing to realize that people like me, with small pitiful noses unsuited to life in this high, dry, dusty air, have been winnowed from the local populace over the course of generations by natural selection. And now I'm being winnowed myself, suffocated not just by incidental illness but by inexorable natural forces that find me ill equipped. Under such pressure, my nose wheezes and drips. It cries out for pity and attention. Weeks later, at gatherings of "internationals"—as Western aid workers, diplomats, smugglers, and spies are known—I spot the telltale tissue clutched in the palm or thrust up the sleeve of the newly arrived. Some never get well. They always look pained, their eyes narrowed against the grit and glare, their noses dripping, their tissues close at hand. I am among the lucky ones who somehow adapt, against all odds, to the new environment; like some fishy creature that learns to live in air, I develop the ability to breathe after all in dust.

Before the Russians invaded Afghanistan in 1979, a pair of French photographers, Roland and Sabrina Michaud, roamed the country for fourteen years, documenting the land and its people. You can look back now at the pages of *Afghanistan: The Land That Was* and see a panoramic shot of Kabul, taken in March 1968 from the height of the Bala Hissar (the High Fort) and spread across two pages of the book. The caption offers this description: "The city rolls around the Kabul River. In the area south of the Pul-e Khesti (Brick Bridge) mosque, bazaars alternate with labyrinthine narrow streets interrupted by a great commercial avenue, Jada-e-Maiwand."[3] The river is there, wide and full, zigzagging across the pages. In the foreground stands a maze of

small mud-brown houses, while the broad avenue beyond this residential quarter is lined with three- and four-story buildings, the
facades painted in shades of blue and umber and cream. The air is
so clear that you can count the windows in the miniature houses,
distinguish nearly twenty cars—green, white, black—and half a
dozen buses on the streets, see the dark-clad people strolling the
riverbank, and even make out the tiny clustered villages far in the
distance beyond the outer limits of the city. You can identify some
buildings that still survive in Kabul—Pul-i Khesti Mosque, the
mausoleum of Timur Shah, Shah-do-Shamshira Mosque—but
you couldn't make the same photograph today. On a good day,
even with the best equipment, the picture would appear blurry
and smudged, shot through the soft focus lens of smog and dust.

Kabul in winter is the color of the dust, though the dust is no
color at all. It's a fine particulate lifted by winds from old stone
mountains and sifted over the city like flour. It lies in the streets and
drifts over the sidewalks where it compacts in hillocks and holes.
Rain and snowmelt make it mud. Mountain suns bake it. Cart
wheels break it down. Winds lift it and leave it on every surface—
on the mud houses and the mud walls that surround them, on the
dead grass and trees of the park, on shop windows and the broken sign of the cinema, on the brown shawls of men in the streets
and the faces of children. Dust fills the air and thickens it, hiding
from view the mountains that stand all around. Dust fills the
lungs, tightens the chest, lies in the eyes like gravel, so that you
look out on this obscure drab landscape always through something like tears.

The city stands alone in thin air, ringed by mountains. Some
small outcrops intrude upon the city itself, scattering houses on
their lower slopes; and the bed of the Kabul River, emptied by
longstanding drought, slips between them to wind through the
heart of town. The sun falls behind the Paghman range to the
west of the city and rises again from peaks known vaguely as

the Eastern mountains. (In all my time in Kabul I never came across a decent map that could tell me the proper names of things. The best maps were printed in Polish—Kabul's own Polish joke— but I don't read Polish, nor did anyone else I met.) These neighboring slopes are secondary ranges of the Hindu Kush, the massive mountain chain that extends some seven hundred miles eastward across the heart of Afghanistan, climbing all the while to culminate in the heights of the Karakorum and the Himalayas. To Kabulis, the city sheltered in a broad, shallow bowl at six thousand feet seems to be the center of everything.

In truth, it stands on the way to everything else. One road leads north, over the Hindu Kush, to the Turkistani steppes of Central Asia stretching away toward Russia. Another tracks south to Kandahar, and west across the desert to Herat and Iran. Another heads east, following the old course of the Kabul River as it plunges between the sheer rock walls of Tangi Gharu gorge and runs on toward Pakistan and the Indian subcontinent beyond. Commerce goes out along these tracks, and trouble comes in. At the eastern edge of the city, atop a rocky promontory, stand the ruins of the old Bala Hissar, demolished more than a century ago by British forces to avenge the murder of a British envoy. In return for performing such services, General Frederick Roberts became Lord Roberts of Kandahar, a hero so famous in his own country that when his bust was later placed in London's St. Paul's Cathedral it was inscribed simply "Roberts." The old stone walls that once shielded the fort still soar above the river, commanding a view of the long approach to the gorge where the waters spill into the steep descent. They recall a watchful time when Kabul had some means to protect itself, some power.

The walls date back to at least the fifth century, to the time of the Hephthalites, the White Huns, who swept southward from central Asia and swamped the once-great civilization of the Kushans. In its glory days during the second century, the Kushan empire exploited

its fabulous location midway along the Asian caravan route—
known as the Silk Road—to gain wealth and political power, doing
business with the Caesars in Rome and the Han emperors in
China. At that time the Kushans' great King Kanishka maintained
two capitals: a winter retreat to the east in Peshawar in what is
now Pakistan, and summer quarters at Kapisa just north of Kabul
near the modern military base at Bagram, built by the Soviets and
now occupied by twenty thousand Americans. French archaeolo-
gists working at Kapisa in 1939 unearthed an amazing Kushan
treasure trove amassed through trade: stacks of exquisite ivories
from India, lacquers from China, bronzes from Rome, and bas
reliefs and glass from Alexandria. After King Kanishka died, power
struggles brought civil war, while developments in Rome and China
disrupted trade; and soon the declining Kushans fell under the
authority of the Sasanian Empire of Persia (now Iran) to the west.
Then came the ravaging Hephthalite horsemen who built the great
walls of Kabul's Bala Hissar, strong and thick, to ward off other
anticipated invaders. The Kushan treasures long displayed in
Kabul's National Museum were thought to have been lost or
destroyed in recent wars, but they were resurrected again after the
fall of the Taliban and the American invasion of 2001. Museum
workers had hidden them away.

I learned most of this ancient lore reading *An Historical Guide
to Afghanistan,* a locally famous guidebook published in Kabul in
1970 by the Afghan Tourist Organization and written by Nancy
Hatch Dupree. She was already known in Asia for her work with
education and rural communities when she married Louis Dupree,
the foremost anthropologist working in Afghanistan in the 1960s
and 1970s and an important chronicler of its past. With her husband she traveled to remote regions of the country and lived for
months at a time in obscure villages near archaeological digs where
prehistoric pot shards were sifted from the dust. In that way she
learned nearly everything there was to know about the past and

present of this small piece of the planet—about the size of Texas—that had come to be called Afghanistan. How she must have loved it then, an adventurous woman with a scholarly bent, dazzled by new discoveries, sitting up at night under the stars with her husband, talking. I can't keep it all straight, the dynasties— the Ghaznavids, the Ghorids, the Mongols, the Timurids, the Moghuls, the Safavids, the Durranis—rising and falling in succession, shifting the seats of power here and there across the map of Central Asia and the Middle East, expanding empires and the very map itself beyond the former edges of the world only to see it trimmed anew as power fragmented in family quarrels or crumbled under hoofs of unknown horses. In all those centuries, what we call Afghanistan was never a nation, really, but a tract of landscape, or rather scattered valleys of habitable land amid deserts and impassable mountains, like a chessboard upon which political games were played by forces from afar who wandered in to wreck the place and pass on. No one knew from which direction the next wave would come.

The guidebook follows Afghan roads once traveled by Alexander the Great and Genghis Khan and Marco Polo, the last of whom luckily was merely sightseeing. The history all reads more or less like the history of the Kushans who also actually came from someplace else—forced from their grazing lands along the Chinese border—and because they were nomads shifted the seat of government from Afghanistan to Pakistan and back with the seasons until their whole enterprise imploded in civil war. The history all reads more or less like recent events too. It is full of eerie resonance.

Like this: "Turning south, covering 75 miles in two days, he quickly subdued . . . rebels [in Herat] and moved on . . . along the Hilmand and from there relentlessly pushed on into . . . Kandahar and Ghazni, on to . . . Kabul-Charikar, up the Panjsher Valley and over the Khawak Pass to . . . Kunduz. The two chief cities . . .

Tashkurghan and . . . Balkh, surrendered without resistance."[4] This blistering campaign might have been waged only recently by the brilliant mujahidin commander Ahmad Shah Massoud, or by the conquering Taliban, but in fact it was led by Alexander the Great of Macedon in the spring of 329 B.C. The description of another later dynasty—that they "stood for law and order, orthodoxy in Islam, and a return to cultural traditions"—might also refer to the Taliban, but in fact it concerns the Samanids who ruled in northern Afghanistan in the city of Balkh at the turn of the tenth century.[5]

After the Soviets invaded Afghanistan in 1979, there were no more guidebooks. So when the international humanitarian community in Kabul expanded after the fall of the Taliban, a local bookseller bought up the stock of Nancy Hatch Dupree's book and put it back on sale. It was still indispensable, though it had become a ghostly book. So many of the sites described had been destroyed. In the summer of 2002, two humanitarian aid workers assembled a sixteen-page pamphlet of information essential for internationals, labeled it *A Survival Guide to Kabul,* and gave it to the boys who sell newspapers in the streets for distribution. (The boys got to keep the money from sales.) By 2003, that pamphlet had expanded, acquired a glossy cover, and become *Kabul: The Bradt Mini Guide.* A new section on sightseeing began: "There's a lot to see in the city, even if most of it is wrecked."[6] But still you need Dupree. You wander through the ruins of Kabul, with your old musty-smelling copy of her book in hand, examining the black and white photo-illustrations of what things used to look like in the old days, when there was peace.

AFTER THE BOMBING, NEWLY PROSPEROUS ENTREPRENEURS, truckers, traders, smugglers, opium dealers, traffickers, and other suddenly flush locals and returned expatriates began to build again amid the ruins of Kabul, so that by 2003 the great expanse of wreckage was randomly punctuated by tall new houses adorned with curves, columns, and spiraling staircases and finished in garish tiles of purple, green, and orange, like exotic castles in some tropical theme park. The style is known locally as "Pakistani Palace" though it's said to have originated in the Gulf States among drug dealers with a need to launder profits and a taste for domestic pretension. In Kabul, the palaces draw attention to themselves, shouting of money, and overshadow the mud-colored rubble so familiar to Kabulis by now as to be scarcely noticeable. You can drive through the wreckage, as foreign journalists used to do so often before Iraq eclipsed Afghanistan in the news, and hardly register that your mind is growing numb. They're still there—the blasted buildings that appeared in newspaper photos and on TV as graphic backdrop for flak-jacketed reporters who couldn't find words to describe what they saw in that ruined city that seemed to them as lonely as the moon. *Surreal* was a word they used a lot. They compared the devastation of Kabul to that of Dresden after the fire bombings of World War II. They had not personally witnessed the destruction of Dresden, of course, but it must have made them feel vaguely better to be able to locate the catastrophic damage in this way, as something familiar, something quite natural in human history, something that just happens in war.

As ruins go, most of those in Kabul aren't particularly dramatic—not like the snarl of twisted steel and concrete slabs that once was New York's World Trade Center. Kabul wasn't built of steel and concrete, but mostly of mud bricks. So the city's ruins are bare-boned skeletons, like the building that housed the Department of Traffic: floors and roof collapsed inward and stacked like pancakes aslant thin brick pillars that lean into air. Or fragmentary facades of business establishments, block after block of storefronts that open into nothing. At what was the finest cinema the circular iron staircase still winds upward, visible through shell-shattered walls. At an old teacher training institute, the roof spills over the entrance. At the monumental mausoleum of King Nadir Shah, high on a hill overlooking the city, the sun shines through holes in the dome that still balances atop shell-pocked columns. The broken marble sarcophagi of the king's family lie scattered in the grass below. You notice these details, but then they begin to blur as the wreckage goes on, block after block. The rubble of tumbled neighborhoods still has not been cleared away, except in patches as someone finds money and a reason to do it. You drive the city streets, perhaps sightseeing as a morbid postconflict tourist, or just trying to get to a meeting, and you see the smash-up stretching on forever—whole districts leveled as if struck by some great quake that cracked the Richter scale.

I LIVED IN A CENTRAL DISTRICT OF KABUL CALLED SHARE NAU, the "new city." The area was shabby and dust-covered and not at all like the classy upper crust neighborhood it once had been, but for the most part it was still intact. My tiny room was located above the office of Madar ("Mother"), an organization founded years before by an American woman named Caroline to help the widows of Kabul. I'd come across it on the Internet and offered myself as a volunteer. Caroline had lived in the country off and on for almost forty years, so I figured that she would know better than most would-be helpers what to do. She'd started her life in Kabul in the sixties—the almost mythical good old days—as an American wife, part of a lively circle of expats scattered about town, living in comfort with Afghan servants, riding horses for fun, and doing exactly as she pleased. Her children had long since grown up and gone back to America. Her husband too. But Caroline had come to be at home in this place where she could live easily in the moral limbo reserved for Western women and where she could still, even in her seventies, do exactly as she pleased and do some good besides. She had become a sort of Afghan: warm, generous, willful, intransigent, combative, and utterly without fear. But she was a kind of Afghan widow herself, living on her own, which may help to explain why she wanted so much to help the widows of Kabul, of whom there were—by the time the mujahidin's factional battles for the city ground down late in 1994—some forty thousand at least. (Four years later, in the heyday of the Taliban, the ICRC numbered the legions of Afghan widows throughout the country at ninety-eight thousand.)[7]

Normally, an Afghan widow and her children would be taken in by relatives, her husband's or her own, but war had decimated families and scattered them. In 1996, when the Taliban captured Kabul, the widows' difficult situation became desperate. The Taliban ruled that no woman should leave her house unless she was escorted by a male relative, but thousands of war widows had no male relatives left. Husbands, fathers, brothers, sons—all gone. Imprisoned in their homes, the widows would starve. (This is the crisis depicted in *Osama,* the award-winning movie by Afghan filmmaker Siddiq Barmak; a widow who lives with her mother, also a widow, dresses her young daughter as a boy—Osama—and sends her/him out to support the household.) Caroline had responded to the situation with programs to teach widows to sew and embroider and weave at home, and she sold the things they made so they could feed themselves. She started secret schools too—many of them—for girls the Taliban refused to educate. The Taliban found out what she was doing. They raided her office and arrested her staff. Never having seen computers before, they beat the staff women for watching "television" and hauled them off to jail; and when Caroline insisted on going to jail with them, the Taliban expelled her from the country. She moved across the border to Peshawar and kept on working until the Taliban fled from Kabul. Then Caroline returned to find the widows still there—still destitute, still hungry, still in need of help. She rented a new office and carried on.

I'd been in Kabul only a few days when Lema, Madar's Afghan office manager, asked me to go along to help hand out old clothes to the poor. I wasn't prepared for the long drive through the rubble or the hovels where we called, but we had a job to do, Lema said. Some American churchgoers had been moved to send aid to Afghans. They'd sent a raft of old clothes to an American army chaplain with instructions to distribute them to the "deserving poor" of Kabul, and he in turn had brought them to Madar and asked us to give them away. (They'd sent electric blankets too, though Kabul had no electricity.) Apparently the chaplain didn't have time to do the job himself, or he didn't know where to find the deserving poor, but the women of Madar knew.

We drove into Karte Se, District Three, where wreckage lay all about us. I felt as if I too had been smashed. But then, as I began to breathe again, I noticed signs of life in the fallen houses: a bit of laundry drying in a window, a kettle on a cook fire in the street, a ragged carpet hung across a blasted doorway. People were living in the ruins—as many do to this day—in houses somehow untouched, or in rooms patched together in buildings only partially destroyed. The businesses were gone, and the stores, so it was hard to see how people managed to live, but these were their shelters.

The car stopped on a dirt road well away from the main street, and Lema and Nasrin, Madar's staff manager, hoisted two bundles of clothes and led the way along narrow paths between broken mud walls to a wooden gate that opened onto a courtyard. Nothing grew in the hard packed earth; a few thin hens pecked the dust around an old cistern. At the end of the yard stood a tall mud-brick house, its broad window holes covered with plastic, its door with a blanket that was thrown aside by a tiny shawl-wrapped woman who hurried to us with outstretched hands. We followed her under the blanket into a foyer piled with fallen bricks and climbed a flight of stairs to a part of the second floor that was still intact. On the landing a small cooking pot simmered over a charcoal burner, tended by a daughter-in-law whose tiny baby lay

swaddled beside the fire like a trussed chicken. At the top of the
stairs, another daughter-in-law gestured to a curtained doorway.
We slipped off our shoes to enter a long bare room. There five or
six children were huddled on the floor under the edges of a quilt
that had been draped over a low table to enclose the space beneath
it. Later, when the cooking was done and the food served, a brazier
of hot coals would be slipped under the covered table to warm the
family as they ate. This arrangement—the *sandeli*—is as close as
most Afghans come to central heating, and even before the coals
are brought, the imagined warmth is a comfort. Still the children
crept out to watch with wide eyes as Lema and Nasrin sorted three
piles of clothes and baby things on the floor, one pile for each
woman.

I hung back, feeling the cold rising from the bare mud floor
through my socks. The plastic at the window flapped in the wind.
Lema gestured toward my digital camera, which she had asked
me to bring along, and signaled that it was time to take pictures.
She directed the mother and her daughters-in-law to squat on the
floor, each one with her pile of old clothes. The three women did
as they were told, stone-faced. They drew the corner of their
headscarves over their faces and raised their eyes to the camera
with the blank look of those who have already endured every
indignity. I turned to Lema. *Humiliating* was the word I wanted,
but it seemed beyond her English vocabulary.

"Do you think they feel bad?" I asked.

"Yes," she said. "Make photos."

"But why?"

"We show we give these things. We show we not steal them.
Very important. Donors want see. Make photos, please."

I too did as I was told, though I tried to lighten the moment. I
coaxed the children into the pictures and passed the camera
around so the women could see the images of their offspring on
the tiny screen. (Where were the men? I wondered, afraid to ask.

So many had vanished.) I asked the women and children to pose for one last photo in the yard, a photo of all the family with Lema and Nasrin too. Lema told them to smile, and they did.

WE DROVE ON THROUGH THE WRECKED DISTRICT, CLIMBING THE slope at the base of a mountain, and looked out over rubble that stretched as far as we could see. "Gulbuddin," Nasrin said by way of explanation. She meant Gulbuddin Hekmatyar, leader of Hizb-i Islami, the party of extreme Islamists that received the lion's share of secret American, Saudi Arabian, and Pakistani aid to the Afghan resistance—the mujahidin—during the Soviet occupation. Gulbuddin and his radical party—like most modern Islamists—traced the origins of their ideology to the Society of Muslim Brothers, a political movement founded in Egypt in the 1920s by a schoolteacher named Hassan al-Banna to protest British imperial rule in his country. The Brotherhood worked peaceably to advance social welfare and justice and the cause of Islam. The British responded with the standard techniques of oppression, alternately trying to court or to crush the organization; and after Gamal Abdel Nasser came to power in the 1950s, he applied even more rigorously the same tactics of cooption and repression. Nasser also turned to the Soviets for aid and arms, prompting the US to send covert assistance to the Muslim Brothers, thereby initiating a Cold War flirtation with radical Islam that would last until 9/11.[8]

The Brotherhood predictably grew stronger and some of its members more extreme. One of them was Sayyid Qutb, a novelist and critic and longtime civil servant in the Ministry of Education who began as a political moderate and devotee of English literature and became the leading theoretician of radical Islam— "the founder of Sunni fundamentalism."[9] Like Mohammed Atta and his 9/11 collaborators, Sayyid Qutb also lived in America for a time. Sent by the Ministry of Education to study at Colorado

State Teachers College (now the University of Northern Colorado) in Greeley in 1948, he earned a master's degree in education, turned down a chance to study for a doctorate, and returned to Egypt in 1951. He had found what we proudly call "the American way of life" revolting—driven by materialism, warped by racism, obsessed with sex, and partial beyond reason to Israel.[10] Our vaunted democracy seemed to him merely an attempt by men to usurp the role of God, who alone has the right to rule. Thoroughly repelled, Qutb turned fully to Islam as a complete ideology, "a total civilization," to be defended by all means, including violence, from enemies within and without: that is, from Egypt's unjust (un-Islamic) military dictators, and infidel Americans like us.[11]

Imprisoned for his political views, he wrote the letters collected as the Islamist manifesto, *Signposts along the Road*—also translated as *Milestones*. The full weight of the repressive secular state pressing upon Qutb and his Muslim Brothers in prison had the effect of forging his thought and firing it beyond his earlier writings on social justice, beyond the nonviolent reformist stance of the Brotherhood, beyond even the influential teachings of the Islamic revivalist Abul A'la Mawdudi, his Pakistani contemporary, who was the first to call for a universal jihad—that is, a revolutionary struggle to seize state power "for the good of all humanity."[12] Qutb agreed with the call for universal jihad, but he sought to go beyond the state to abolish secular systems and governments and find "freedom in the realization of Islam in society under the authority of God."[13] In *Signposts*, he calls upon Islamists everywhere to seize power throughout the Muslim world, and he provides the religious and moral justification for using lethal violence against nonbelievers. Just as George W. Bush claims to use armed invasion and regime change to "spread democracy," Qutb argues that Islam is obliged to liberate people through armed jihad, delivering human freedom by force.[14]

Qutb was executed in Egypt in 1966, but his manifesto had a life of its own. By then Islam was struggling against both communism and capitalism, and King Faisal of Saudi Arabia was worried enough in 1971 to pledge one hundred million dollars to al-Azhar University in Cairo, the oldest Islamic university in the world, to promote Islamic education. *Signposts* must have circulated among the students there. It soon reached Kabul University when young Burhanuddin Rabbani—future president of Afghanistan—returned from al-Azhar as a professor of Sharia law and translated it into Dari, a variant of Farsi (Persian) that is one of the two principal languages of Afghanistan. Gulbuddin Hekmatyar read *Signposts* in Dari at Kabul University. Osama bin Laden studied it in Arabic in classes at Jedda, where Sayyid Qutb's brother Mohammed was one of his teachers. Mohammed Atta must have read it too.

As a student in the American-sponsored Faculty of Engineering at Kabul University in the early 1970s, Gulbuddin Hekmatyar distinguished himself as an extreme ideologue, given to enforcing his faith through violence. An American professor who taught him in those days, or tried to, remembers that Gulbuddin assaulted women students who appeared on campus in Western dress. Some report that he threw acid at their unveiled faces and at the legs of those who wore short skirts. The professor remembers that he more often beat them up. "He's a psychopath," the professor says. "He should have been locked up then."[15] In fact, he was locked up, though only briefly, early in 1973 when he was charged with murdering a Maoist student; and that's why he had to miss the gathering of professors and students who met at the home of Professor Rabbani to form a *shura*—a leadership council—for the growing Islamist movement. Rabbani and his associates were Islamic intellectuals, and though most of them were provincials—not sophisticated Kabulis—they were not regressive fundamentalists like the men of the next generation who would form the Taliban. They were well acquainted with the systems of Western thought that had given rise to the West's advanced technical development—a level of modernization they, like Sayyid

Qutb, both admired and coveted for the Islamic world. They wanted to fashion upon the basis of Islam a thoroughly modern political ethos—a new Islamist ideology capable of both participating in the modern world and countering Western imperialism. When these men met at Professor Rabbani's house to formalize their organization, later named Jamiat-i Islami (Islamic Society), this was the forward-looking project the group had in mind.[16] But they put the murderous Gulbuddin in charge of political activities.[17]

The Islamists were not the only ones making plans. On July 17, 1973, while King Zahir Shah was out of the country, his cousin and former Prime Minister Mohammed Daoud Khan, with help from Kabul's young communist parties, proclaimed a new Republic of Afghanistan and named himself head of state. Soon he began to arrest those who seemed to threaten his power, from both the left and the right. In 1974, when he arrested Ghulam Muhammad Niyazi, dean of the Sharia faculty and leading proponent of the Muslim Brotherhood, and two hundred of his associates, Gulbuddin Hekmatyar fled to Peshawar, along with Burhanuddin Rabbani and most other leaders of the Islamist movement. There Gulbuddin had a decided advantage, for he is a Pashtun, a member of the most numerous and troublesome ethnicity on both sides of the border.[18] (Rabbani, by contrast, is a Tajik, a member of a northern minority.) Gulbuddin appealed to pro-Islamic, pro-Pashtun contacts in the Pakistani government that soon named him official liaison for all exiled Afghan Islamic parties. And there, in 1975, he broke with Professor Rabbani's Jamiat-i Islami to start Hizb-i Islami (Islamic Party), his own far more radical faction.[19] There would be seven principal parties in Peshawar when all the lines were drawn. By the time the Soviets invaded Afghanistan in 1979 to rescue the heavy-handed communist regime that had replaced Daoud, and the United States stepped up secret aid to help the Afghans whip the Soviets, Gulbuddin and Hizb-i Islami were already the darlings of

Pakistan's Inter-Services Intelligence (ISI), the brother agency through which the CIA would funnel billions in American aid to Afghan "freedom fighters."[20]

No one suspected at the time that the Afghan resistance—the mujahidin—might actually defeat the Soviet army. The Americans seemed to know very little about Afghanistan and successive administrations had no Afghan policy to speak of, except to make things tough for the Soviets. So the CIA simply doled out money and weapons to the ISI, which skimmed a generous fee and passed on the rest to the mujahidin.[21] The ISI spread the rewards around among several factions, apparently to incite competition and discourage Afghan unity—which might have inspired Pakistan's own radical Islamists to rise up—but Gulbuddin and Hizb-i Islami always came out way ahead. He became the favorite of America as well, and of America's good chums the Saudis and Saddam Hussein.[22] He used their aid to sabotage his fellow mujahidin parties, even as they fought against the Soviets; and he undermined especially his archrival, Ahmad Shah Massoud, the military commander of Jamiat-i Islami. Another Afghan leader said of him, "Gulbuddin's problem is that he kills more mujahidin than Soviets."[23] Gulbuddin never appeared to care much for the Soviet war. He fought his biggest battle against fellow Pashtuns for control of the poppy fields in Helmand Province.[24] He apparently cared most about advancing himself, his prosperity, and his own notions of radical Islam.

After ten years of fighting the resistance, the Soviets gave up and went home, leaving a passel of mujahidin parties squabbling over plans for peace. In the absence of a common enemy to inspire at least the occasional illusion of unity, the resistance split along the fault lines of ego, Islamist ideology, and especially ethnicity. The dominant Pashtuns of the south and east (who speak their own language, Pashtu), the northern Tajiks and Uzbeks, and the Hazaras of the central highlands, Shi'a Muslims whose

Asiatic features, attributed to descent from the Mongol troops of Genghis Khan, make them the most identifiable and universally persecuted minority—these are merely the largest groups, each with its own internal rivalries arising from subtribal structure, geography, and history. The Soviets left the communist puppet President Najibullah, former head of the secret police, in charge of the government; and to shore up his presidency they handed over all their heavy weaponry to his army, and three billion dollars in annual aid as well. President Najibullah himself was changing his stripes, trying to make his governance acceptable to both the resistance parties and the international community. Professing a policy of "national reconciliation," he embraced Islam, dropped Marxism/Leninism altogether from the platform of the communist People's Democratic Party of Afghanistan, and gave the PDPA a new and appealing name: the Homeland Party. He offered Ahmad Shah Massoud the job of minister of defense.[25] The jihad against the Soviet invaders was over. Why couldn't the mujahidin lay down their arms and go home? Why couldn't his government stand—devoutly but moderately Islamic, a bulwark against crazy Islamist extremists like the psychopathic Gulbuddin? These were good questions.

The answers lay with the CIA and the ISI. They shifted their sights from the Soviets to the stooge they left behind, determined to oust President Najibullah. Pakistan wanted to replace him with a stooge of its own, Gulbuddin; and the United States, bent on carrying its covert anti-communist war to the bitter end, went along.[26] The scheme also matched Gulbuddin's ambitions, and he still had plenty of weapons left over from the jihad to turn upon Kabul. In 1990, with the connivance of ISI, he teamed up with Shahnawaz Tanai, President Najibullah's own secretary of defense, to stage a coup. The far-left communist diehard seemed an odd comrade for the far-right religious fanatic, but they shared the tribal heritage of Ghilzai Pashtuns in a country where identity counts more than

ideology. Besides, Gulbuddin was never one to sacrifice an opportunity for a principle. In preparation for the coup, he tried to buy
off President Najibullah's army, bribery often being the surest
way to victory in Afghanistan. He got money to do it from
Osama bin Laden, who was working at the time in Peshawar, in
collaboration with ISI, to overthrow two presidents, Afghanistan's Najibullah and Pakistan's own Benazir Bhutto, both designated enemies of Islam.[27] But in the event, most of Najibullah's
army stood by him and the coup failed. Furiously, Gulbuddin
turned once again upon his rivals in Jamiat-i Islami and murdered thirty of the party leaders, including some of Ahmad Shah
Massoud's top military officers. He was still casting about for
more enemies when, in 1991, the UN came up with a plan for
President Najibullah to relinquish power to an Afghan interim
government to be selected at a gathering of all the resistance parties headquartered in Peshawar. Remarkably, the leaders of the
parties agreed—though not, of course, Gulbuddin.

Then the Soviet Union dissolved, and with it went the Afghan
state. On January 1, 1992, by prior agreement, the defunct Soviet
Union and the United States ended their proxy war on Afghan territory by stopping all military aid to both the Afghan government
and the mujahidin. Soviet shipments of food and fuel to Kabul
stopped as well. Things fell apart. All that was left of Afghanistan
was, in the words of historian Barnett Rubin, "hyperarmed net-
works of power."[28] The stage was set for the internecine battles of
parties and tribes to erupt in civil war for control of the capital
and the country.

In April 1992, President Najibullah vanished into hiding while
resistance leaders in Peshawar still dickered over plans for the
Afghan interim government to which he was supposed to surren-
der power. Gulbuddin moved upon Kabul again to seize it for himself. Massoud's forces entered the city to turn him back. Massoud,
fighting in alliance with another northern army, the Junbish-i
Milli-yi Islami (National Islamic Movement) militia of the Uzbek

General Abdul Rashid Dostum, claimed Kabul for the resistance leaders of the government. Their new agreement, reached the next day, called for a council of leaders from all the parties to serve with an acting president. That post was to be filled for two months by the moderate Islamist Sibghatullah Mujaddidi, followed for four months by Professor Rabbani. After that, a shura was to be convened to choose an interim government to serve for the next eighteen months, at which point elections would be held. (Never able to work together, the Peshawar parties had settled for government by rotation.) Massoud, who had declined to claim Kabul for himself, was named secretary of defense. On April 28, 1992, members of the Islamic Jihad Council arrived from Peshawar in a caravan of battle-gray pickup trucks (provided by Saudi Arabia) to proclaim the new Islamic State of Afghanistan.[29]

But the state embodied in the person of President Najibullah had already disappeared; and the would-be Islamic state of the Peshawar Accords quickly shattered in a power struggle among the four most powerful factions, split largely along ethnic lines: Rabbani and Massoud's Tajiks of Jamiat-i Islami, Gulbuddin's Pashtuns of Hizb-i Islami, Dostum's Uzbeks of the Junbish militia, and the Shi'a Hazaras of Hizb-i Wahdat (Unity Party). They laid claim to different parts of Kabul and preyed upon the citizens, looting homes and government buildings. And all through the summer of 1992 Gulbuddin bombarded the city with rockets, still trying to claim the capital as his own. In due time, Acting President Mujaddidi handed over his impotent office to Professor Rabbani, but Rabbani in turn declined to give it up. Instead, he convened a shura of dubious authority to ratify the continuation of his government for another eighteen months.[30] So the fighting continued. It was a civil war of sorts—Gulbuddin against Rabbani and Massoud, Pashtuns against non-Pashtuns—but it was a civil war stirred by outsiders (Pakistan's ISI, the Saudis, Osama bin Laden) in the vacuum created by the abrupt departure of outsiders (the Soviets and the Americans) and subject to infinite deadly variations as commanders shifted sides and sold their services. Before the year was out, more than five thousand civilians were dead, and close to a million Kabulis had fled the city.[31]

Afghans were shocked that an Afghan would destroy an Afghan city, and the capital at that. All these years the mujahidin had tried to fight by traditional rules, keeping their firefights well away from towns and villages so that civil life might go on even in the midst of war. People went about their business and tended their farms as best they could. Even the mujahidin fighters went home to plow and plant and harvest as the seasons came around. When they had to kill an Afghan—some informer or government collaborator—they did it in the street. Even in wartime they wouldn't enter a man's house to search or to seize him, for every man's house was his own. Yet here was Gulbuddin month after month, year after year, lobbing rockets into the mud-brick houses of Kabul. Massoud's forces too ran amok in neighborhoods of the Hazara minority, raping, mutilating, and murdering without mercy. Was it something about all that foreign aid, all those years on the armaments dole, or was it incessant war that changed the rules of engagement? According to the ICRC, about 20,000 people were killed between April 1992 and December 1994 in the fighting that followed the "liberation" of Kabul from its "communist" government.[32] Other sources put the death toll at 50,000 and claim as many as 150,000 wounded.[33] Almost three-quarters of those who survived had to flee from their neighborhoods to other parts of the city or the refugee camps of Jalalabad and Peshawar. The state had disintegrated and the urban center shattered, scattering citizens like bits of shrapnel. Gulbuddin's rocket attacks from the outskirts of the city went on.

Then it was the turn of the Taliban to storm Kabul. They didn't come, as it sometimes seemed, from nowhere. They came from Kandahar, in the south, from the heart of Pashtun country. They had that historic claim to the capital and the country, for Pashtuns had held power in Afghanistan for more than 250 years; but they made their case and won converts at first on moral grounds. Some of the leaders had fought as mujahidin, and many had been wounded during the long wars. Pakistani journalist Ahmed Rashid notes that the Taliban leadership was "the most disabled in the world," and visitors facing a gathering of its one-eyed, one-legged, fingerless officials did not know "whether to laugh or to cry."[34] The Pashtuns from Kandahar had fought the Soviets and the Najibullah regime under the leadership of their traditional tribal elders, and they had never received the wealth of arms and money doled out to the ideological Islamist parties in Peshawar. After the Islamic government took charge of Kabul, they went home, and many of them who were mullahs went back to their madrassas to study and to teach; but they could not escape the anarchic in-fighting, banditry, rapacity, and corruption of heavily armed mujahidin commanders—warlords—run amok. The warlords preyed upon the caravans of powerful Pakistani truckers— the so-called transport mafia—and wrecked their plans to extend their traditional smuggling ventures in Afghanistan, via Kandahar, to Iran and Central Asia. Mujahidin leadership had failed to bring peace, and traditional leadership that might have put things right broke down—the old leaders dead or discredited or driven off or bought. So the one-eyed, one-legged mullahs discussed these matters and chose a leader of their own, the pious Mullah Mohammad Omar, a thirty-five-year-old wounded jihadi veteran of landless peasant stock who ran a tiny mud-hut madrassa in a Kandahari provincial village. Then, with divine guidance, they came up with an agenda: to "restore peace, disarm the population, enforce Sharia law and defend the integrity and Islamic character of Afghanistan."[35] They called themselves Taliban— students—for that is what most of the leaders were.

The Pakistani government of Benazir Bhutto had a different but related agenda: to open a safe trade route through Afghanistan for the transport mafia. So it was not exactly coincidental that the Taliban's amazing first victory took place at a truck stop. In

October 1994, some two hundred Kandahari Taliban took Spin Baldak on the Pakistan border from the hands of the Pakistani Frontier Corps; and they went on to seize a nearby mujahidin arms dump that held, among other treasures, eighteen thousand Kalashnikovs. The Taliban thanked Allah for this bounty, but most commentators credit Pakistan for the faked conquest—a ruse by which the ISI began to assemble behind the little band of righteous mullahs a massive modern military operation.[36] A couple of weeks later, the Taliban rescued a hijacked Pakistani truck convoy, hanged the local warlord who'd held it up, and went on to take control of Kandahar, the second largest city in the country. Tens of thousands of young Pashtun students rushed out of refugee camps and ISI training camps in Pakistan and out of Saudi-financed fundamentalist madrassas along the border to join the triumphant Taliban. These young boys were, as Ahmed Rashid describes them, the flotsam of war, thrown up on "the beach of history" with no memory of country or clan or family or village life, no occupation or skill, no education but the Quran, no past but war, no identity but in Islam, no acquaintance with women or girls, and no hope but in reclaiming their homeland for the Islamic caliphate.[37] They moved on Kabul, but in March 1995 Massoud drove them back, delivering the Taliban's first defeat. Massoud turned them back from Herat too, the city that anchored the western end of the trans-Afghanistan truck route. But in September 1995, they took it. And then they moved again on Kabul.

In Kandahar, Mullah Omar donned a robe said to have belonged to the Prophet and proclaimed himself Amir-ul Mominin, or Commander of the Faithful. Osama bin Laden gave him three million dollars to buy off mujahidin commanders who stood in his way. Then for ten months the Taliban laid siege to the capital, shelling it from the south just as Gulbuddin had done. They were holy warriors no more, restoring "peace" to lawless Kandahar, but a well-armed, well-trained juggernaut—Pakistan's proxy army in Afghanistan—bent on conquest of the country.[38] President Rabbani used the time to build alliances with other leaders, including Gulbuddin, in hopes of concluding a peace settlement. But just when it seemed he might succeed, the Taliban, backed by Saudi Arabia and Pakistan (who always lied and said they had nothing to do with it), launched an attack more massive and more swift than any ever planned by any Afghan. Gulbuddin, realizing that his old benefactors in the ISI had thrown him over for the Taliban, had struck a deal with his longtime enemy Rabbani to join the government, and with Massoud to help defend Kabul. But in the event, in September 1996, having drawn Massoud's forces south of their defensive line in the city, Gulbuddin's men stood aside as the Taliban advanced against them. Seeing the trap too late, Massoud withdrew his forces to his northern stronghold and let the dying city go.[39] The Taliban entered Kabul, took Najibullah and his brother from the UN compound where they had hidden, beat them, castrated them, dragged them behind a jeep, shot Najibullah, strangled his brother, and hanged them both from a post outside the presidential palace for citizens to see. The city had been, for a second time, liberated.

Kabulis say that in leaving the city Massoud, at long last, took pity on them. Of Gulbuddin they ask, "What kind of man shells his own people?" Standing that cold winter day with Nasrin on the hillside above the city, I wondered what kind of foreign aid makes it possible. Nasrin gestured beyond the ruined neighborhoods before us to the location of gun emplacements in the far distance. Her face looked fierce. She had a way of drawing her eyebrows down into one sharp black line when she felt pained, as she often was by memory. A Gulbuddin rocket had hit her house when she was a girl and killed her father. She had lost most of her hearing in the blast. "Gulbuddin," I said loudly, looking out, to show I'd got the message.

Everything about the Afghan civil wars—the interminable internecine battles for power, sparked, sponsored, and prolonged by foreign powers—leaves the observer perplexed by inexplicable aims and baffled by shifting alliances. So many leaders. So many parties. So many doctrinaire varieties of "true" Islam. Here in Kabul the lines are clearer. There was Ahmad Shah Massoud, a man of prayer and a reader of poetry, greatest of mujahidin commanders, leader of the Northern Alliance, "Lion of the Panjshir Valley," nemesis of the Soviets, and—unheard of among Afghans— a man who had declined proffered power. Many revered Massoud as a national hero, and after his assassination in 2001, arranged by bin Laden, as a *shahid,* a martyr. Others swept up in the storm feared him and displayed his image as a kind of talisman, a badge of allegiance announcing: "I am on your side. Please don't shoot me." In Kabul his picture was everywhere: in shop windows, in homes, on windshields and car bumpers, on the plastic fob dangling from the office key I'd been given. Massoud's intense, deep-set eyes gazed over the city from an enormous billboard high on the mountain near our office. At night it was illuminated, and as I lay in my bed I could see his bright tragic face rising over the capital like the moon. Historical complexities dissolved in a simple proposition. Massoud was the good guy. And on the other side was Gulbuddin.

We left the car, carrying bundles of old clothes. The next house lay up a steep, narrow passageway, icy and slick with sewage. A wooden door in the wall opened into a yard from which a staircase led to an upper room. I slipped off my shoes and ducked under the door quilt. In the dim light, I could just make out the forms of two women who stood against the wall. A small voice rose from the sandeli that occupied the center of the room, and looking more closely, I saw the brown, beaked, toothless face of an old woman who huddled there in the quilt that draped the table. She spoke to Nasrin about the two women who were her daughters-in-law, and about their children, who were there too, huddled under the table, and about her son who had fought with

Massoud and later been imprisoned for a long time and tortured by the Taliban. "That is why he now has gray hair," she said, gesturing toward the doorway where he stood. Nasrin and Lema sorted the clothes. I took the required photographs. "Winter kills the old woman," Lema said in English. The gray-haired son—tall, erect, dignified, silent, and barefoot—escorted us over the frozen ground to our car.

Heading back to the office, we stopped to buy bread at the *silo*. Or next to it. What Afghans call the silo (pronounced "see-low") is an immense multistoried granary and bakery built in the 1950s by the Soviets in a Cold War foreign aid campaign to win the hearts and minds and bellies of Afghans who, as it turned out, much preferred their own traditional naan to heavy "modern" bread. The Soviets built silos in other big cities too, in Mazar-i Sharif and Kandahar, perhaps preparing even then for the appetite of an occupying army. The tall yellow silo in Kabul stands on a broad avenue, and it was here, Nasrin says, that fighters sometimes set up their guns to mow down citizens in flight from rocket attacks. The windows are shattered now, and the walls are full of shell holes. I know without Nasrin having to tell me. Gulbuddin. But somewhere in the gutted silo someone still bakes heavy loaves of dense brown bread. A metal shipping container in the yard serves as a shop where we select a few loaves from a stack on a makeshift table. Then near dark we drive back to the office in silence along the drought-dried riverbed, filled with flimsy flea-market stands, across the Pul-i Khesti bridge, and through the city center, past the shell-shattered Kabul Hotel, closed indefinitely for renovation—where in 1979 Afghan police "rescuing" the American ambassador from kidnappers "accidentally" killed him—to the broad, broken streets of Share Nau. All the way I hold in my arms the big, round, comforting loaves of bread. At the office, I leave the bread in the kitchen and go upstairs to my own tiny room and light the sawdust fire.

THE LITTLE NGO I BEGAN TO WORK FOR, TRAINING HIGH SCHOOL
English teachers, was just one of many. Some NGOs had worked
in Afghanistan throughout the Soviet occupation, the civil wars,
and even the reign of the Taliban, providing food, medical care,
schooling, and other services to suffering citizens failed by a succession of competing governments. Others, like Madar, had moved
during the Taliban time, on principle or under duress, to work
with Afghan refugees in Pakistan or Iran. But with the fall of the
Taliban and the promise of massive international aid, NGOs
returned to Afghanistan and multiplied. By 2002 there were about
eight hundred of them in Kabul. Two hundred were international
organizations, including some big ones with familiar names like
CARE, Red Cross/Red Crescent, Médecins Sans Frontières, and
the International Rescue Committee, but most were smaller out-
fits with acronymic monikers that gave no clue to their purpose or
function.[40] About six hundred NGOs were Afghan organizations
that relied on the UN and the aid programs of foreign governments for the money and technical support to carry on their
work. ACBAR, the Agency Coordinating Body for Afghan Relief,
is the organization charged with keeping track of all the others. It
prints an alphabetical list of all the NGOs, with contact names
and numbers, fat as a big city phone book.

The agencies of the UN and foreign governments, international NGOs, and independent for-profit "contractors" occupy
big houses, the former homes of upper class Kabulis, in prime
neighborhoods such as Share Nau and Wazir Akbar Khan. Project directors and visiting consultants use the rooms as offices and
living quarters; they set up desks for their staff in the spacious hallways. Huge generators installed in the yard power the computers,
printers, copiers, fax machines, and cell phone rechargers vital
to their work. (As improvements are made to the dodgy electrical grid and rains revive the river, power appears in Kabul, but

intermittently and always by surprise.) In winter, generator-powered heaters and blowers warm rooms and corridors alike to temperatures suitable for Americans and Europeans. Afghans entering these buildings for the first time are amazed, believing that houses are not meant to be so unnaturally overheated, nor Afghans either, who are accustomed to keeping their jackets on indoors. Afghans are used to their own institutions, like the high school where I soon began to teach: without desks, without chairs, without blackboards, without sanitary facilities, without electricity, and without heat.

The foreigners with the biggest budgets pay unheard-of rents for the privilege of occupying the finest houses in Kabul, with the result that more and more landlords evict their Afghan tenants in favor of deep-pocketed outsiders. The ousted tenants tumble to the next level of housing, and so on down the line until those tenants at the bottom of the rent market are forced out to squat in the ruins or join the city's roving homeless. Sooner or later everyone has to move house. Workers jeopardize their jobs by leaving the office early to make the rounds of rental agencies, searching for a new home. Yet they need their jobs to pay for the housing. It is a delicate balance. Each new lease negotiation with the landlord forces tenants to fork up or move on. Civil servants and teachers, at the low end of the salary scale, are pushed farther and farther from their offices and schools. They ride the unreliable buses to work—men in the back, burqa-clad women piled like laundry bags in the few seats reserved for them at the front—and every year the trip grows longer. One hour, two hours. It's only a matter of time before these white-collar professionals try to leave their essential jobs in the schools and universities and government ministries and find work at international agencies.

The internationals pay high salaries—high by Afghan standards anyway—so that an uneducated man driving a car can make more money than a professor at Kabul University or the head of a hospital, the chief of police, or a cabinet minister. The man who drove me to my teaching job every day made three times the salary of the high school teachers in my class, all of whom were on the downward slide in the game of moving house. I was not surprised when they asked me to show them how to write Western-style resumes. Of all the educated men and women competing for menial jobs with international agencies, those who have English and computer skills are most in demand. The English-speaking husband of one of my students leaves his administrative job in the Ministry of Education to work for the UN as a driver. A deputy minister becomes a dispatcher, a school principal becomes a translator—not the work they hoped to do in life, the work they trained for, but at least they don't have to move again. They can pay the rent. The lucky ones, they float upon the sea of international benevolence—hundreds of millions of dollars of promised foreign aid—while others are swept under. Administered through the UN, USAID, and assorted governmental and nongovernmental organizations, international assistance inflates an artificial economy, parallel to but well removed from the economy of everyday Afghan life. (The drug trade is an even more powerful engine, pumping up the artificial economy, but it's a homegrown, traditional moneymaker that doesn't pretend to serve the average citizen.) Some of the new money finds its way into the pockets of Afghan shopkeepers, tradesmen, and provisioners. A sign on an Afghan-owned grocery store popular with internationals reads HAPPY ALL THE TIME. But living in the midst of such plenty, most Afghans are poorer than ever.

MEMBERS OF THE GREAT ARMY OF FOREIGN INVADERS—THE ex-pat aid experts—are always going somewhere. They drive around Kabul looking for meetings, looking for each other, looking for a decent meal. At times in Kabul, when work is stymied, the very act of driving around can seem to lend some purpose to life. For those on the go, Kabul offers an immense fleet of yellow and white taxis, mostly beat-up Toyota Corollas, some with the driver's seat on the left and some—for an additional challenge— on the right, and many equipped with ski racks for reasons incomprehensible in a country where nobody skis. But taxis are subject to breakdowns, and taxi drivers who don't understand instructions in English cause frustrating delays. For fearful internationals there is the additional question of security: how do you know a taxi is really a taxi? So aid agencies maintain their own vehicles—white Land Rovers and Toyota Land Cruisers are very popular—and their own full-time drivers, all men. Hundreds of these vehicles, neatly emblazoned with acronyms, take to the streets of the capital each day—streets already crowded with bicycles, horse carts, donkey carts, pushcarts laden with fruits and vegetables or old clothes, big wooden flatbed trailers pulled by tough old men, money changers flaunting wads of bills, touts peddling mobile-phone cards, legless panhandlers on makeshift go-karts, beggar women in dirty burqas, and poor boys flogging newspapers or waving tin cans that waft the smoke of burning asafoetida to ward off evil and to elicit tips. The streets themselves are bad, full of potholes and piles of rubble and garbage. After a snowfall they grow slick with ice or mud.

Guiding vehicles through these clotted streets is the job of Kabul's traffic police. Each wears a handsome, broad-shouldered woolen coat and trousers the color of army blankets, spiffed up by a Sam Browne belt of white vinyl. They have white vinyl hats to match, like members of a marching band, and red and white paddles, suitable in size and shape for ping pong, each equipped with a big red reflector and the words STOP POLICE printed in red in English. Under the terms of international agreements that divvied up the task of reconstructing Afghanistan, it fell to Germany to train the police, but when I first arrived that project was just getting under way. The police were still improvising. They'd wave their paddles to urge on traffic in one direction while vehicles stuck in cross traffic honked their horns. When they let the honkers go, the newly halted motorists would hit their horns. The din was unrelenting. Drivers rolled down their windows as they crept past to yell curses at the policemen, and occasionally an officer would swing his snazzy STOP POLICE paddle into some snarling driver's teeth. But mostly the traffic cops seemed remarkably restrained, even unconcerned. They dragged easy chairs and sofas to the middle of the traffic circles, where they could often be seen lounging, passing the time of day, while all about them swirled chaos, unattended. Eventually a few traffic lights were installed in the center of town, and every now and then the cops would rev up the generators that powered them and sit back, laughing, to see what the drivers would do. It seemed a kind of revenge.

Kabul is a big city—at least a couple of million people and growing fast with the influx of returning refugees. It sprawls around, between, and behind a number of steep, rocky hills. A few key roads connect the disparate parts of the city, but many of these arteries are still in ruins or closed for purposes of "security." So making your way around town can be supremely difficult and often impossible. Drivers try a likely route and if they reach an impasse, they turn around, retrace their path, and try another. To prevent traffic-snarling U-turns, the traffic police put large chunks of concrete down the center of the main streets, but drivers team up to wrestle them aside so they can double back. As things are, you can spend hours driving to and fro, looping this way and that, or stuck in stalled traffic, never actually arriving at any destination.

I drove around mostly with a man named Sharif. I'm a better driver than Sharif, but I was not allowed to drive myself. Sharif and I were doomed to twindom by the Afghan national ethos of sexism that requires the male presence almost everywhere, particularly behind the wheel of a car. Wherever I went, Sharif went too; and often we went together nowhere at all. I declined to sit in the back seat, where women belonged, but always sat up front with Sharif so I could take in the sights of the busy streets. Stopped dead in a traffic jam in the middle of the street, Sharif would lean back, adjust his testicles under his long perahan, and pop a cassette into the tape deck. Islamic prayers. Sharif is devout. Sharif also speaks pretty good English, having spent time as a refugee in Pakistan.

I liked him—in between prayers, we chatted—and he seemed to like me, though he refused to believe that back home in the States I drive a truck. Trying to illustrate the odd concept of driving regulations, I once told Sharif, "In my country we drive in lines." He said, "In your country is very many foreign customs." He preferred to tell me about Kabul. "In Taliban time," he said, "was no cars. No taxis. Nothing in streets. Now many, many cars." Unlike most Kabulis, Sharif thought this was a happy development. He himself owned three cars and a truck, all of which were part of the daily parade around Kabul, so Sharif made a very good living even when he was stalled at an impassable roundabout or caught in a snarl of pushcarts, playing his pray-along tapes or listening to patriotic country crooners on the US military radio station.

Like Thursday mornings, for example, when we were always stopped dead by the procession of certified war casualties making their way to the Ministry of Martyrs and the Disabled to collect their weekly stipends. Early in the morning they straggle through the streets: women in tattered burqas faded to a dull dove gray and men wrapped against the cold in *pattus* of military brown. They come from the side streets singly or in twos and threes, assembling themselves into a grave parade of the lame, the halt, and the blind, like some medieval pilgrimage to the shrine of a healing saint. One-legged men, victims of land mines, hobble on their Red Crescent crutches. This is the country of one-legged men. These, the officially disabled, drag their shattered bodies over the rough pavements of the wrecked streets, stopping traffic at every crossing. They press on amid the honking horns, seeking no miracles, no cures, but merely a small handout: the

wherewithal to make it through another week. Every day the
mines that salt the roadsides and the dead orchards and the fal-
low fields explode to create new martyrs and new casualties, officially disabled. Every *Naw Roz* (New Year's Day) thousands of
Kabulis visit a hillside shrine in the midst of the city and somebody steps on a mine. That year it was an eighteen-year-old boy
who lost both legs. And every week the Thursday procession to
the Ministry of Martyrs and the Disabled grows longer and more
belligerent. They are Kabul's most aggressive pedestrians.

But not the only ones. One bleak December morning, when
Sharif and I were thoroughly stuck, I watched an old man approach,
walking toward us at the edge of the street. He was tall and
upright, and handsome with his white beard and fine silk turban.
Another man bicycled past us from behind and proceeded toward
the old man. Just as they were about to pass each other, a car
lurched sideways, forcing the bicyclist to swerve. He ran into the
old man, who stumbled but regained his balance and stayed
upright. He spun around quickly and smashed his fist into the
cyclist's jaw, knocking him into the street with his bicycle on top
of him. At that, a young man passing by socked the old whitebeard, who went down backward with his feet in the air and his
fine turban in the dust. A traffic policeman, waving his paddle
overhead, rushed out from among the stalled cars and clubbed
the young man, who reeled backward, caught a heel on the curb-
stone, and sat down hard. In a moment he was up again, yelling
at the policeman. A fifth man, who had been casually leaning
against a garden wall taking the feeble morning sun, strode forward. He stepped between the young man and the traffic policeman with his arms extended, palms outward, holding the two
apart. It is the pose of the peacemaker. It is also the pose of cruci-
fixion. The old whitebeard picked himself up and delivered a brutal blow to the proud, unprotected chin of the peacemaker, who
flew back into the wall against which he had been lounging
only moments before and slid down to sit in a deflated heap at

the bottom. The whitebeard licked his knuckles, set his turban straight, stepped over the fallen bicycle, and went on his way. It was all over in seconds. Sharif was laughing. "Mujahidin," he said. And all at once Afghanistan, which had seemed so baffling, began to reveal itself.

AFGHANS ARE FAMOUS FIGHTERS. FIERCE, IMPLACABLE, RUTHLESS, bold, savage, brutal—these are the adjectives attached to them in history books. Their reputation seems exaggerated considering how many times the land was overrun and the cities sacked—by Alexander, coming and going, Genghis Khan, Tamerlane, and other less memorable marauders—but all that is ancient history. In more recent times—1747 to be exact—modern Afghanistan began to take shape as a kind of tribal confederation when one Ahmed Khan was elected shah, more or less democratically, by an assembly of Pashtun men. Taking the name Ahmed Shah Durrani, he established the Durrani dynasty that was to last, with one brief inter- ruption, until the communist revolution of 1978.[41] Hamid Karzai's presidency, advertised in America as the advent of "democracy," seems rather to Afghans to be a Durrani restoration, for Karzai comes from a powerful Khandahari Pashtun family of the Popolzai line, the lineage of Ahmed Shah Durrani himself. The Pashtun tribes lived then and now mainly in the south and east of Afghanistan and in even greater numbers in northwest Pakistan, their lands having been divided in 1897 when Sir Mortimer Durand, then foreign secretary of the government of India, drew the notoriously permeable border line that bears his name. Generations of Pashtuns dreamed of establishing the unified country of Pashtunistan; many still do. But instead they remain the largest and most influential ethnic group in Afghanistan—the center of Kabul is Pashtunistan Square—while over the line in Pakistan's Northwest Frontier province, Pakistani Pashtuns threaten to rejoin their Afghan brothers and take with them a substantial chunk of

Pakistani landscape.[42] There are at least twenty—some say more like fifty—other ethnic groups in Afghanistan: Tajik, Uzbek, Hazara, Turkoman, Nuristani, Aimaq, Farsiwan, Baluch, and so on. But for centuries the names Afghan and Pashtun have been used interchangeably. Afghans are equated with Pashtuns, and Pashtuns are tough.

The British diplomat and historian Martin Ewans, once head of chancery in Kabul, describes "the main characteristic of the Pushtoons" as "a proud and aggressive individualism, practiced in the context of a familial and tribal society with predatory habits, a part feudal and part democratic ethos, an uncompromising Muslim faith and a simple code of conduct."[43] That simple, hard-edged code—the Pashtunwali—obliges them to be hospitable, even to their enemies, and to provide sanctuary for strangers. (These, the more generous provisions of Pashtunwali, help to explain the Taliban's refusal to hand over their paying guest Osama bin Laden.) But the code also obliges them to seek revenge for the slightest affronts to their honor—for insults, real or imagined, to their name or their property, a category that includes women. Revenge, of course, breeds revenge, so that murderous feuds, vendettas, and battles involving individuals, families, and clans have long been the stuff of everyday Pashtun social life. The most important political body is the *jirga,* or assembly, in which every man is entitled to an equal say, or an equal insult. Pashtuns grapple for power, yet they think so little of authority that the descriptive phrase "fiercely independent" has become a cliché. They'll follow a clan-head or khan as long as it serves their purposes and no longer, so that a leader is stuck with the task of ceaselessly demonstrating his fitness to be followed. Factor in Islamic inheritance practices that divide a man's property equally among his sons, giving none a clear economic advantage, and you have the basis of democracy, or in a rugged landscape of scarce resources, constant fighting and factionalism and "brother-war."

In the past, about the only thing that gave Pashtuns pause in their incessant quarreling was the appearance of an outside enemy. Nothing inspires Pashtun unity like the need to expel an invader, and given the global politics of the last couple of centuries that usually meant the British. Historians like to speak of modern Afghanistan under the Durrani shahs as a "weak buffer state" of little significance except as a no-man's-land between major players in the global political game—rather like the mangled calf carcass that powerful horsemen struggle to possess in the Afghan sport of *buzkashi*. From the north, the Russian tsars ogled Central Asia and beyond it, British India. Afghanistan lay in the way. The British, who had set up shop on the subcontinent with the East India Company, countered with a "forward policy"— tilting toward something like George W. Bush's pushy "preemptive war"—designed to keep Afghanistan dangling from the British horse. During the nineteenth century, Russian and British emissaries, spies, adventurers, and soldiers danced back and forth for decades in what historians call the Great Game, and it was they, not the Afghans, who drew the borders of Afghanistan. (One early British emissary noted that Afghans didn't even have a name for their country, but near the end of the nineteenth century Amir Abdur Rahman began to refer to it as "Yaghistan," a name variously translated as "land of the free" or "land of rebels."[44])

For their part, the Afghans fought among themselves for the right to succeed Ahmed Shah Durrani, and the shahs and khans who came after him, in one city or sector or another. Few were as efficient as Zaman Shah, a grandson of Ahmed Shah Durrani who grabbed power after his father's death in 1793 by all at once locking up his more than twenty brothers and blinding the eldest. For most would-be successors, the brotherly battle was messier, bloodier, and more prolonged. What Western historians describe as "anarchy" prevailing in Afghanistan—"anarchy" that sometimes "justified" a "forward policy"—was mostly tribal Pashtuns being Pashtuns.

Early in the nineteenth century, a bold and popular Pashtun leader named Dost Mohammed came to power in Kabul and

gradually expanded his rule to other Afghan cities and regions.
But the Russians were expanding too—supplying the shah of Persia
with military advisers and urging him to advance against Herat
and Kandahar. The Russian threat was matched by the British.
Unable to enlist Dost Mohammed to serve their interests, the
British determined to reinstate their own puppet on the throne in
Kabul; and Dost Mohammed, like so many subsequent Afghan
leaders, found himself in the middle of the foreigners' fight. In
1838, 20,000 troops of the Army of the Indus—together with
38,000 camp followers, 30,000 camels, a big herd of cattle, and a
pack of foxhounds—invaded Afghanistan, and by August 1839,
they had restored to his palace in Kabul a Pashtun reject: the
deposed, exiled, and aged Shah Shuja (a lucky brother who had
escaped the efficient Zaman Shah). According to George Eden,
Earl of Auckland and governor general of India at the time, the
British meant not only to block Persian (and Russian) encroach-
ments from the west, but also "to establish a basis for the extension and maintenance of British influence throughout Central
Asia"; but in an official manifesto, they justified the invasion in
loftier terms. They said that once the new ruler was installed "by
his own subjects and adherents" and once he was "secured in
power, and the independence and integrity of Afghanistan established, the British army will be withdrawn." Historian Martin
Ewans notes that the words they chose for this pronouncement
are "uncannily similar" to those the Soviets would use to justify
their invasion in 1979.[45] (The Soviets too meant to stay only a few
months.) They also smack of the spin of the Bush Two administration that installed its own Shah Shuja in the person of Hamid
Karzai.

Perhaps it's too obvious—too cheap a shot—to mention here
the old saw about those who don't know history being doomed to
repeat it, for everybody knows that Bush the Lesser doesn't read
history or much of anything else and thus may remain to this
day the only person in the world who doesn't know that what

followed the British invasion of Afghanistan in 1838–39 was the greatest military defeat in all of British history. Having won the war—"mission accomplished"—the British seated an unpopular puppet. In the interest of "security," they maintained in Kabul a full brigade of troops, soon seen not as liberators but as an occupying army. The troops swaggered about, drank in public, used and abused Afghan women, and consumed food supplies while Afghans went hungry. There was unrest among the Afghans and uprisings here and there, but the British remained steadfast and cheerfully optimistic about the eventual success of their noble venture. Then in November 1841, Alexander Burnes, an officer in the Bombay Artillery and special emissary to the Afghan throne, was murdered together with his brother by a mob that overran his Kabul house. Three weeks later, during truce negotiations, Kabuli insurgents murdered William Macnaghten, who, as senior adviser to the governor general of India, was the chief representative of the British crown in Kabul. Macnaghten was mutilated and beheaded, and his body was put on show in the Kabul bazaar.

The British agreed to withdraw, for they had too few troops on the ground to defend themselves against a full-scale insurrection. The Afghans promised the soldiers, their families, servants, and hangers-on safe passage through the wintry passes leading out of Afghanistan, then harried them through the snow and slaughtered the last of them at a place called Gandamak. A brigade of 4,500 soldiers, followed by 12,000 civilians, marched out of Kabul on a January morning. Three thousand are said to have died the first day of exposure, even before the Afghans attacked. By the fourth day, only 120 soldiers and 4,000 followers were still pushing on through the snow. Two days later there were only 80. When they turned to make a last stand at Gandamak, there were 20. It is said that 6 mounted officers raced on from Gandamak, but only one man, badly wounded, the army physician Dr. William Brydon, rode in to the garrison at Jalalabad.

As things turned out, there were other survivors; the following year, a mighty British "Army of Retribution" that set upon the land to rape and murder and pillage returned with more than two thousand rescued captives and defectors. But it makes a better story if you don't know that, if instead you focus on the misery and terror of the English people straggling through the snow—the handsome young soldier, the woman clutching her baby, the pathetic little boy clinging to the hem of her cape—as the pitiless Pashtun tribesmen fire at them, such easy targets, from the rocks above. It makes a better story if you imagine poor, brave Dr. Brydon, bleeding badly, as good as dead really, hanging on the neck of his dying horse as it stumbles on toward Jalalabad, and somehow surviving to tell the terrible tale. That's the version the British have never forgotten. From an Afghan perspective, of course, the story is different.

When the British returned to even the score, they burned the Kabul bazaar and ravaged the countryside. Then in 1842, having reestablished Britain's reputation as a fearsome military power, they declared the Anglo-Afghan War at an end and left the country much as they had found it, with Dost Mohammed back in power. He ruled for another twenty years, dreaming of Afghan unity in the midst of fratricidal Pashtun power plays that climaxed in anarchy again at his death. Apparently having learned little from their experience, the British launched—only forty years later—a Second Anglo-Afghan War as fruitless and costly as the first. The aim once again was to counter the Russians and advance British "influence" in Central Asia. When it was all over in 1881, the British secretary of state for India described an outcome that again sounds eerily familiar. "As the result of two successful campaigns, of the employment of an enormous force, and of the expenditure of large sums of money, all that has yet been accomplished has been the disintegration of the State which it was desired to see strong, friendly and independent, the assumption of fresh and unwelcome liabilities . . . , and a condition of

anarchy throughout the remainder of the country."[46] There was a
Third Anglo-Afghan War as well, in 1919, that lasted only a
month. Afghan King Amanullah had proclaimed a jihad, demanding full independence from British suzerainty; and the weary
British, weakened by the First World War, scarcely put up a fight.
Handing Amanullah what looked like a diplomatic victory, they
cut Afghanistan loose. But they also cut the subsidy the king
needed to bring his country into the modern world. Afghanistan
would be independent, but still poor.

There was another result of the Anglo-Afghan wars. As British
journalists, politicians, and historians retold again and again the
bitter story of the bloody retreat from Kabul, Afghans seemed to
grow ever larger and more savage. They acquired in the minds of
the British, and by extension the West, an abiding reputation as a
race of barbaric and treacherous fighters, without scruple or mercy,
inhabiting forbidden territory. Afghanistan's "principal claim to
fame throughout history was as a passageway and death trap
for invading foreign armies," wrote one American journalist.[47]
The Afghans, left with a bitter distrust of outsiders, withdrew into
isolation and fought among themselves, sometimes with a ferocity
that confirmed the world's opinion. It was a hundred years before
any great power invaded Afghanistan again, only to meet the
same fierce and canny fighters. When the Soviets gave up, in their
turn, after a decade of bloody war and crept slowly north again
toward home, Afghan mujahidin of the Northern Alliance—
Massoud's men—made them fight for the road through the
heights of the Salang Pass and picked them off (such easy targets)
one by one.[48] But by then the Western perspective had changed;
the Afghans were whipping our enemy, and we were on their side.
When Peter Jouvenal, the BBC cameraman who won awards for
his coverage of the Afghan wars, later set up a small hotel for journalists in Kabul, in a house where Osama bin Laden was said to
have visited one of his wives, he wryly named it Gandamak Lodge.

Most Western reporters covering the wars lacked the long view of history, but from the comfortable, frustrating distance of their hotel rooms in Peshawar, they were oddly drawn to the notorious savagery of the Afghan guerillas. To many young journalists high on adrenaline, the height of reportage was to travel "inside" with the mujahidin. Smuggled across the border from Pakistan, snuggly bundled in ski jackets, they'd slog along with the Afghans, now known as "freedom fighters," moving at night to avoid detection. Encumbered by gear and unused to the altitude, they had a hard time keeping up with the lean, hardened fighters who traveled light and moved fast. Some confessed that the Afghans packed them in on mules, like any other heavy baggage. But somehow their own inability to keep up—their own softness and flab—made them all the more enamored of their superhuman hosts. One journalist wrote, "In them we saw a stronger, more heroic version of ourselves."[49] Reportage sometimes read like fan mail, tinged with a kind of homoerotic glorification of manliness, yet safely homoerotic because these tough, fierce, idealized bearded warriors seemed the very pinnacle of macho masculinity. Who wouldn't take a chance to hang out with such boys? Charlie Wilson, the womanizing, coke-snorting, alcoholic Texas congressman credited with extracting from the US Congress multimillions in covert aid to the mujahidin, claimed as his reward a short hike with the freedom fighters during which he was allowed to fire a rocket launcher all by himself.[50] As George Crile tells the story in *Charlie Wilson's War,* it was the high point of Wilson's sorry life, though it's possible that his Pakistani handlers, unwilling to risk a klutzy congressman's neck in Afghanistan, actually staged the event in Pakistan. Pakistan's ISI had played the same trick on CIA Director William Casey, taking him by jeep in the dead of night to a fake Afghan mujahidin camp not far from Islamabad.[51]

So the Afghans, all through the Soviet war and the civil wars that followed, handily maintained their historic reputation as the most ferocious fighters on the planet. But facts sometimes got lost or skewed in this romantic vision. Poverty, for one thing. Lots of mujahidin traveled light because the clothes they stood up in were all they had. They lived "like Spartans," reporters said, when in fact they lived like Afghans. Islamism, for another. Those fierce freedom fighters, trained and armed with Stinger missiles by the CIA, were Islamic jihadis. And at least 35,000 of them were not Afghans at all but volunteers from 43 Muslim countries in the Middle East, North and East Africa, Central Asia and the Far East—Algerians and Egyptians, Saudis and Kuwaitis, Pakistanis and Uzbeks, Filipinos and Uighurs—eager to die for their faith in Afghanistan, or elsewhere on another day.[52]

The Afghan fight was always about ideology. But American policy was stuck in the Cold War and skewed—as it is once again—by righteous religiosity. Bill Casey, CIA director from 1981 to 1986 and a devout Catholic, welcomed Islamic militants as natural allies of the Catholic Church in the battle against godless Soviet communism.[53] Soviet Foreign Minister Eduard Shevardnadze asked George Shultz, secretary of state in the Reagan administration, for American help in limiting the spread of Islamic fundamentalism, but nothing came of the request.[54] Instead, throughout the Soviet occupation, the CIA went on training those "Arab-Afghan" Islamic jihadis in Pakistani camps—at a cost of about $800 million.[55] It brought their Pakistani and Afghan teachers to camps in the United States to be schooled in many lethal skills.[56] So the Arab-Afghans imported to fight in Afghanistan were nothing like the native mujahidin who were described by Robert D. Kaplan in *Soldiers of God* as "neither complicated nor fanatical."[57] The Afghans fought for their families, their villages, their land, while the exotic Arab-Afghans fought for a cause. As one former homegrown mujahid put it to me, "We Afghans were fighting to live. They were fighting to die for Islam." Moderate Afghans warned the United States: "For God's sake, you're financing your own assassins."[58] And indeed, almost all the leaders of militant Islam worldwide and of every subsequent major terrorist attack can be traced to the Afghan war.[59] But America—more vengeful and devious than any Pashtun and too clever by half—secretly armed the righteous anticommunist cause and created a godly monster.

The homoeroticism was real enough, though it was a rare Western male journalist who reported propositions received from manly Afghans. How could you square *that* with official notions of military manhood? (What would it do to Charlie Wilson's appropriations if Republican congressmen got wind of it?) But a male Australian journalist friend (very straight) confessed that when he traveled with the mujahidin, he could scarcely sleep for the sound of soldiers bonking. He said the way the mujahidin carried on gave new meaning to the terms "mountain pass" and "strategic advance." It scared him to death. It scared and demoralized the Russians too. Stories abounded of Soviet prisoners of war gangraped by the manly men of the mujahidin, though the mujahidin switched to raping women once they hit the streets of Kabul. Stories of rape and sodomy of abducted girls and boys were common as well, and they are writ large in the founding myths of the Taliban. Mullah Omar and his men are said to have won over the citizens of Kandahar when they rescued a "dancing boy" from the clutches of two rival warlords and again when they hanged a Kandahari mujahidin commander responsible for the abduction and multiple rapes of two teenage girls.[60]

The widespread rape of women wasn't much noticed officially, for many of the rapists in Kabul were thought to be Massoud's men; and by that time—the time of the civil wars—Massoud was the lion of Western journalists.[61] (In an idolatrous biodocumentary on Massoud, a French filmmaker dares photograph only the bare feet of wives and daughters serving the dinner they've prepared. "They have their traditions," says the English voiceover, as if keeping women locked away is merely a quaint custom and their servitude an effect of nature.) But then, throughout the wars, women were scarcely mentioned at all. Wartime journalism in Peshawar was "a self-consciously macho activity," according to Robert D. Kaplan, and Pakistan's Northwest Frontier "a Wild West, sepia-toned outpost of masculinity." Inside Afghanistan, Kaplan remarked upon some "moving tents with narrow holes for the eyes," but another observer reported that women were "not even in the background . . . just not there."[62] So you can read book after book about Afghanistan in which the term *Afghan* clearly means only "adult male Afghan"; and many reputedly excellent books of contemporary reportage and history written by men contain not a single sentence about women or children.

Sometimes those Western male reporters tracking the mujahidin seemed to suffer subliminally the absence of women. One saw in the mountains the shape of "a young girl's breasts." Another, reporting for *Harper's,* described a mountain pass that looked to him like a vagina. Afflicted by similar spasms, Soviet journalist Artyom Borovik describes an Afghan road that "like a hooker, swung its curvaceous hips back and forth."[63] But most seemed content with the company of men and the invisibility of women. After arriving unexpectedly, long after dark, at a modest home in a remote village, British author Jason Elliot writes: "An ample meal appeared. How these minor feats are conjured into existence without any apparent interruption in the rhythm of affairs—no matter the number of unexpected guests—is one of the perpetual and mysterious delights of travel in Afghanistan."[64] What kind of journalist can't trace this mysterious delight to its source behind the curtain? To those barefoot women who carry out, night and day, the hospitality of Pashtunwali that makes the Afghan men such famous hosts? (Answer: The same kind of journalist who doesn't realize that the real function of this Pashtunwali hospitality is to detain him, to consume his time, to keep him from looking around the village.) And what Western woman would describe such hospitality—preparing an "ample meal" for unexpected guests in the middle of the night without running water or electricity or refrigeration or a decent lamp, without even Minute Rice or a tin of beans—as a "minor" feat?

In our time the fierce, implacable, ruthless, savage, treacherous Afghan man is irresistible. Western women fall for him too. When I told friends in humanitarian aid work that I was going to Afghanistan, they all smirked. "Get a good driver!" one said. "So what does that mean?" I asked. "You don't know? My god, where have you been?" And then I got the stories—perhaps apocryphal—of this woman or that, working for CARE or Save the Children or the American Embassy, whose assigned driver was just so gorgeous that—well, what would you do? Everyone knew the story of the newly married wife in the State Department power couple (or was it USAID?) who went to Kabul on a brief mission and ran away with her driver. All the stories end there, like romantic movies, with the chemically charged couple dashing off. Nobody knows, or nobody tells, the "ever after" part. I met one American woman—a fortyish, twice married, independent businesswoman—who'd arrived as a charitable volunteer and married an Afghan man in Kabul. I invited her to join me in language lessons I was taking from an excellent male teacher. "My husband would never let me talk to another man," she said. "He loves me too much." I could see she was pleased. He was very good looking. A few weeks later I heard that her husband had taken a second wife in Dubai. I met another American humanitarian who was obsessed with a slim, handsome (married) Afghan driver. For weeks he did his best to avoid her and escape to other work. She wrote into her project budget a staggering fee for car and driver, and when a lax donor agency handed her the cash, she bought herself the man of her dreams.

I DON'T KNOW IF AFGHANS ARE ANY BETTER OR WORSE THAN ANY other guerilla soldiers anywhere. I don't know whether they're any more fierce or more ruthless, more courageous or more relentless than any other men under any circumstances fighting for their lives. I do know that the Afghan men I knew, many of whom had fought with the mujahidin—men I taught, men I employed or worked with or worked for or met in passing—were polite, soft spoken, solicitous of their families, considerate, and kind. To a man, they were hungry for peace. And as for my driver—there was the placid, chubby, hardworking, and devout Sharif. He often brought us eggs from his mother's chickens.

But give a man like Sharif a vehicle and he will drive like a commando. Give a man a horse and he will ride headlong into a wild game of buzkashi, beating off opponents to snatch at a bloody calf. Give him a Kalashnikov or a Stinger missile and he will take to the mountains with the mujahidin. The impulse is the same— some desperate scramble for survival grounded in the certainty that despite the claims of kinship and *qawm*, family and friendship, religion and party, each man is on his own. This is his psychic state: solitariness, an aloneness, deep and abiding. It's a state of mind bred perhaps by generations of struggle with an exacting land, brutal poverty, and murderous enemies, and confirmed by the recent quarter century of unremitting war. Perhaps because there have never been any lasting sources of authority in Afghan life— no durable monarchy, no clerical hierarchy, no reliable aristocracy of intellect or wealth—each man seems to feel that he is on his own against impending chaos. Alone, he will attach himself, if the opportunity presents itself, to some benefactor, some khan or commander—some landowner or warlord—some man in charge, to guard against impending violence.

But khans and *commandans* have only as much power as they can amass in their lifetimes. The landowner's wealth is divided among his sons, so that none is the equal of his father and all are thrown into combat with one another. As for the commandan with his private militia, his power is as ephemeral as his life is short. Even the mullah who may exert some small influence in village life represents no established seat of power, no papacy or bishopric, but is rather a kind of freelance artisan tending to local religious needs the way the village carpenter attends to the need for furniture. The Afghan's nation isn't even a nation really, but a failed state, a mere passageway, a battlefield, a *buz*—a goat torn between horses in geostrategic games. As for the men who've tried to rule it in the last century, five were assassinated, four were exiled, two were executed, and one—the Taliban's Mullah Omar—rode off on a motorbike and disappeared. The last time a ruler died peaceably in office of natural causes was in 1901, and since then only two men have handed over power, grudgingly, to another lawful ruler, and one of them, Sibghatullah Mujaddidi, had no real power to give up. So nothing lasts: no authority, no institution, no man. Life is always starting over, like another round of buzkashi, and each man must grab again and again for the goat. Perhaps he would like to be gentle, but the game is rough and only one man can win. Perhaps he would like to be loyal, at least to his family and friends, but the pressure of circumstance makes him ever watchful for the main chance. Perhaps he would like to be at peace, but danger lies all about.

Some Afghans, sometime, must have led lives of quiet harmony and discipline, for who else planted all the orchards and the vineyards, tended all the mulberry trees, dug with infinite patience the endless irrigation *jouies,* fenced all the fields with stones, built the high mud-brick walls of the farmsteads throughout the land—now shattered and destroyed? But what chance had those small people against the powers of the outside world? Outsiders offered Afghanistan political "expertise" and above all military "aid," and the more aid Afghans got, the more they fought. It's a simple equation. Historian Barnett Rubin puts it this way: "Because the number of mujahidin depended on the number of weapons available—the supply of volunteers was endless—more military assistance meant more mujahidin."[65]

The Carter administration sent $30 million in military aid to Afghanistan in 1980 and $50 million in 1981. By 1984, Reagan had upped it to $120 million and secured a secret promise from General Zia ul-Haq of Pakistan to help the mujahidin. In exchange

Reagan waived a US policy banning assistance to countries with nuclear research programs, sent Pakistan the third biggest chunk of the foreign aid budget, and turned a blind eye while bombs were built.[66] (Years later, after the war against the Soviets was over, the administration of Bush Senior suspended aid to Pakistan, claiming to be dismayed that its ally had somehow become a nuclear power.) In April 1985, as the Soviets prepared to withdraw from Afghanistan, Reagan signed National Security Directive 166 authorizing a more aggressive policy: that we use "all means available" to drive them out, and Congress jumped on the war wagon with $250 million. All the while the US cleverly paid the Chinese to make Soviet-style weapons for the mujahidin, so that captured weapons would not give away American involvement in the dirty Afghan war. (Mujahidin commander Abdul Haq once complained of the waste of having to fire off a lot of SAM-7 missiles to get the hang of how they worked, because they'd come with instruction manuals written in Chinese.)[67] The US also secretly diverted hundreds of millions of dollars worth of weapons allocated as Afghan aid through the back door to Iran as part of Reagan's Iran-Contra scam, but plenty of weapons still reached the Afghans as well.[68] Aid climbed to $470 million in 1986, and for the first time the US shipped laser-guided Stinger anti-aircraft missiles into the Afghan arms pipeline—state-of-the-art weapons that had never before been distributed outside NATO. (The frantic effort to buy them back from people who could use them to shoot down our airplanes is still going on.)[69] In 1987, even as Soviet troops were making their way out of the country, American military aid reached $630 million. The Soviets completed their withdrawal in February 1989, but US military assistance rose to $700 million for the year.[70]

Only then did the administration of Bush Senior take a look at the politics of our aid beneficiaries—particularly our longtime ally, Gulbuddin—and call for a speedy political settlement "sidelining extremists." Belatedly the US cut off aid to Gulbuddin's radical Islamist organization, but the Saudis and other Arab states picked up the slack. All along Saudi Arabia—birthplace of regressive Wahhabi Islam and the most conservative theocratic Islamic state in the world—had been matching American aid dollar for dollar and then some, bringing combined aid to the mujahidin to about $1 billion a year. The Saudis also picked up the tab—about $1.5 million per month—for transporting weaponry across the Pakistan border into Afghanistan, using Saudi Red Crescent offices in Pakistan to handle the money. US aid allocations to other mujahidin factions dropped—only $280 million in 1990—but they kept coming, while the Soviets continued to send aid to the Afghan government of President Najibullah in Kabul. Barnett Rubin tallies the assistance: "If we add the approximately $5 billion in weapons sent to the mujahidin during 1986–90 and a conservative estimate of $5.7 billion worth sent to Kabul, Afghanistan's total weapons imports during the period eclipsed those of Iraq and were at about the same level as those of Japan and Saudi Arabia—with the difference that personal weapons accounted for a much higher proportion of imports to Afghanistan." The country probably received more personal weapons than any other country on earth, and more than Pakistan and India combined. But maybe that wasn't quite enough. In June 1991, two years after calling for a swift political settlement, Bush Senior authorized an off-budget transfer to the mujahidin factions, then engaged in civil war, of $30 million in Iraqi weapons captured in the first Gulf War.[71] Perhaps George Senior simply wasn't paying attention. A CIA official later told Steve Coll of the *Washington Post* that when he mentioned the Afghan war to the president in passing, Bush Senior "seemed puzzled" and "surprised." The president asked, "Is that thing still going on?"[72]

Once the Soviets left Afghanistan, the jihad was at an end. Iran advanced the position of moderate Islam: that the fighting must stop. But the US was still embarrassingly on the side of the Islamic extremists and against the sovereign government of Afghanistan, which it still regarded as a Soviet tool. So it made sure the warfare would go on. It backed an ISI scheme to rally all the mujahidin factions in one big push to capture Kabul and oust President Najibullah. Pakistan wanted to install its own friendly puppet (still Gulbuddin) in Kabul, while the single-minded Americans thought only of piling more humiliation on the battered Soviets. Mujahidin field commanders, including Massoud, said they couldn't capture Kabul—they were guerilla fighters, untrained for frontal assault and siege, and they didn't attack cities or civilians. But the ISI and the CIA claimed they could do it, if only they received a little more military aid and a little practice in urban warfare. So the US sent still more arms through the Peshawar pipeline, while in Islamabad, US ambassador Robert Oakley sat down with Pakistani officials, and not a single Afghan, to plan an attack on Jalalabad, the largest city on the way to Kabul.[73] Meant as a warm-up for the assault on the capital, the slow-motion siege of Jalalabad was a prolonged disaster, as the mujahidin commanders had predicted, with thousands slaughtered on both sides and among the civilians caught in between. But by that time the mujahidin party leaders, who had spent far too many years squabbling over the arms buffet in Peshawar, seemed to have forgotten all about the people they were supposed to be fighting for. Cut loose like kites with severed strings, they drifted ever upward into the thin air of extremist ideology and personal ambition. Then on the first day of 1992 the US and Russia shut down the buffet, leaving all those hungry party leaders, all those desperate men, and all those weapons. What did they expect? It's easy to blame Afghanistan's "backwardness" and tribal ferocity for the bitter civil wars that followed Soviet withdrawal, but in the quality and profusion of their armaments the Afghan brothers were thoroughly modern and up to date.

THE AFGHANS FOUGHT, AND THE AMERICANS WENT HOME. WITHIN two years, the new Clinton administration, under pressure from congressional Republicans to stop wasting money on miserable little chaotic countries, shut down all humanitarian and development aid to Afghanistan. At the CIA Afghanistan receded into the background.[74] Then the black-turbaned mullahs of the Taliban barreled out of the Pashtun south in their Saudi pickup trucks, and students came in their thousands out of the Saudi-funded madrassas of Pakistan, and they crept over the country—welcomed at first for the "security" they brought to wild and wartorn towns of the south, for opening the roads so food could get through, for the "peace" that entered war-weary lives when they hanged another warlord from the turret of a tank. But then, right away, they cracked down on music and television and kite flying and women and girls and white shoes and nail polish and men whose beards were not long enough to grip in your fist and those whose turban tails dangled at an improper length. Theirs was not the modern Islamist ideology the intellectuals of Kabul University had envisioned. It was a volatile mix of dictates pinched from such arch-conservative Islamist sources as the Muslim Brotherhood of Egypt and Pakistan's Jamaat-i Islami, from Sayyid Qutb and Abul A'la Mawdudi, from the ultraconservative version of Indian Deobandism taught in Pakistan, and the radical Wahhabism of Saudi Arabia promulgated in Pashtunistan by Osama bin Laden and *his* Afghan mujahidin commander, Abdul Rasul Sayyaf—all stirred into an idiosyncratic fundamentalism that looked longingly backward to the seventh century and the exemplary life of the Prophet. It was a totalitarian theology that banned toothpaste, all brands, as a product unendorsed by Muhammad and unmentioned in the Quran. All over Afghanistan, people resisted this onslaught of fervid religiosity, and Massoud offered his Northern Alliance as a bulwark against it; but the United States, which had meddled so long and so recklessly in Afghanistan, declared a new policy of neutrality in what it called a "civil war" between the Taliban and Massoud.

    At first, the US actually welcomed the Taliban and their fierce brand of law and order. This is where oil comes into the story, in an episode demonstrating that even a country with no oil at all cannot escape the machinations of "American oil interests." They led the Taliban welcoming committee.[75] They had long been scheming to funnel the oil reserves of the Caspian area—perhaps the last great oil deposits on earth—to Pakistani seaports by way of a pipeline laid across Afghanistan. (In the football parlance so dear to Texas oilmen, this is the equivalent of making an end run around Iran.) The big problem was security. It doesn't pay to lay an oil pipeline through a war zone, and the bloody warlords kept on fighting and holding up construction.

Luckily for the oil interests, the Taliban seemed well on the way to liquidating the mujahidin and making way for one sweet deal. Twice in 1997 Taliban leaders visited Washington to meet with officials of the State Department and the American oil conglomerate Unocal. The oil company confesses to having spent between $15 and $20 million on the project, a sum that includes the salaries of plenty of ex–State Department officials hired to help negotiate the deal. Among them was Afghan-American Zalmay Khalilzad, a longtime Pentagon planner and adviser to Donald Rumsfeld, later named by oilman George W. Bush to be special envoy and subsequently ambassador to Afghanistan and then Iraq. (Another player at the table was Hamid Karzai, representing Unocal in negotiations with the Taliban.) At the time, Khalilzad urged the administration to "engage" with the Taliban, arguing that "The Taliban does not practice the anti-US style of fundamentalism practiced by Iran—it is closer to the Saudi model."[76] Never mind that the Saudi model—the Wahhabism followed by Osama bin Laden—thoroughly oppresses women and ignores basic human rights; it's a model American oil profiteers can do business with. So they tried hard to do business with the Taliban. Eventually the project fell through, largely because the Taliban could not perfect "security" while Massoud went on fighting and bin Laden was busy blowing things up. But hope dies hard. After the Taliban fell, the US sent as ambassador to Afghanistan one Robert Finn, an expert on Caspian oil. He was replaced in 2003 by Khalilzad, who soon came to be regarded in Kabul as the real boss behind Karzai. But when he left for Iraq in 2005, security in Afghanistan was still a joke, and the pipeline was but a pipe dream.[77]

While the US was courting the Taliban, Massoud turned to Iran and India for help, and he arranged to buy military equipment from the vanquished Russians and the Russian mafia. Meanwhile the fortunate Taliban had only to hold out their hands for money, arms, supplies, training, and intelligence from America's peculiar allies—Pakistan and Saudi Arabia—and Osama bin Laden and his al-Qaeda movement. In February 1998 bin Laden called a press conference at his Afghanistan base to announce the formation of an international radical Islamic coalition—the International Islamic Front for Jihad Against Jews and Crusaders—resolved to carry out violent attacks on the United States. The group's manifesto, written by bin Laden, was signed by radical Islamic leaders from Pakistan, Egypt, Bangladesh, and Kashmir. On August 7, 1998, teams of Islamic suicide bombers funded by bin Laden and trained in Afghanistan attacked the US embassies in Kenya and Tanzania; and in the same week in Afghanistan, the Taliban, aided by Pakistan's ISI and 28,000 "Arab-Afghan" suicide soldiers from the Saudi-funded madrassas of Pakistan, captured Mazar-i Sharif and massacred thousands of its citizens.[78] Soon after, Ahmad Shah Massoud wrote a letter to the US Senate.

Massoud protested that Pakistan and its Arab allies had handed over his country to "fanatics, extremists, terrorists, mercenaries, drug mafias and professional murderers."[79] He asked America to break its old habit of letting Pakistan run its Afghan policy and help him instead in his war against the Taliban, Pakistan's ISI, and Osama bin Laden. (Later, after 9/11, Afghans would ask why the US wasn't bombing Pakistan, or Saudi Arabia, instead of them.)[80] But the US—the Clinton administration now—thought Massoud an unsuitable ally because he made money in the poppy trade, though mujahidin leaders, notably Gulbuddin, had been doing so all along. (Indeed, the Afghan-Pakistani drug business had exploded along the mujahidin supply lines from a little regional opium traffic to the world's biggest heroin operation—with the tacit blessing of the CIA.)[81] And Pakistan—the military dictator Pervez Musharraf now—also told Clinton to "engage" with the Taliban. Clinton, like the string of presidents who preceded him, did what Pakistan said, perhaps because the advice so perfectly coincided with what he'd been told by the Unocal folks at home. By "engaging" with Taliban "moderates," he hoped to persuade them to hand over bin Laden. In the aftermath of the African embassy bombings, he'd lobbed some missiles at bin Laden, but the Monica Lewinsky scandal left him powerless to act again. And so American policy remained in thrall to Pakistani intelligence, which trained and protected the Islamic radicals America feared, and to Saudi Arabia, which funded the enterprise. The Saudis sent millions to bin Laden and the Taliban, while the Pakistani ISI made a show of turning over a few small, expendable al-Qaeda operators now and again whenever American patience seemed to be wearing thin.[82] The only political voices in the United States raised against the Taliban were those of feminists who complained that Afghan women had been stripped of all human rights. But for a long time that was not enough to cause the Clinton administration to choose the other side. Women in America, it seemed, didn't have much clout.

Despite the official policy of neutrality, Richard A. Clarke, national security adviser on counterterrorism to four presidents, proposed that the CIA support Massoud against the Taliban on the grounds that "if Massoud posed a serious threat to the Taliban, bin Laden [who supported them] would have to devote his arms and men to the fight against the Northern Alliance rather than fighting us."[83] But the CIA found the work "very, very, very risky" to their safety and reputation, should such a secret operation ever come to light.[84] The CIA also now claimed to be low on cash. So it delivered only some small token payments to Massoud, and radio equipment to encourage him to listen in on the Taliban. In exchange it pressured him to deliver the big prize, Osama bin Laden. Legal niceties prevented the CIA from asking Massoud to "kill" bin Laden—the Clinton administration felt obliged to play by the rules of international law and diplomacy—so they tried instead to persuade Massoud to capture alive a man who was continually surrounded by one hundred heavily armed jihadi bodyguards. But Massoud was weary of America's self-absorbed policy. (They thought only about bin Laden; he thought about his country.) If his men undertook this suicidal mission, he asked, what was in it for the people of Afghanistan? After so many years of fighting, Massoud must have been weary of America's fastidiousness, too—of its refusal, after twenty years of meddling, to take sides, declare the Taliban an enemy, and set aside the legalities that protected bin Laden. Massoud said American policy was myopic and bound to fail. By 1999 al-Qaeda was already operating in sixty countries, including the United States, and the plot that produced 9/11 was under way.[85]

Massoud holed up in the north, as he had done at times during the Soviet occupation, and waited. Around him he began to gather allies: formidable mujahidin commanders such as the Herati leader Ismail Khan, the Uzbek Abdul Rashid Dostum, and Abdul Haq, a Pashtun in exile whose wife and children had been murdered by bin Laden and the Taliban; and Hamid Karzai, sometime Unocal negotiator and scion of a powerful, exiled Kandahari Pashtun family that had backed the Taliban in 1994 and then in 1999 rallied Pashtuns against them. (Hamid's father, Abdul Ahad Karzai, who led the defection, was assassinated in Quetta in 1999.) Even former King Zahir Shah joined the alliance as Massoud gradually assembled something rare in Afghan history—a moderate Islamic royalist multiethnic coalition. It seemed it might be the groundwork for a nation. *Washington Post* editor Steve Coll, trying to pin down Massoud's place in history, argues that "Afghanistan

after 1979 was a laboratory for political and military visions con-
ceived abroad and imposed by force. . . . A young, weak nation,
Afghanistan produced few convincing nationalists who could
offer an alternative, who could define Afghanistan from within.
Ahmed Shah Massoud was an exception."[86] Kabulis who survived
the anarchy and destruction of the mujahidin's brother wars,
Kabulis who remember the rapes and atrocities and executions of
the mujahidin years, Kabulis who long for nothing more than peace
may take a dimmer view of the man who wouldn't stop fighting.
Yet even people who remember all those things will tell you that
Massoud was different.

When the second George Bush slid into the White House,
Massoud was still waiting for America to spot its enemy. He could
not have been optimistic. Bush the Lesser was himself a born-again
religious fundamentalist who believed in imposing his beliefs on
the world by force, the mirror image of bin Laden, and clueless—
the first American president in memory to boast of his own ignorance, parochialism, and religiosity. Condoleezza Rice, then his
national security adviser and a Cold War specialist, seemed to think
the Taliban was armed by Iran, which was in fact sending aid to
Massoud. Richard Clarke immediately sent her an urgent counterterrorism agenda, including again his proposal to aid Massoud
and even bomb Taliban infrastructure, but his proposals went
nowhere. The whole Bush neocon team—Rice, Dick Cheney,
Donald Rumsfeld, Paul Wolfowitz, and the rest—were so focused
on star-wars missile defense and oil and snatching Iraq that the
urgent security briefings of outgoing Clinton antiterrorism experts
seemed not to register at all. Nevertheless, during the first six or
seven months of the new administration, US intelligence services
noted such dramatic increases in threatened terrorist attacks that
at last the suggestion to make tentative provisions to send covert
aid to Massoud sneaked into a proposed national security plan. It
took many months to get everybody together for a meeting—the
new president was so often on vacation—but at last the plan was

adopted.[87] Miraculously, it seemed that the administration of Bush the Lesser might consider giving Massoud the help he needed. Massoud and his allies, of course, were the same moderate forces the US might have backed a decade earlier had policy not been parceled out to Pakistan by administrations given to indifference or greed—the kind of greed that doesn't want to bust up profitable friendships with the Saudi royal family or blow a chance to lay hands on Central Asian oil. It's an irony of this long sad story of slapdash American foreign policy that the Bush Two team—who knew nothing about Afghanistan and cared less, except of course for the oil pipeline—would be the ones to back the better man. But it's not the last irony. Five days after the new national security plan was adopted an al-Qaeda suicide bomber aimed a fake TV camera at the chest of Ahmad Shah Massoud and hit the detonator. Two days after that was 9/11.

Massoud was still a presence in Kabul, and from my window I could see him looking out over the city from the mountaintop billboard. I could study his face—the deep lines of the furrowed forehead and the eyebrows drawn down into knots above dark, deep-set eyes of blistering intensity. It was his tragedy to see more than others who dictated the fate of his country from offices far away. On one side of our divided world stand the privileged nations, especially our own, exercising the discipline of "whatever it takes" to buy some illusory sense of security; and on the other, the miserable little failed states that serve as battlefields for our proxy wars, their patriots our puppet soldiers, their civilians our collateral damage, their societies the rubble through which our "democracy" marches ever onward to the open market. Barnett Rubin says it well: "The developed country does not, as Marx thought, show the backward country its future; the fragmenting countries show the integrating ones the dark side of their common present. The violence and decay of Afghanistan is the reflection . . . of the violence that created and maintains our security."[88]

Massoud must have dreamed of security too. His hair was salted with gray and his back was bad, and his life had been spent at war. Among men who glamorize war, he had become the greatest hero; but he must have known that among women, who scavenge the shards of war, he seemed another gunman, like the rest. In his last years, he designed and built a modest home for his family with a library for himself. The library had big windows that looked out over the Panjshir Valley and bookshelves to hold the works of the Farsi poets he loved. I read somewhere that he laid the carpet himself. He was a weary soldier who must have wanted to go home. He lived with his wife and children in that new house for only twenty days. Then he was murdered by outsiders in the pay of an outsider, another "former protégé of the United States," Osama bin Laden.[89] He hadn't even finished unpacking his books. Whose fault was that?

IT WAS FEBRUARY WHEN CAROLINE AND I AND ANOTHER VOLUNteer named Helen set off for Mazar-i Sharif, and no time to travel in the mountains of Afghanistan. But the winter had been long in Kabul, and we needed a change. Caroline wanted to go to the fabric bazaar in Mazar-i Sharif to search for new materials for her projects. An early warm spell in Kabul convinced us that the worst of winter was over, and we learned when Caroline sent her driver, Hasan, to inquire at the truck stop that the road over the Hindu Kush was open. "They'll be playing buzkashi now," Caroline said. "If we're lucky, we can see the real thing." That settled it.

Caroline's little NGO owned no vehicle that could make the long climb over the mountains. We would have to hire one. So we set off before dawn for the marketplace on the northern outskirts of Kabul where trucks and private vehicles-for-hire waited for passengers. Hasan insisted on coming with us, all the way to Mazar-i Sharif, to look after Caroline and provide at least the appearance that we were properly escorted by a man. (An excellent driver, he'd operated a private long-distance travel service until

the Taliban beat him up and stole his bus.) For half an hour he
went up and down the line of vans and SUVs for hire, negotiating
with drivers until he struck a deal for a Toyota Town Ace—
Afghans pronounce it "Tunis"—and a dreamily handsome driver
named Marouf. We climbed in, arranged our water bottles and
our bags of bread and hard boiled eggs and tangerines around us,
and settled in for a lovely drive. It was to be our little holiday.

In the gray light of dawn we drove north across the Shamali
plains, past the rusted tanks and overturned personnel carriers
along the roadside, the barren farmlands and broken vineyards,
the orchards of skeletal trees, the mud-brick walls of farming compounds melting into the land. Dust to dust. At Jabal ul-Saraj, where
the road forks northeast to the Panjshir Valley—where Massoud
had stood again and again against the Soviets: six times before he
reached the age of thirty—we crossed the river on pontoons laid
beside the shattered brick piers of the old blown bridge, within
range of the rusty gun of a Soviet tank half submerged in the
stream. We kept to the main road, heading due north into the foothills along the Salang River, and the land began to rise. The river
ran clear and glacially blue. At each bend, flat-roofed mud houses
clustered on a south-facing shoulder of mountain. There the
stream was edged by terraced patches of garden, and where it
pooled into eddies, dotted with duck decoys cut from sheet-metal
and fixed in place. The sun overhead was bright in the clear air,
the sky a brilliant cobalt that deepened as we climbed higher and
higher into snow.

Marouf gripped the steering wheel with both hands, fighting
the rough road, and moved the Town Ace right along, as if he had
not a moment to lose. On the dashboard red plastic roses tossed
their heads with every bump and lurch. From the middle of the
windshield, Ahmad Shah Massoud looked down at us, wearing
his familiar, bemused sidelong smile. Occasionally Marouf reached
out quickly to touch the photograph, whether for luck or in hom-
age I couldn't tell. Like Massoud, Marouf was a Tajik. He wore

the same woolen vest, the same rough woolen cap. He'd had his own bad luck. He'd driven over a land mine, he said, and it blew him apart. He spent six months in the hospital and then went back to driving. "What else can I do?" he said. Whenever he left the vehicle you could see that he was oddly short, as if when the doctors put him back together there'd been a piece missing from the middle of his torso. He walked funny too, one leg goose-stepping, and the other flopping along behind. But when he took his seat behind the wheel, you couldn't tell. Since the mine accident he'd had four children in six years. He said he was in a hurry to get home to his wife.

When we'd left Jabal ul-Saraj, about two o'clock in the afternoon, Hasan had said we'd reach the Salang tunnel in an hour. Built by the Soviets in 1964 to ease the flow of goods (and soldiers) between Afghanistan and the Soviet republics of Central Asia, this highway, crowned by the tunnel, was the main route between Kabul and the north, and in winter the only one. War with the Soviets had nearly wrecked it, and later, in 1997, Massoud blew up the southern end of the tunnel to trap fleeing Taliban troops who had captured Mazar-i Sharif only to have the people rise against them. Most of the rubble had been cleared, but the tunnel hadn't been fully repaired. Traffic moved officially in one direction only: north one day, and south the next. Now the road we traveled grew rougher, slowing us down, and the traffic thickened ahead of us. One hour. Two. "There it is," I said, when I saw that at the top of the long snowy slope before us the road disappeared behind a wall of concrete posts. But that was only the first gallery, Hasan said—the first of many stretches where the road had been cut into the side of the mountain and covered with a concrete roof supported at the outer edge by concrete pillars. The galleries were meant to protect the road from avalanches, which in theory at least, could spill over the roof, but we came upon one gallery that had been completely swept away only the day before. A few surviving pillars canted out at odd angles over the slope, and far down the mountain others lay scattered near two upended trucks protruding from the snow. *"Barfkuch,"* Hasan said. He was always ready with a lesson in Dari, the language Helen and I struggled to learn. *Barf,* we knew, meant snow. But *kuch*? *"Kuch, Kuchi,"* Hasan said. Kuchis are Afghanistan's wandering nomads. *Barfkuch* is snow on the move.

We climbed higher, switching back and forth with the twisting road, skidding now on snow and ice between deep drifts banked along the roadside. We swung around the last turn below a long gallery and slid into a traffic jam. Frightened cows looked down on us, peering over the hand-painted sign on the tailgate of a Pakistani truck: KING OF THE ROAD. Marouf fixed his eyes on those bland bovine faces—or was it on the sign?—and all his vibrant energy suddenly blew skyward as if the cone had lifted off some boiling internal volcano. He leaned out the window to scream at the truck driver. He punctuated his remarks by spitting at the cows. The truck driver screamed back. Marouf jumped out and stormed toward the truck as best he could with his curious lurching stride. But he must have seen that beyond the cattle truck was a tanker, and beyond that a line of lorries and brightly painted Pakistani trucks, minivans, and SUVs, white Land Rovers emblazoned with UN acronyms, Taliban wagons (pickup trucks with tinted windows), and battered Toyota Corolla taxis. All stuck in a traffic jam bigger than any I'd seen in the streets of Kabul.

He retreated, grumbling and howling curses. Ahead of us, many drivers were putting chains on their vehicles, and Marouf did the same with Hasan's help and mine. Against Hasan's advice, Marouf lashed the chains tightly in place with nylon rope. The vehicles ahead began to inch forward, and Marouf was ready. He punched up a tape at top volume—some double-time pummeling of drums— and revved the engine. He swung wide toward the edge of the road, gunned the Town Ace forward, and spun the wheel hard to cut in front of the cattle truck, leaning from the window to curse the other driver. Someone in the back of the cattle truck threw a rock that thunked on our roof, but Marouf was already skidding past the fuel tanker into the dark gallery. A little Corolla sped around the other side of the tanker into our path, cutting us off, and Marouf howled with rage. "Look at this," he shouted. "There is no one in charge. It is shameful." He bashed the rear of the Corolla and laughed when it skidded and sideswiped the gallery wall. I glanced at Helen, who was clutching the seat. Caroline shook her head and said apologetically, "They like to be first, these men."

And so we went up the mountain in constant combat with a hundred other guys all determined to arrive before anyone else at the same place. Men leaped from their vehicles and ran up and down the line yelling directions and curses at other drivers. Then they jumped back in, bent on filling the next open space in line, wherever it might occur. Two vehicles forged ahead, blocking each other and the road, and while the two drivers raced their engines, drivers trapped behind them ran forward on foot to shout conflicting orders about who must do what. "A melee," Helen said. Caroline said, "Mountains can be so peaceful," and got out to walk with Hasan tagging after her for propriety's sake. Soon one of our tightly lashed tires came off the rim, just as Hasan had warned, and Marouf launched himself into a paroxysm of rage, as if he had truly lost his mind. I got out and started the tough job of disentangling things while Marouf pounded the road, screaming and waving his fists in the air. I looked up to see the cows go by. KING OF THE ROAD.

We entered the last gallery just as the sun dropped out of sight, turning the high peaks luminous white, then pink. Inside the gallery it was already black as night. The air was thick and gray with exhaust. Headlights couldn't penetrate it. They cast only a pale and eerie glow through which dark silhouettes loomed and vanished. Snow had blown into the spaces between the pillars and frozen there in ominous arcs that hung over the vehicles like great waves about to break. Men on foot emerged from the murk— strange, looming shapes, shouting.

When at last we left the gallery, it was night and the stars were brilliant in the black sky, the air thin but clean and cold. Soon we were stuck again. Before us the road disappeared in a long pool of water that stretched away between sheer walls of snow and ice as tall as a house. It was the entrance to the tunnel, blocked by a Corolla that had sunk to the door handles in the icy wash. Drivers stood all around, barking orders at the Corolla driver. "Help me, my brothers," he cried. "In the name of the Prophet, Peace Be Upon Him, give me a push." The men hollered back, "Push yourself." At last three passengers crawled out the windows of the Corolla, sank to their hips in the icy water, and pushed until the car rose up and disappeared into the tunnel. Marouf gunned the Town Ace and we plunged into the little lake. The water covered our headlights and we sailed on in darkness until the Town Ace rose again, slithering up a ridge of ice, and dropped into the tunnel.

There the road was almost smooth, though pocked with deep craters filled with sand and slush. Fifteen minutes later I caught a flash of stars overhead, shining through a hole in the ceiling—a "Massoud hole," Hasan called it—and then we were out again in the still, cold night. The inside lane of the narrow road ahead was filled with hundreds of trucks headed south, parked now with the engines swathed in tarpaulins for warmth, waiting for morning and their turn at the tunnel. Forced into the outside lane, we crawled downhill in the dark, creeping from one icy switchback to the next. The other drivers, perhaps exhausted by combat or fearful of the drop that lay at the edge of the icy road, fell into something like a line to inch down the mountain.

We stopped at the first *chaikhana,* collapsed on the floor of a little room upstairs, and slept for a few hours. Before dawn we were on the road again with Hasan driving to give Marouf, and all of us, a rest. The mountains pressed upon us in the darkness, their great gray shapes more felt than seen, until at first light they fell away into rolling farmland. Gradually the earth grew dry and stony, and cliffs rose to enclose us again. We wound through a long narrow canyon—Hasan said this pathway through the last mountain had been magically made by the Caliph Ali himself— and then there were caravans of camels in the road and domed houses of red earth and at last the broad Turkistani plains that stretched away in one long, clean line to Mazar-i Sharif.

We women checked into a hotel. Caroline paid Marouf something extra to take Hasan back to Kabul, and they left at once to catch the southern traffic through the tunnel. Two weeks later, when we got back to Kabul, we learned that Marouf had abandoned Hasan halfway up the mountain. He asked Hasan to get out and check the tires, then drove off alone, taking Hasan's blanket with him. Hasan hailed a truck and paid the driver for a ride, but they got stuck overnight in a gallery near the top of the mountain. He bought a few pieces of wood from another driver who was chopping up his truck bed with an ax; he made a little fire, but he couldn't get warm. They finally reached the tunnel only to find that the military commander in charge had closed it indefinitely because of the threat of avalanches. The drivers, in a fury, attacked the commander's soldiers and seized their weapons. They broke down the door of the commander's office and beat him nearly to death. The soldiers produced the frozen bodies of three men who had been caught in the last avalanche, the one that had swept away the tumbled gallery we had seen. The drivers were not impressed. They beat the soldiers. Then they got back in their trucks and drove through the tunnel. The next day Hasan reached his home in Kabul where his wife restored him by massaging his frostbitten feet and legs with salt. That same day a series of avalanches closed the Salang Pass, and it remained closed for a month. Later I asked Hasan if he knew why Marouf had tricked and abandoned him. He shrugged and smiled and said, "It is our custom."

Ignorant of Hasan's homeward journey, Caroline, Helen, and I were stuck in Mazar for a couple of weeks, waiting for a plane. After Caroline finished the business she had come to do, she said,

"Would you like to see some buzkashi? Or did you have enough of it on the drive up here?"

Helen said, "I'd like to see the kind they play with horses." And so we walked out to Dasht-i Shadian to watch men on horseback pull a dead animal to pieces in the course of a cold afternoon.

WHEN WE REACHED THE PLAYING FIELD, THE CALF HAD ALREADY been killed. It lay on the ground, still stretched west, toward Mecca. Its head was gone, and its legs splayed at impossible angles. The hoofs had been hacked away. An old man was inscribing a circle in the dirt around the carcass with the heel of his boot. The wind spiraling out of a gray and sunless winter sky lifted the tail of his faded cloak. Behind him, turbaned men were already gathering in the concrete bleachers, greeting their friends with a hand to the heart and a barrage of salutations. "How are you? How is your health? How is your family? How was your night?" They clutched their brown woolen blankets around them to keep out the winter chill and turned their hatchet faces toward us, swiveling row by row to watch our ascent as we climbed to the top of the stands.

Horsemen materialized in the dusty air. Singly and two by two and ranked like cavalry shaping up for war, they rode out of the distance. They emerged from the dusty streets of the city that lay beyond the far side of the field and from the barren land that fell away on either side. They came on at a walk, so as not to tire the horses, dark figures moving steadily, converging on the field of play; and as they drew near, so that we could distinguish from the stands their turbans, their bright saddle blankets, the tassels tossing on the bridles of the eager horses, the air grew electric as if they rode to us enveloped in the force field of their own excitement. Some began to circle in front of the stands—trotting, jostling one another, racing away and back again. Caroline clapped her hands. She said, "This is the real thing."

I glanced behind us to see a white horse trotting toward the stands. His rider wore a turban of pale silk and a padded winter *chapan*—the long cloak of the northern tribes that live here beyond the Hindu Kush. It was striped in dark colors that had faded with age to a uniform gun metal gray. President Karzai wears a chapan on state occasions, in his trademark bright green and purple stripes, always looking starched and pressed; but Karzai wears it in ceremonial style, draped from his shoulders with the extralong sleeves falling free like the tails of a cutaway. The rider wore his chapan like a coat, with the long sleeves pleating into folds along his arms, and the hem of the garment spread across the rump of the white horse that was well dressed itself in tassels and silver buckles and a bright striped Uzbeki saddle blanket.

The rider goaded the horse with his heels but held him back with hard hands so that the animal had nowhere to go but up. He danced up and down while the rider affected nonchalance.

"He's the *tooi-bashi*," Caroline said. "He's like the master of ceremonies, or something."

"So what does he do?" Helen asked. Helen was a nurse, perpetually organizing things. She liked to know how systems worked.

"Well, what you see. He rides around. He runs things for the *tooi-wala*—the khan who sponsors the games—so the khan can sit back and look important. I suppose it's a ceremonial thing, but somebody always has to be seen to be in charge."

I pulled my camera out of my pocket as the tooi-bashi approached just below us. He saw it at once. He snatched at the reins and kicked the horse sideways to face me. Through the lens I watched the horse brace his neck and open his mouth wide, grappling with the iron-barbed bit. He reared, carrying the rider aloft as pedestrians scrambled to get out of the way. For a moment they hung there in the air, the exotic horseman and the wild-eyed airborne horse framed against the dull expanse of dusty plain and far distant mountains, and then the rider relented and released his grip on the reins. Caroline was thrilled. She'd been a horse rider herself in earlier days and imagined that she was one still. After

I'd volunteered to come to Afghanistan to help with her work, I'd sent her an e-mail to ask about the weather. "What's the winter like in Kabul?" I was packing. I had practical choices to make. "Do I need boots?" The answer, when it finally came, said nothing about the weather or the vexing issues of footgear and the proper weight of a winter coat. It said, "Please bring some good potato peelers and mouse traps for very small mice that are eating the kitchen towels. If you want to ride, bring your own saddle." As the winter wore on, a dozen potato peelers disappeared from the kitchen in the cook's pocket along with a dozen traps for very small mice, while Caroline, lost in nostalgia, spun tales of thrilling horseback rides she'd taken in the fields of Kabul forty years before. Then meadows lay all about and the grass was green and the brimming irrigation jouies just right for jumping. That was before the land was laced with mines, of course. Before the rocket attacks and the bombs. Huddled by the woodstove in the darkened office on winter evenings, sharing a meal of leftover rice and bread, Helen and I would listen to the voice burbling out of the shadows. It came to me then, slowly, that Kabul in winter is a state of mind, a mix of memory and desire that lifts like dust in the wind to hide from view the world as it is.

"Isn't he wonderful?" Caroline said.

The tooi-bashi was performing, kicking his horse around, hauling on the nasty bit until the animal reared again and lurched back to earth. I put my camera in my pocket, and he soon rode on.

"You didn't show him his picture," Helen said.

"He didn't ask. He didn't want to see it," I said, thinking no photo would match the image he must hold in his mind of himself when his chapan was new and bright-striped, and his beard dark and fierce. "He just wanted somebody to be impressed enough to take his picture."

"No," Caroline said. "He wanted everybody to see him having his picture taken. It shows how important he is. When people talk about this match, they'll mention his name."

"And will they mention the photographer?"

Caroline laughed. "Afghans are very creative," she said. "Very poetic. Wonderful storytellers." No one loved Afghans more than Caroline. They could do no wrong. She too would carry in her mind the image of the proud tooi-bashi on his prancing horse, cutting a sharper figure—bigger and more handsome—than he appeared in the digital photograph where I could clearly read the frayed edges of saddle blanket and chapan, the scarred face of the horse, the grizzled look of the old man's beard. You could not be in Afghanistan very long without learning that facts are feeble things. Never mind that you are old and poor, and your horse too is thin and wheezy. Presentation is everything, a display of the dauntlessness that keeps an old man, or a crippled country, going through the darkest times. Make your horse stand on its hind legs and dance, and you may make a name for yourself, a name that may be mentioned when Afghan men gather in the evenings to tell tales.

The tooi-bashi reappeared on his white horse, parading along the edge of the playing field to the center of the stands, to a kind of covered pavilion, carpeted and strewn with cushions. There he turned to salute a fat-bellied, bearded mogul who had just arrived in a white Toyota sedan and taken his place upon the platform's lone easy chair. Lesser dignitaries and followers disposed themselves on the carpets at his feet.

"There's the tooi-wala," Caroline said. Just then he lifted his hand, and at the signal the tooi-bashi goaded the white horse to rear once again and spin to face the playing field. A rank of horsemen disengaged themselves from the pack and rode forward to salute the khan. They were big hard-faced men, dressed in dark tunics and high leather boots and leather skull caps edged in fur, the outfit of professional buzkashi players, the *chapandazan*. Most of them probably were farmers for much of the year, doing the heavy work of farmers, but when the cold weather came on and the crops were gathered and the buzkashi season began again,

a local landowner would send out a message to his fellow khans
who in turn would summon their best riders, and the farmers
would put on their spurs and their leather hats and ride away
to vie for the prizes—silk turban cloths and piles of money—
provided by the generous host. Now, at some invisible signal the
chapandazan ranged themselves close to the circle where the dead
calf lay, while all around them closed a pack of a hundred or more
eager horsemen—the khans for whom the chapandazan rode and
the khans' followers, the *sawarkaran*. The chapandazan drove
their big, strong horses forward, chest to chest, and everything
seemed to stop as horse met horse.

"Can you see what's happening?" Helen said.

"They're trying to get hold of the calf," Caroline said. "See
them jostling?"

"I can't see anything but dust," Helen said.

A horse rose on its hind legs. It lifted its head and chest for a
moment above the struggle. Another horse squealed. Whips rose
in the air and thwacked horses' rumps. The whole pack seemed to
move as one, inching forward and back across the circle where
the carcass lay. I caught sight of one *chapandaz* only to see him
disappear, reaching down, I supposed, among the hoofs of the
struggling horses. Then all at once the mass seemed to loosen and
a few horsemen broke free. They raced down the field, and we
could see the calf dangling by one leg in the grip of a chapandaz
riding a fast black horse. A second chapandaz closed in and
leaned from his saddle to snatch at the carcass. ("Every calf has
four legs," says an old Afghan proverb: there is more than one
way for a canny man to win.) The two riders, with the calf suspended between them, galloped beyond the edge of the field, up
the bank at the far end, and circled back into the mass of horsemen. They broke from the pack again at midfield. The black horse
was still in the lead. The rider leaned far back over the horse's
rump, then threw his body forward and jerked the calf from the
grip of the other chapandaz. He raced toward the stands. Free

and clear now of the pack and even of the rival rider, he dropped the calf in front of the tooi-wala's pavilion and spun his horse away.

"He made it!" Caroline cried.

The victorious chapandaz accepted his prize money from the tooi-bashi. Then he tugged at the saddle girth, snugging it for the next mad dash, and turned the black horse again to the spot where the mangled calf carcass lay. Around him closed the other chapandazan and the great mass of sawarkaran while boys on bony cart horses trotted around the edges, ready to give chase when the calf grabber burst from the pack at a gallop.

"I can't see a thing," Helen said. "It's like trying to watch a stampede."

Caroline laughed. "It's buzkashi," she said.

IT'S KNOWN AS AFGHANISTAN'S NATIONAL SPORT, IF THE KALEIDO-scopic array of clans and tribes can be said to share a "national" pastime.[90] Here, north of the Hindu Kush, where the mountains of central Afghanistan give way to the steppes of Central Asia, generations of nomadic horsemen raced across unbounded plains, barren but for the seasonal stand of grass that fed their animals. Some say these wild riders invented the game of battling on horseback for possession of a carcass, while others say they merely adapted it from the sport of Genghis Khan's Mongol invaders who played a kind of equestrian soccer with a human head. The northern horsemen fought over a goat, the *buz* of buzkashi. The sturdier calf used today holds together better and prolongs the game, and its greater weight—perhaps a hundred pounds—puts a premium on the size and strength of both rider and horse.

Afghan landowners and warlords have long enhanced their popularity and power by sponsoring buzkashi matches, just as the fat tooi-wala in the easy chair was doing now, but in former times the meets might last for many days. The local khan recruited friends and neighbors to help him organize the festivities and host distinguished guests. He issued invitations and arranged feasts. He put up the prize money and appointed an official to oversee play, while he sat back to watch the games, like a general gazing upon the field of battle, in full view of his admiring guests. If the games were a success—that is, if lots of players came and no contingent rode home in a huff—the sponsoring khan would grow in reputation as a worthy leader who knew how to handle things. Riders returning to their distant homes would spread his fame.

So important was buzkashi to the political life of certain regions of Afghanistan that an American Foreign Service officer stationed in Kabul in 1972 chucked his diplomatic career to write an academic dissertation about it. G. Whitney Azoy was attached to the US Embassy when, at a social gathering at the Afghan Foreign Ministry, an Afghan friend revised his life with a single suggestion: "If you want to know what we're really like, go to a buzkashi game."[91] Azoy abandoned his diplomatic desk for American academia and soon returned as a newly minted anthropologist to the fields of play. Research, he called it. I'd come across a copy of his dissertation, published in 1982, on the bookshelves in our office, affectionately inscribed to Caroline, a fellow horse lover. Tucked up in bed, with the quilt pulled up to my chin, I'd read by the light of a kerosene lamp *Buzkashi: Game and Power in Afghanistan,* as had every other foreign journalist trying to make sense of the place, and I thought of it now as I sat in a chill wind on a cold concrete bench among straight-backed, silent men riveted to the rush of horses in the rising dust.

The struggle going on before us was merely the superficial show—a power game of "the first order"—in Azoy's scholarly analysis. Behind the clash of chapandazan lay power games of higher orders where the political fate of khans and even kings and communist dictators might be decided. The winning chapandaz gained fame and more silk turban cloths than he could possibly use, while the successful khan gained more followers, more power over his neighbors and his region. In 1953 it occurred to Mohammed Daoud, then the ambitious prime minister of Afghanistan, that the government headed by his cousin and brother-in-law, King Zahir Shah, could consolidate its power by sponsoring in the capital the symbolic spectacle so popular in the country's northern reaches. To celebrate the king's birthday, the government brought buzkashi south over the mountains to Kabul.

But it was country buzkashi come to town—transformed from wild game to regulated sport. It was played in the eighteen-thousand-seat Ghazi Stadium—where more recently the Taliban conducted public executions—confined by concrete walls. It began at a set time. It proceeded according to newly written rules. Traditional buzkashi required a rider only to carry a carcass free and clear of all other riders to win the round, but the new sport required him to race around a flag on the far side of the field and deposit the carcass within a scoring circle. The sport was dubbed *qarajai* buzkashi, the term *qarajai,* or "black place," suggesting the new spatial limits that traditionalists found very black indeed. Spectators complained that the rules reduced the game to repetitive back and forth, more like tennis than rodeo. The great mass of mounted khans and sawarkaran, who might join by the hundreds in a riotous northern meet, were banned from the playing field. Kabul buzkashi was to be restricted to chapandazan—and worse, the chapandazan were to play in *teams*. In the wild country matches one chapandaz might block another's rival, but such cooperation among competitors was a thing between men, one to another, that had to be earned. It was voluntary and fleeting. A team was something else again that seemed to encumber a man with prescribed allegiances. The Afghan National Olympic Committee selected chapandazan to represent each province and issued them flashy matching uniforms—but the peculiar concept of teamwork never took hold. Why assist another man when you might grab the calf and the prize for yourself?

In 1973 that question apparently struck Mohammed Daoud,

whom the king had eased out of the office of prime minister. While the king was away in Italy, Daoud proclaimed the new Republic of Afghanistan and named himself president, prime minister, foreign minister, and minister of defense as well. Five years later Daoud himself was shot down in the Saur (April) Revolution that installed Noor Mohammed Taraki as head of a communist regime. Taraki's portrait replaced Daoud's in the stadium, and the annual buzkashi tournament was staged as usual in another public demonstration of the power of the state.

Taraki was a lifelong political activist and sometime agent of the KGB. He had founded the communist People's Democratic Party of Afghanistan (PDPA) in 1965—only a few years before the Islamist intellectuals of Kabul University began to organize their contradictory vision of a future Islamic state. But Afghan communists, being Afghans, could not agree among themselves. Early on, they split into two parties: Taraki's hardline Khalq (The People) and the more moderate Parcham (The Banner). They sabotaged each other's coup attempts. Kabulis joked that the difference between them was merely modish: Khalqis sported bushy black mustaches while Parchamis were clean-shaven.[92] Perhaps it was true, for at last they managed to reunite and seize power. Now, subsidized by the Soviets, Taraki was impatient to create the new, thoroughly up-to-date Afghanistan of his dreams, organized along Marxist/Leninist lines. But as Louis Dupree remarked, Marxism in Afghanistan was doomed to be "more Groucho than Karl." The PDPA comrades were mostly intellectuals, educated in the United States, the Soviet Union, Europe, and Egypt, and members of the small Kabuli urban middle class. Their country had no industrial proletariat—85 percent of Afghans were nonliterate peasants and nomads—so they had to impose a "grassroots revolution" upon the masses from the top down, and from the relatively sophisticated capital to the tribal villages of the hinterlands. They turned to the army to get the job done and to enforce upon the peasantry the new "working-class ideology" promulgated by government officials.[93] (In Italy, years later, exiled King Zahir Shah observed that sending young Afghan men to be educated in the Soviet Union had been "a mistake."[94] He might have said the same thing of those who went to Egypt and returned as Islamists.) Resistance began at once and spread across the country. In Herat thousands died in protests against new government policies, especially the revolutionary proposal that a compulsory nationwide literacy education program should include girls and women.

The Soviets were determined that the Afghan experiment in communism should not fail. Quickly they sent in "advisers" to dilute PDPA policies so that citizens might swallow them. But by that time the factions of the PDPA had fallen out again. Taraki's Khalqis used their moment in power to obliterate potential opponents: functionaries of the old regime, political activists, Islamists, mullahs, Maoists, teachers, students, army officers, bureaucrats, disaffected ethnic groups, and the clean-shaven comrades of Parchami persuasion. The reign of terror brought mass arrests, disappearances, betrayals, torture, executions, and a prison for thousands—the notorious Pul-i Charkhi, ringed by mass graves. Whole clans were executed, whole villages massacred.[95] This was political buzkashi played dirty and for keeps.

President Taraki was next. Within a few months his own vice president, Hafizullah Amin, who had organized the violent communist coup that overthrew Daoud, organized the murder of Taraki as well—and many more executions as he speeded up the drive to get to the bottom of the enemies list.[96] PDPA membership was small, never more than 5,000 men, but before the comrades were through they had killed, by their own report, more than 12,000 people imprisoned at Pul-i Charkhi. Later, reports prepared by others put the number executed between the April 1978 revolution and the Soviet invasion of December 1979 at 27,000. Add to that the number of murdered and missing persons in the countryside, and the total number of citizens who "disappeared" under the Khalqi regime climbs to somewhere between 50,000 and

100,000.[97] Despite Amin's murderous efficiency—or perhaps because of it—the Soviets concluded that the American-educated Amin was "working towards a defeat of the revolution and . . . serving reaction and imperialism."[98] They suspected then, as many Afghans do to this day, that he was in the pay of the CIA. By that time, the American national security adviser Zbigniew Brzezinski was also "working towards a defeat of the revolution" by starting a secret program to aid the Afghan counterrevolutionaries, the Islamist mujahidin. His devious plan was to draw the Soviets into an unwinnable war in Afghanistan, to give the Soviets "their Vietnam," and it seems to have worked.[99] On December 27, 1979, three months after Amin came to power, airborne Russian troops stormed Amin's palace and killed him. They took control of Kabul and installed another PDPA puppet president, Babrak Karmal. The next day Russian motorized divisions crossed the Amu Darya river—the Oxus of ancient times—on Afghanistan's northern border to take over the rest of the country.

Buzkashi went on as usual. The 1980 Kabul Buzkashi Championships were staged as a celebration of the Saur Revolution that had first brought the communists to power. The puppet Karmal dressed up for the press like a chapandaz. His vice president gave a resounding speech proclaiming buzkashi "a manifestation of the spirit of the struggle of our people."[100] But all over the country the people struggled against the Soviet invaders. From Dasht-i Shadian in Mazar-i Sharif, the real home of buzkashi—the venue Azoy calls the Yankee Stadium of the game—came word that some fifty Soviet soldiers, invited to attend a meet, had been slaughtered on the site. By 1982 the Kabul tournaments had been canceled and assemblies of men on horseback banned throughout the country. From helicopters, Russian snipers picked off mounted men.

If Zbigniew Brzezinski is to be believed, America can take credit not only for secretly stoking a ten-year-long war in somebody else's country but for starting it in the first place.[101] Stansfield

Turner, CIA director at the time, reportedly worried that the US intended to "fight to the last dead Afghan," and he questioned whether it is right to "use other people's lives for the geopolitical interests of the United States."[102] But cold warrior Brzezinski seems to have been free of such qualms, and Turner too went along with the program. And then, once the Soviet invaders were gone, the US, like some fat tooi-wala, stood the mujahidin to a few more rounds of play. By the time the Americans opted out of the game and quit Afghanistan in 1992, nearly two million Afghans had been killed, according to the UN, and another 600,000 to two million maimed. More than six million Afghans had fled to Pakistan and Iran to become the world's largest population of refugees of a single nationality. Another two million Afghans had become internal refugees, in flight within their own country. And at least a million and a half had been driven insane by ceaseless war. Considering that there had been only about sixteen million Afghans to begin with, at the time of the Soviet invasion in 1979, the UN figures meant that in the midst of the brother wars half the people of Afghanistan had already been killed or wounded, or driven from their homes or out of their minds. And still the battles went on.

ON THE WAY BACK FROM THE STADIUM, A MAN OFFERED US A LIFT to our hotel. He said he had graduated from Education University in Kabul and become a teacher in Mazar; but when the Taliban came and burned the schools and killed many of the teachers, he fled with his family to Pakistan. He'd returned to start a construction business, rebuilding schools, apparently at a profit. He drove a big sedan. (The source of capital was always a mystery.) "We need the international forces to take charge," he said. "We need them to keep us in order until we can disarm the country. We must disarm the country, but sadly we can not do it." He paused for a moment, reflecting upon this conundrum, and then he went on to explain. "We all killed people, you see." He said it matter-of-factly. "Someone's father, sister, daughter, brother. So we are all subject to revenge. We can not put down our arms because we are all guilty. I am a Tajik, not a Pashtun, but this is a problem for us all. It is our code. What can we do?"

I thought of the half-dozen young, scared American soldiers who had wandered into our buzkashi game. Wearing flak jackets and full combat gear, they had walked into the tooi-wala's pavilion carrying their automatic weapons at the ready. The Afghan men around us sat perfectly still, but they watched as the soldiers exchanged some words with the tooi-wala and his men. Then three of the soldiers handed off their guns and strolled onto the field. At a sign from the tooi-wala, three Afghans dismounted and led their horses to the soldiers. One soldier struggled to mount, with the help of an Afghan, while the horse spun in circles. He was barely in the saddle when the horse took off at a gallop. An Afghan gave chase on horseback, grabbed the reins, pulled the runaway to a stop, and helped the soldier get down. A second soldier was carried off in another direction and dumped in the dirt. The third soldier thought better of the whole thing, turned the horse he'd been offered back to the Afghan owner, and strode to the pavilion to pick up his gun.

"Oh dear," Caroline said. "I'm afraid they've made a very bad impression."

Helen defended them. "Look what good sports they are," she said. The first two soldiers had made their way back to the pavilion, swaggering in their funny-looking too-tight uniforms, and now they were laughing, too hard, with the khan's men.

"They're such youngsters," Caroline said. "I don't think they knew what they were getting into."

Later we saw them again in the marketplace, stationed in a wide semicircle among the shops and stands, and they did indeed look like youngsters, aiming their guns at a crowd of Mazari women clad in white burqas who stood together in silence like a gathering of ghosts. The soldiers had established a perimeter in the heart of the bazaar around a store where their lieutenant was shopping for carpets. They were in charge.

BACK IN KABUL, WHERE EVERYONE WAS TALKING OF BUSH'S THREAT to invade Iraq, we persuaded Caroline to rent a television set so we could watch international news. She went off with Hasan and returned with a portable set and a satellite dish. We installed the TV in the big unused sun parlor on the second floor above the office. It was a high-ceilinged room, lined on two sides with tall windows to take advantage of the winter sun. A *gulkhana,* the Afghans call it. A flower room. It was meant to be our office, but since the Kabuli smog so often dimmed the sun, the room was rarely warm enough for work. So we all worked downstairs, near the woodstove, while this room stood empty. It was my favorite place. It looked to the west, over the low rooftops of Share Nau and an old citadel just beyond, to the distant mountains of the Paghman range. I'd often come here at sunrise to watch the snowy slopes turn the color of flamingoes and then pale again to pearly white. In the late afternoon I'd come here to read, wrapped in a woolen pattu, curled in one of the big red easy chairs, glancing up now and again at the darkening mountains until the light grew dim and I closed my book and lost myself in watching them slowly slip away into the night.

Then it would be nearly time for the news, and Helen would join me. We'd fire up the generator on the balcony just outside—we rarely had city electricity—and turn on the set. We watched the BBC World Service and EuroNews and Al Jazeera and Al Arabia and Deutsche Welle and the English-language broadcasts of Iranian television and whatever else we could get. Hungry for news, we became skilled channel surfers, swooping between highlights here and there, catching the wave that seemed to be rolling, on every channel, in every language, toward certain disaster. From another quarter we heard the voice of the mullah, amplified and projected into the street below from the big mosque on the corner, condemning (according to a neighbor's translation) the infidel warmongers, the bloodthirsty crusading Christian devils, the Great Satan Bush.

One evening we chanced upon Fox News and the official American spin: Afghanistan, now at peace, had been rebuilt. For hours we cursed and swore at the TV set, but for once we couldn't change the channel. Fox News told us that America had bombed Afghanistan to save the people from the evil Taliban regime and that the Taliban had been totally defeated.[103] But at that point, in February 2003, Taliban were still fighting near Kandahar and in the east around Jalalabad. And to repel the American enemy, they had long since teamed up with al-Qaeda and—would he never go away?—Gulbuddin Hekmatyar. (When I left the country in 2005, they were fighting still.) The Taliban had been, after all, a power-ful movement that swept through the country and wiped out or co-opted almost all the mujahidin commanders the US had been so crazy about. Neither demonizing the "regime" nor changing it could make the Taliban evanesce. Many Talibs had shaved their beards and changed the color of their turbans and melted into the population. Some were still in the government. A lot of Taliban propaganda had seeped into the minds of men and stuck. Fox News also told us that Afghan women had been liberated, that they had thrown off their burqas and gone back to school. Yet the chief justice of the Supreme Court—one of those Taliban types still in the government—had just publicly condemned equal educa-tion as "evil." In Herat the warlord/governor Ismail Khan had forbidden men to teach girls, and the girls' schools had closed. In Jalalabad, bombs had demolished two girls' schools in the pre-vious week, and a woman teacher had been murdered. Caroline still maintained the neighborhood schools for girls she'd started in the Taliban time because parents felt it wasn't safe to let their girls walk to public schools. Every week brought news of girls abducted from Kabul streets. Only the day before, in broad daylight, Hasan had seen two Afghan soldiers drag a flailing burqa into a car.

As for the peace that America had brought to Afghanistan, the American Embassy in Kabul was a forbidding fortress, hidden behind walls of concrete and sandbags, bristling with razor wire and armed guards waiting for attack. (That was before the US started building its new billion-dollar fortress embassy, largely underground.) And everywhere in Kabul the streets were full of armed men: Afghan soldiers, American soldiers, ISAF soldiers— Germans, Brits, Dutch, Turks—of the international security force. The ISAF troops moved through the streets fast in convoys of armored vehicles; helmeted soldiers manned the gun turrets. Sometimes they accidentally ran people down. Then there were the unknown men, many in odd uniforms—gray, green, blue, brown—and many in plain black clothes and shades. Who were they? Who did they answer to? Who knew? Months before, the Karzai government had vowed to disarm the private militias of warlords all over Afghanistan. That included the militias of General Dostum, the Uzbek leader in the north, and his Tajik rival Atta Mohammed; but only the week before a Dostum man had gunned down the wife and daughter of one of Atta's right-hand men. The two "disarming" sides had found enough weapons to go to war again, and who would stop them? Both Dostum and Atta were members of the Karzai cabinet. This is the same Dostum who fought by the side of Massoud in 1992 to save Kabul from Gulbuddin Hekmatyar, and then in 1994 teamed up with Gulbuddin against Massoud and the Rabbani government to shell the ruined city one more time. Over the years he'd fought beside and against nearly everybody else, and in the end they'd all been defeated and run out of the country by the victorious Taliban to the applause of many Afghans who'd had enough of mujahidin anarchy, atrocity, and exile. But the US, getting things wrong again, had rehabilitated the discredited commanders by inviting them to a conference in Bonn in December 2001 to reconstitute themselves as the new

Afghan regime. (In March 2005, President Karzai—the same President Karzai who had vowed repeatedly to disarm the warlords—would name Dostum chief of staff of the army; and US ambassador Khalilzad would commend the choice.) The presence of men like Dostum in the cabinet—men who might just as well be tried for war crimes—was a peculiar feature of the Afghan peace.

Afghanistan, we learned from the TV, had been "rebuilt" thanks to millions of dollars of international aid pouring into the country. Where was it? That was the question we'd heard asked of American ambassador Finn only weeks before. At a big meeting of international aid agencies at the Ministry of Foreign Affairs, the Afghan head of an Afghan NGO had stood up and barked his rude, ungrateful question at the ambassador who was even then going on about all that American aid was doing for Afghanistan. "Where is it?" the Afghan said. "We have not seen it." The room went quiet with embarrassment. All the internationals present knew how aid works: that most of it goes to support the experts and contractors and bureaucrats of the "donor" nations, providing cover (and more tax dodges) for the rich in the guise of helping the poor. Ambassador Finn explained to the impatient Afghan that the "lion's share" had been spent on necessary "start-up costs" such as renting and refurbishing "appropriate work facilities"—all those nice big houses—and equipping them for "appropriate standards" of international living and work. Perhaps next year, he said, the benefits of aid would "trickle down" to ordinary Afghans. (Two and a half years later a candidate for the Afghan parliament would run on the slogan, "Where did the money go?") But at the time there was an unofficial freeze on humanitarian activities in Kabul; no one knew whether funds appropriated to rebuild Afghanistan would actually be delivered, or whether programs once started could be finished. International aid, such as it was, was on hold or drying up—diverted to the looming war in Iraq.

Fox News went on describing a mission accomplished in a place they called Afghanistan, a country utterly unlike the one in which we lived. One night, as we sat in the dark to save generator power for the TV set, we heard some no-name right-wing think-tank prowar neocon talking head explain that America could speedily repair any incidental damage to Iraq's infrastructure, just as it had done in Afghanistan. Security, water, electricity—all those things Kabulis had learned to live without—he said had been restored in Kabul "in no time." Even in the dim glow of the TV, I could see that Helen was weeping. "Please can we go back to the BBC?" she said, and we never watched Fox News again.

We had no way then of knowing that for almost a year the White House had been snatching from Afghanistan the US spies and special forces once aimed at al-Qaeda and secretly mustering them for the crusade against Iraq. The number of Americans on the ground was never large—little more than a hundred CIA agents and three hundred special forces personnel—but by then the CIA was gone from Herat and Mazar-i Sharif and Kandahar; and the manpower of Task Force 5, the covert commandos supposedly hunting for Osama bin Laden along the Pakistani border, had been cut to the bone.[104] But at night we heard the planes. The deep drone of the big cargo carriers rattled the windows and woke us from sleep, and then we heard the whoosh of fighter jets, high up. There seemed to be more now, every night, just before dawn. Before long, I would be sitting in front of the television in the dark, wrapped in my pattu, watching bombs drop on Baghdad.

THE MORNING AFTER THE BOMBS BEGAN TO FALL I WENT DOWN TO the street as usual and found Sharif sitting in his car at the curb. How could I say "*Salaam aleikum*"—Peace be with you—when my country had just started a war? I said instead, "*Chittur asti?*"— How are you?—and climbed into the front seat. He didn't answer. He didn't return my greeting. This in a language and a country where ritual greetings are a prolonged ceremony as essential to life as air. The shock of Sharif's silence took my breath away. He threw the car in gear and we bumped down the street past the mosque where the loudspeaker was blaring another message from the mullah, though prayer time was long past. "This day is different," I thought, though the pale sun soaking the dusty morning air seemed to cast the same thin gray light as yesterday and the day before. Sharif pointedly turned on the radio news in Dari and cranked the sound way up.

I looked at him more closely, this man with whom I'd shared the morning drive each day for months. He'd done well for himself. But I knew the price he'd paid. Sharif had told me the story, and one day Caroline had taken me to visit the site of his family's farm near Paghman, the cool hillside village where once King Amanullah had built his summer palace and picnicked with the Kabul elite. We had walked to the end of the village and climbed the low rise in the foothills, just under the mountains of the Paghman range, where the old family farmhouse had stood. It was a beautiful site, watered by flowing jouies, sheltered by the mountain, warmed even in winter by the eastern sun. There one day during the Soviet occupation, Sharif's father was blown up by a mine planted next to a mulberry tree in the orchard behind the house. The Soviets knew that Afghan farmers liked to squat next to a tree to relieve themselves, and that's where they put the mines. Later, when the Soviets had agreed to leave the country, they rolled the tanks through Paghman village one last time and shelled the abandoned villas of Kabul's upper class just for spite. Part of the little farmhouse was blown away. And later still, when the Soviets were gone and the Afghans were fighting among themselves, a solitary rocket came whistling out of the bright sky one sunny winter's day and fell into the garden at the back of the house where Sharif's older brother stood talking to their grandfather while a little girl, a neighbor, sat on the garden wall and chatted to the family's milk cow. After the blast Sharif's grandfather was disoriented and dazed. The cow and the girl and Sharif's older brother were dead. When he told me this story, Sharif said: "Then I must leave school. I must be grandfather and father and old brother." He was about fourteen at the time, and he'd taken care ever since of what was left of his family.

He'd come to Kabul to work for Caroline, who'd known the family from the old days, before the Soviets, when she'd been part of the expat elite who summered in the hills of Paghman. During the Taliban time, the police had arrested Sharif fifteen times because he worked for the infidel American woman. Each time he paid them money to be released, and each time the price went up. He gave them fifteen thousand Afghanis—all that he had. The next time Caroline put up two thousand dollars to free him. But they arrested him again and held him for twenty days. They accused him of being a Christian. To make him confess they beat his feet with steel cables and broke the bones. His feet still hurt, he said. He wore big, wide shoes. But all this time he'd looked after his little brother, Kabir, supporting him in school, taking him to English lessons, keeping close watch on him, prodding him to do the things Sharif might have done himself if things had been different.

I reached over and turned down the radio. "You're very angry this morning, Sharif," I said. "It's about the bombing, isn't it?"

He was silent for a long time, chewing the ends of his mustache. Then he said, "You bomb Afghanistan. Many people killed. But we also happy Taliban go away. You say you help us. Now you bomb Iraq. Go get oil. Next maybe Iran? Syria? Will you bomb our brothers everywhere?"

"I don't know," I said.

"Already you forget Afghanistan," he said. "Just like before. Russians go. Americans go. What you care about Afghanistan? Nothing. Let them fight. Let them kill each other. You can watch. Like chicken fight in Babur's Garden." Sharif pushed a tape into the deck and a high, keening voice filled the silence with unutterable grief. It was a familiar Shi'a lament about the slaying of the Caliph Ali's son Husain and infant grandson on the plain of Kerbala sung by a woman whose voice seemed to groan with pain. He had played it before one cold, rainy day when he'd driven me to the Panjshir Valley to see the place where Massoud lay dead. It was the saddest music I have ever heard.

"You Americans," Sharif said. "You are children. You think of today only. What about years to come? What about promises you made in year last?"

So there it was. He had believed in the American promise—that this time we would not abandon his country, and we had betrayed him. We promised aid that most did not see. We promised reconstruction that didn't happen. We promised a new democratic government and installed the same old warlords. We promised peace that didn't come. We promised loyalty that lasted no longer than General Dostum's alliances. Yet Sharif would have been loyal to America, and to President Karzai, if we had given him the chance.

"I'm very sorry, Sharif," I said. "I'm angry too." The music soared around us, bringing tears to my eyes. "Please don't be angry with me, Sharif. This man Bush who does this, he is not my president."

Sharif had stopped the car, trapped by traffic behind the Italian hospital. He turned to me, wordlessly, a face full of sorrow and disdain, and I knew that he saw me plainly for what I was: another American who would not take responsibility for what my country did to the world. I saw him too: another very old young Afghan man, standing alone, on ruined feet, in a wintry garden where who knows what might fall out of the sky.

PART II

IN THE PRISONS

A wooden door sheathed in steel, anchored to the stone wall by iron chains. A padlock as big as my fist. "There's no doorbell," Beck says. She pounds on the steel plate. The chains rattle. Thudding blows echo from the dark innards of the women's prison. We wait. The long, low prison building lies at the back of a walled compound housing the provincial administration: the Welayat. The compound is crammed with shabby office blocks: the governor's office, the court, the men's detention center, the headquarters of state prosecutors and investigators. It takes up two or three square blocks near the center of Kabul, yet it is inconspicuous; almost every building in Kabul crouches behind anonymous walls. I'd passed it many times, vaguely wondering what it was, before I drove through the gate that cold January morning with Beck and her Afghan colleague Marzia. The guards had waved us in and the car had slipped along the icy drive to the back of the grounds. Narrow planks led over a ditch strewn with trash to the entrance of the women's section. Beck grasped the iron chain and beat upon the door.

This was my first visit to the women's prison with Rebecca

Bradshaw, the director of operations in Afghanistan for Frauen die Helfen, a German NGO. Beck was British and young, but she'd worked for years in Croatia and Kosovo and then moved on to open the office in Kabul in February 2002. Over the years Frauen die Helfen had developed a macabre and necessary specialty: assisting traumatized women in postconflict situations. That is, women afflicted by the violence of physical, sexual, or mental assault in the midst of the violence of war, victims of violence compounded exponentially. FDH psychologists and doctors were especially skilled at sorting the dark strands of multiple traumata and helping women reweave something like a life. But how is that to be accomplished in the aftermath of war that lasted nearly a quarter century, in a country where women and girls are by custom routinely confined, raped, beaten, sold, and murdered? Drowning in such violence is a kind of dying, fast or slow—depression, anxiety, suicide, violence and more violence visited upon the self. Physicians for Human Rights tried to assess the damage and reported that in 2001 "more than 70 per cent of Afghan women suffered from major depression, nearly two-thirds were suicidal, and 16 per cent had already attempted suicide."[1] But what exactly troubles this woman with wracking pains, that one with numbness and lethargy? Why does this one scream so much and that one tear out her hair? What makes this one run away from home, and that one set herself on fire? How can they be helped? In Afghanistan there was no end of such women, and some of them were here in this prison.

"They're always in the guards' room," Marzia said. "They never can hear." She put her face to a large hole in the door and called out in Dari, "Hello. Hello. Are you there?" She laid her fist against the door.

A cold wind lifted papers from the ditch behind us and pasted them against our legs. It rattled the dead limbs of trees that stretched away in a row along the shell-pocked face of the prison and enveloped us in a little localized cloud of dust, as if we had been singled out for attack. Marzia drew one end of her scarf over her face, and using the other end to wrap her fist, she thundered on the door. At last I heard the sound of slippers shuffling on stone, and a sharp face appeared in the hole in the door. The woman stared at me, then shifted her gaze to Beck and to Beck's hand that held a large duffel bag.

"Oh, it's you. What did you bring us?"

She thrust a brown woolen sleeve through the hole and inserted a key in the padlock. The door swung open. Before us a corridor plunged into darkness. I held my breath and stepped inside. The guard secured the padlock again and led us down the cold stone hallway that smelled of mildew and damp. I stumbled on the uneven floor and stepped into unseen puddles. Afghanistan follows the Islamic calendar that counts the days from the Prophet's flight to Medina, so that in Afghanistan at that time the year was 1380. Until that moment the different calendar had seemed to me a cultural curiosity, like an alternative system of bookkeeping, but in the Welayat the fourteenth century became real.

The corridor opened into a courtyard where a circular hut squatted amid mounds of rubble and trash. Worn shirts hung from a clothesline, frozen stiff. Three prison wings enclosed the yard, but the rooms in the wing to the right lay open and useless, and the wing on the far side was falling in upon itself. We turned toward the front wing of the building, the only section that seemed to be in use. The guard drew back a blanket covering a doorway and we stooped to slip inside. Two iron bedsteads covered in army blankets stood against opposite walls. On pegs near the door hung a row of blue burqas—the guards' I guessed. Even a prison guard might not feel safe without a burqa in the streets of Kabul. I sat down on one of the beds, as Beck and Marzia had done, and as my eyes grew accustomed to the dim light I saw that a tea kettle was simmering on a propane burner in one corner of the room. Next to it, under the windows, were what appeared to be bundles of rags or laundry piled on the floor. Then I saw that each bundle was a woman wrapped in a shawl and huddled against the wall with her knees drawn up under her chin. Each bundle was a prisoner.

All the while Marzia had been chatting amiably with the guard, and now she turned the full beam of her warmth and confidence on the prisoners. She greeted each one by name, and picked up the scattered details of their lives. "How is your baby, Zara?" she asked, crossing the room to kneel on the floor, peel back the edge of a blanket, and peer at a knotted face. "Are you giving her the medicine? Does she sleep? And you, Merhu, have you seen the doctor? Fariba, did your mother come to visit you?" The women timidly mumbled their replies, as if they were afraid to get the answers wrong. The baby seems a little better, thank you. The doctor has not come. Nor the mother. Thank you very much.

"It is hard for your mother to come so far," Marzia said, "and then to have to stand in the cold." Family members weren't permitted to enter the prison but had to wait outside and speak with the prisoner through the hole in the outer door. "She will come when she can. I'll see about the doctor. Do you still have the pain?"

Marzia was little more than a girl herself—a student who'd learned English as a refugee in Pakistan and joined FDH as a translator—but she went on gathering information and meting out comfort like a kindly aunt, efficient and concerned. Then she turned to Beck to report what she'd learned and to translate Beck's questions to the guard. Had anyone actually summoned the doctor from the men's prison? (The women's prison had no doctor of its own, no nurse, no infirmary, no medicines.) Should FDH send a car to take Merhu to the women's hospital? Would tomorrow be all right?

The blanket in the doorway was lifted time and again as other guards and other prisoners slipped into the room. The guards greeted Beck and seated themselves on the beds. The prisoners slumped to the floor at their feet. There were more greetings, more questions, more arrangements, but all eyes focused on the duffel bags that Beck and Marzia had brought. At last it was time to open them. Bars of soap and bags of raisins were handed around, one gift for each woman. The raisins vanished first. Then woolen sweaters appeared, bought in the second-hand bazaar but freshly washed, and Beck quickly snapped up the best ones and presented them politely to the guards. "They'll take the best stuff anyway," she muttered, "so we might as well give it to them in the first place."

"Are they so mean?"

"No, they're so poor. They make less than twenty dollars a month. Often they don't get paid at all. Then journalists and NGO people like us waltz in with gifts for the prisoners. How would you feel?"

The prisoners sidled out with their booty, and the guards hit Beck up for cigarettes. They sat on the beds smoking and fingering their new sweaters. Quickly the little room filled with smoke. Beck told them I'd come back soon to interview some of the prisoners. "You know we're writing a report for our donors about the Welayat," she said, "and Ann is going to help us. So please let her in when she comes." Marzia translated the request and a guard's quick comeback: "Does she smoke?" Beck handed over the rest of her pack of cigarettes. "For later," she said, as we got up to leave. In the hallway she asked to have a look at the prisoners' rooms, and the guard led us farther along the dark corridor, pulling back a blanket at each doorway to reveal another small bare room—six in all—crowded with iron bedsteads upon which women sat cross-legged, hugging their new sweaters. The rooms were cold, with the damp penetrating chill of old stone, and lit only by the afternoon sun slanting through dirty windows. It fell upon a row of little plastic bags hanging on the wall, each one holding all that a single prisoner possessed at that moment in the world.

"We first came to check on the prisoners' legal rights," Beck said, "but as you see, their needs are more basic. We gave them heaters right off, but the guards sold them. Anything portable seems to walk right out the door, I'm afraid."

"The blankets too," Marzia said. "The guards said the prisoners sent them home to their families. As if they had families worth sending gifts to."

"Have we seen enough?" Beck asked.

Then we were back in the car, passing through the gate, pulling out into Kabul traffic—free women going freely where we wanted to go. My feelings must have been written on my face. Beck said, "I thought you were used to visiting women's prisons."

"I am. But I've never been in a prison like this." I'd spent a lot of time in women's prisons in the United States, interviewing the inmates—battered women, mostly—jailed for murder. I'd told their stories in a book. That was twenty-five years ago, a long, long time in a country incessantly modernizing itself. At the time, each of those American prisons was grim and terrible in its own way, as all prisons are, but even then every one of them was equipped with running water, central heating, electricity, lights, toilets, hot showers, hot meals, medical care, rehab programs, extension classes, TV, radios, bedding, cigarettes, shampoo, legal aid, library books, telephones, chaplains, counselors, playing cards, hair-dryers, Coke, candy bars. Every woman had a cell—a harsh and lonely room, but her own. The worst moment, always, was walking out the door, hearing it clang shut behind me, knowing that I had just exercised a privilege the women I'd left behind, on the inside, might not know again. I left them, on the inside, to their private anguish. But this was worse. These women, huddled on cheap, filthy beds, some clutching swaddled babies as small and silent as loaves of bread, crowded together in dank, freezing rooms like steerage passengers in the hold of some dismal ship, adrift. This was misery.

"It's good you're going back to talk to them," Beck said. I was staring out the car window at the blurred swirl of traffic: a line of

SUVs, the windows darkened with self-importance, going somewhere fast.

"Yes. I suppose it is."

THE WOMEN IN THE WOMEN'S PRISON WERE NOT MURDERERS. NOT
many of them anyway. Most of them weren't even criminals, not
by any standards you would recognize today in the West. Most of
them were girls and women charged with committing offenses
against public morality. Many were charged with *zina*, a term
that indiscriminately covers extramarital sex, both consensual and
coerced. Some were charged with entering into "illegal" marriage.
Some were charged with elopement, or running away from home.
One had been picked up by the police and brought to jail because
she was lost.

There were only sixteen women in the prison at the time—not
many in a city of two million people. The guards said there were
rarely more than thirty-five. Was this the best Kabul could do for
criminals? After so many years of warfare and destitution, of desperate times when people take desperate steps, surely more women
must have sought survival outside the law. Where were they? Kabul
had many district police stations, each with its own lockup, and
there were roadblocks everywhere manned by soldiers or gunmen
in ambiguous uniforms, and private houses nearby into which the
apprehended might quietly disappear. The police said they never
detained women in the districts but always delivered them to the
central prison. The soldiers and the gunmen said nothing at all.
Yet women and children disappeared every day. Only recently
two adolescent boys in separate but nearly identical cases had
been sentenced to long terms of imprisonment for murder. Each
had been seized at a roadblock and held in a private jail where he
was abused and used sexually by the policeman who had snatched
him. Each of the boys in time had turned on his abuser and killed

him. It was a serious crime to kill a policeman—never mind the
reason—and the boys were locked away in the men's cellblock
just across the yard. Once in a while a woman who was brought
to the women's prison said that she too had been seized and held
by unknown men in such a private jail, or in a district police
office. The police denied it. Where was her proof? No one
believed her. Everyone knows how women lie.

Yet even if you added some hypothetical numbers of women
possibly held illegally by police or freelance gunmen, the total
count of women in detention was not very large. You had to wonder how many other women suspected of zina or elopement or
illegal marriage or other offenses to moral standards were simply
judged and punished at home, by their families. In Kabul Welayat,
thirteen of the sixteen inmates held at the time were charged with
crimes of zina. A year later, in 2004, an international agency investigated the women's prison in more conservative Herat and found
that 78 percent of the women detained there were charged with
zina. But in Jalalabad, in Pashtun country not far from the Pakistan border, there were no women imprisoned for zina at all.
Officials explained to an investigator that such "problems" were
handled "in the family." This was the inescapable burden of Afghan
girls and women: the family honor. Under the terms of "tradition" and of "Islamic" practices that "protect" them, girls and
women had come to bear responsibility for the moral life and
reputation of the families that owned them. This is not a new
trick; in the West, Victorians boosted women to a pedestal that
required moral "purity." But the Afghan code is narrower, and more
rigidly enforced. The "fallen" Victorian woman lost her reputation.
The fallen Afghan woman loses her life in an "honor killing" unof-
ficially condoned to preserve the morality of women. No one knows
how many girls and women, said to have brought shame upon the
family, are killed by their fathers and brothers. How many are
driven to suicide. How many are locked away. How many are "disappeared."

ALL DURING THE MONTHS OF JANUARY AND FEBRUARY IN 2003, I went often to the prison to visit the women incarcerated there. I went with an Afghan schoolteacher named Zulal who translated one story after another until the patterns of Afghan justice for women began to come clear.

We talked first to a woman who would later be listed in Frauen die Helfen's official report, for the sake of her privacy, only as C. She was charged with both zina and elopement. She and I settled ourselves opposite each other with Zulal at my side, sitting cross-legged under the windows in the guards' room. It was the only reasonably warm room in the prison, or at least it felt so to Zulal and me if we kept our coats and scarves on. The chief guard hustled everyone else from the room and seated herself on a bed near the propane cooker to listen to our conversation. C told us she thought she was about nineteen years old. (Few Afghans keep birth records, so most can only estimate their age.) Four years earlier, she said, when she was about fifteen, her family had married her off. Now, remembering, she knotted her fingers together and stared at the floor, and I watched her thin face darken as she spilled out her story to Zulal. Her husband's house was "not good." Her husband's mother was a "bad lady" who committed "adultery" many, many times at his command. He told C that she must do the same. (Zulal turned to me, her face a mask to hide rising emotion. "I think it is not adultery," she said. "She has no word for it, but I think in English it is 'prostitution.' Her husband got money.") C said that eventually she escaped from her husband and went back to her father's house; but her husband sent his brother to fetch her back, and the village elders declared that she must go. She couldn't say how long she remained there, locked in her husband's not-good house, doing as her husband commanded—the inability to account for elapsed time is part of the malaise of war and sexual violence—but at last she escaped again and somehow made her way to Pakistan. There she found work as a house servant, but she missed her family, and after some time she returned again to her father's house. The family was no longer there. She went to the police to ask after them, and the police arrested her and brought her to prison. Here she had been detained for many days, and here she would remain indefinitely while the official state investigators looked into her case.

Then we talked to D. (She's D in the official report that Beck wrote, but let me give her a name, a false one to protect her, but a real name to match the real face I still see these two years later. Dustana then. It means "friend.") Dustana said she was about twenty, though her sallow skin and sunken cheeks made her look older. She had been in prison for six months. She too had been married off, but only a few months after the wedding, her husband's brother came to her house and ordered her to leave it because her husband had divorced her. The brother showed her an official-looking paper, but being illiterate, she couldn't read it. She asked to talk with her husband, but the brother said she could not. Instead he delivered her to the house of her aunt. There, after some time, the aunt introduced her to a man from Bamiyan and said that she must marry him. She did as she was told, but the marriage was a fake, and the next day the new "husband" disappeared. The brother of the original husband, having come into a little money, also disappeared. (Zulal turned to me: "Is this not also in English 'prostitution'?") Then, to Dustana's surprise, her husband showed up. He brought the police and insisted they arrest Dustana on charges of adultery and bigamy. After investigators reported their findings to the prosecutor, she was brought to court, convicted of "illegal marriage," and sentenced to five years in prison. Dustana was still bewildered by what had happened to her. She had come to believe that she'd been tricked by her husband's brother. But what part her aunt or her husband might have played in the scheme she could not make out.

Then there was N—Najela—who could not even guess at her age. She said she had been very happy when her family arranged her marriage to a cousin because secretly she loved him. For three months or so after the wedding, she enjoyed a happy marriage. Then her husband began to bring home "foreign" men and force her to "commit adultery" with them. When she could bear it no longer, she went to the police and accused her husband of forcing her into prostitution. Both Najela and her husband were taken to prison. When the investigators finished their work, the prosecutor agreed with Najela that her husband was a "very bad and immoral" man. The judge sentenced him to five years in prison. But the prosecutor noted that Najela had "worked" for her husband "for a long time" and that she had failed to complain "immediately" to the police, who at the time were Taliban. So she was judged guilty of prostitution and sentenced to three years.

E—Ejar—gave her age as "about twenty-two." She said she'd been married young to a man who often beat her; and one winter night he threw her out into the street. Seeking the protection of a male relative, she took refuge for the night in her uncle's house; but her husband went to the police and charged that she and her uncle had committed adultery. She was convicted of zina and sentenced to six years. She had already been in prison for nine months, but because no one in her family ever came to see her, she didn't know what had become of her uncle.

J—Jamila—said she was between twenty-two and twenty-five years old. As we talked she held to her breast her baby girl, born in the prison where she'd been locked up for eight months. She said she'd been married for a while, but one day her husband told her three times that he divorced her, and that according to Islam, she must leave his house at once. (In fact, the divorce procedure described in the Quran requires the husband to state his intention to divorce his wife in the presence of two witnesses and to repeat this witnessed declaration two more times at monthly intervals; during these months the husband is required to maintain his wife in his home as his wife in all but conjugal relations. But Jamila believed what her husband told her: that his condensed, expedient version of divorce was "Islamic.") Jamila declined to talk about where she went or what she did after she left her husband's house, but some time later she willingly married another man with whom she was quite happy. When her first husband learned of her marriage, he went to the police and charged her with bigamy. She was arrested for "illegal marriage." Her first husband swore he had never divorced her, and as there were no witnesses to prove otherwise, she was convicted and sentenced to eight years for elopement and zina.

L—Latifa—told us the same story. She had been sentenced to five years for the same crimes. She too had a baby. She was eighteen years old.

ZULAL AND I SAT THERE DAY AFTER DAY ON THE LUMPY TUSHAKS on the floor of the guards' room as the light failed and the gaunt face of the prisoner before us receded into darkness. Then it was time to say our thank yous and goodbyes. We were always careful to explain at the beginning of each interview that we could do nothing to assist the prisoner with her case, that telling us her story would bring her no benefit at all, but that it might help other women in other times—this was our hope—if what we learned persuaded lawmakers and courts and police to change the way they did things. Still the prisoner always clung to our hands as we said goodbye. Hanging on. At these moments Zulal always looked stricken.

When I'd first proposed that she accompany me to the prison as my translator, she'd been shocked at the impropriety of it. She'd been given a proper Islamic upbringing, and an Afghan's regard for upright behavior.

"Why will you talk with such women? They are very bad."

"What makes you think they're bad? Do you think they were born 'bad'?"

"They are in prison!"

"But why? How did they come to be there? What if they don't belong there? What if they are not 'bad' at all? What if they are just like you and me?"

"That cannot be. I don't think so."

In the end I persuaded her with sophistry: that only by talking to bad women could we help the law learn to treat them correctly and thus protect the good. Zulal, with greater difficulty, persuaded her parents that my work was quite proper and that she should be allowed to help me. (As an unmarried woman, even at age thirty, she could do nothing without the approval of her father and brothers.) In the beginning, with C, the first prisoner we interviewed, she'd been diffident and formal. She'd translated my questions with a stiff professionalism, but she'd leaned closer to catch C's quiet answers, and then, in the middle of the story she had turned to me with the independent judgment that must have surprised even herself: "*I think it is not adultery.*" After that, day by day, she softened and I knew she had begun to see in these women the likeness of women she knew, the shadow of her friends, her sisters, herself, so that now, at leave-taking, when a woman clung to her hands, Zulal would embrace her gently and say, "May I go now?" It is an Afghan politeness, a propriety. "May I have your permission? Please, forgive me. May I go?"

AFTER SUCH STORIES IT WAS NO GOOD TALKING OF WOMEN'S rights. In the West we like to think that human rights accrue to the individual by virtue of being human. But in Afghan society the individual counts for little, and woman amounts to less than that. It's the collective society that matters—the Islamic *umma* (the community of believers) or the tribe or, more intimately, the family.

The women of the Welayat were accused of having disrupted society by violating the moral code that holds it together. Justice lay in repairing the breach. Justice was not to be found in punishment, for punishing the individual, as we do in the West, produces no social good. If the women of the Welayat were punished—as many would be by being detained for years—it was merely a secondary effect of bringing society back into proper balance. Our justice is individual and punitive. Afghan justice is social and restorative, or is meant to be.

But the concept invites anybody with a grievance to use the legal system to settle a score, just as it tempts the state to abuse its power by rounding up those whose ideas threaten to do it some future harm. Prison becomes a repository for the unwanted wife or the shameful daughter, a convenient Dumpster used by the husband or father too tender-hearted to slit the woman's throat himself. Every woman in the Welayat knew she was in prison because someone in her family wanted her there—her husband or former husband, her brother, her father, her mother-in-law—although in many cases it was hard to figure out the motivation of the accuser, or even the identity of the family Iago who schemed offstage. Jamila believed that her first husband, who accused her of illegal marriage, was jealous of her second husband and of her happiness. Latifa believed that her first husband, who made the same accusation against her, planned to extort money from her second husband. Tormented women like Dustana worried endlessly about who had set them up ("My aunt?"), and why ("My husband?"), and what they had done to deserve this fate. The murkiness of such cases left investigators and prosecutors and judges free to speculate as well, and often to decide cases, in lieu of, or in spite of, empirical evidence, on the basis only of patriarchal attitudes. But this was no more than their duty after all, for making whole the society was their job, and the society was by definition patriarchal.

ONCE A WOMAN WAS ARRESTED, WHAT WOULD HAPPEN TO HER?
How was the family equilibrium to be restored? Officially the legal
system has three tiers: the primary level where early investigations
take place and judicial decisions are handed down, the secondary
level where appeals are heard and additional investigations carried
out, and the Supreme Court where final appeals are brought. The
further up the system you go, the more conservative the justices
become, for by accidents of education and history most of those at
the top were trained exclusively in Sharia law. There used to be a
Family Court system as well, established under the communist
government of President Najibullah, but the Taliban did away
with it; now only Kabul has a family court.

Cases are presented by prosecutors (*saranwali*) to judges who
are meant to be impartial, but even the composition of the court
suggests its bias. Of Afghanistan's 2,006 judges, only 27 are
women.[2] The woman defendant matters so little that often she is
not called to appear in court for her own trial; she is notified later
of her sentence. She may never learn the charge that was levied
against her. And often the charge is not a criminal charge at all;
"elopement," for example, is no crime under the penal code, and
arresting people for eloping is a violation of their internationally
recognized right to freedom of movement, yet women and men
too are arrested for elopement all the time. (A woman judge
explained: "We must not encourage women to escape from home
because we must have a good moral society.") Women witnesses
too are often kept from court, for propriety's sake; and if they do
appear, there must be two to equal the testimony of one man. (The
Quran specifies that two women witnesses are needed "so that if
one of them errs, the other can remind her."[3] The male witness
requires no prompter.) Defense attorneys who star in American
justice were absent from Afghan courtrooms until 2004 when FDH

started a legal aid program, funded largely by the German government, to train a handful of women lawyers to defend the women of the Welayat. But why should an individual have a defense lawyer when it is the society—represented by the state prosecutor and the judge—that matters? When the new defense attorneys appeared in court with prisoners from the Welayat, judges reprimanded them: "What are you doing here speaking for this bad woman? You must be a bad woman yourself." That's the system, and while it grinds on, the accused remains in prison, month after month.

Soon after I started interviewing women in the Welayat, I paid a visit to the legal department of Afghanistan's new Ministry of Women's Affairs. The ministry was something previously unknown in Afghan governance, established in December 2001 under the eyes of a watching world at the Bonn conference that fabricated the Transitional Islamic State of Afghanistan. It held the promise of great changes for Afghan women, though the first minister, Sima Samar, who'd spent much of her life working for women's rights, was discouraged from doing "too much" by her male colleagues even before the plane carrying the new cabinet touched down in Kabul, and she was soon eased out of office without ever being assigned a telephone. Her successor publicly described beating women as a "normal custom" in Afghanistan, but she wasn't one to make a fuss about it; and by the time I showed up at the legal department there was little chance anyone in the ministry would do anything on behalf of women, although a couple of years later they did hang out a banner saying: GREAT LEADERS HAVE GREAT MOTHERS. But even then, the legal department still didn't have a telephone or a heater.

The ministry had become a Kabuli joke: the *Misery* of Women's Affairs. I sat down with three women lawyers in a freezing office and told them about several women in the Welayat who needed their help. Each one had been subject to some kind of violence—

battering, sexual assault, forced marriage, marital rape—and each woman had tried to escape from that violent situation. As a result, each had been charged with a "crime." Some had left home alone, and they had been charged with running away. Others had left home with the help of a male friend or relative, and they had been charged with elopement, illegal marriage, or zina. Each of these women, I argued, could make a good case in court that she had acted merely to save herself from a criminal assault. The lawyers, huddling in their coats and scarves, listened politely, as Afghans do, but their blank looks told me that the barrier between us was greater than language.

"You see, all these women are victims of domestic violence," I said.

"What is that?"

I tried to explain in simple terms through Zulal, but we kept stumbling on words and phrases (like *marital rape*) that had no equivalent in the Dari language, much less in the Afghan law.

"In my country it is against the law for a husband to force his wife to have sex when she doesn't want to."

The lawyers seemed embarrassed by the topic, but they hurriedly discussed it; and then the chief lawyer, who knew a little English, replied: "In Afghanistan not."

"In my country it is against the law for a husband to hit his wife."

Another hurried sotto voce discussion. "In Afghanistan not."

"In my country it is against the law to force a young girl to marry an old man she doesn't want to marry."

"In Afghanistan not. In my country is custom."

It's a rule when trying to lead people to an understanding of women's rights to "start where they are." But where were these women? They seemed to be stuck like the women of the Welayat somewhere in the fourteenth century. Politely they said they enjoyed talking with me and hoped I would return to talk some more, perhaps some day when it was not quite so cold. In the meantime, was there anything they could do for me?

"Yes, of course. You can go to the Welayat and talk to the prisoners. You are lawyers. You can look after their rights. You can take these issues to the government and to the court. Get them treated fairly, or maybe released."

Now the discussion was vigorous and firm. Zulal translated: "They say they cannot look into these cases because these women are bad women." She shot me a look that said, "You see? I'm not the only one."

"Ask them what makes them think these women are bad."

"They are criminals."

"What makes them think they are criminals?"

"They are in prison."

Zulal was stifling a smile now, almost laughing as she translated from the mouth of the chief lawyer the words she had spoken to me herself only a few weeks before. Perhaps the lawyers could undergo a change of heart as Zulal had.

"Ask them if they will go to the Welayat just once."

"No, they cannot go there."

"Why not?"

"It is a prison."

Beck and I would visit the women lawyers of the legal department many times to discuss legal issues and the status of the women of the Welayat. Their job, they said, was mainly to write legal papers, though we could never obtain a copy of a paper they had written. We offered to give them a training course on domestic violence, and they said they would be grateful and eager to do such a course. We set up a weekly schedule and posted the time and place. But each time we appeared for the training, the lawyers were not there. They were attending a required "capacity building" English class or computer course. They had gone to a meeting or a funeral. They were unwell or their children were sick. The chief was having a baby.

THE LAW IS SOMETHING ELSE AGAIN. SOMETHING ELUSIVE. SOME-
thing hard to pin down because there is so much of it. The Afghan
Constitution of 2004 declares that "The Citizens of Afghanistan—
whether man or woman—have equal Rights and Duties before
the Law."[4] But what law? There is a penal code and a civil code and
an amorphous body of traditional practices (varying from one ethnic group or tribe to the next) commonly referred to as customary
"law," and the moral code of Sharia from which various schools
of Islamic jurisprudence or *Fiqh* (chiefly, in Afghanistan, the
Hanafi or the Shi'a) derive bodies of law that classify crimes and
such applicable penalties as *Kisas* (retaliation), *Diya* (blood
money), and *Hadd* (amputations, stoning); and you can get an
argument any day in Kabuli legal circles about which is which
and which takes precedence in any particular set of circumstances. On paper, the legal codes that apply under the new constitution seem reasonably clear, but those who should apply them
are unfamiliar with the new body of laws, and often deliberately
obtuse. Some judges flatly deny the existence of a constitution
and legal codes, claiming instead that Sharia is the only law of the
land.[5] Others point out that the meaning of the words "Citizens—
whether man or woman—have equal rights and duties" is not
equivalent to the meaning of the words "men and women are
equal." Think about that.

The rule of law is the spine of any governance that pretends to
democracy. But without an informed judiciary to apply legitimate legal codes, justice becomes a lottery (usually for sale to the
highest-paying litigant) and the rule of law a joke. Everyone complains that greedy judges turn the tangle of Afghan law to personal advantage; Afghans live under the rule of bribery. But a
number of international agencies have gone to work to sort out
the law and train Afghan judges and lawyers to apply it, particularly as it pertains to women and children, because the whole

world knows that Afghanistan has not done right by its women. Besides, Afghanistan has signed international treaties guaranteeing the human rights of women and children—treaties that are embarrassingly at odds with Afghan law as it is currently administered in all its multitudinous permutations. Some projects train investigators or prosecutors or judges. Some train police. Some train lawyers.

In 2004, about a year and a half after my first visits to the women of the Welayat, I spent a couple of weeks sitting in on a training course offered by an INGO (international nongovernmental organization) and designed by New York City legal aid lawyers, judges, and law professors to teach Afghan lawyers the arcane skills of the defense attorney. I hoped it would help me find a way through the multiple mazes of Afgan law. Hypothetical cases were put to eighteen students—including only one woman— by the instructor, a high-powered, fast-talking, quick-thinking New York woman who seemed to me a model of success in her profession and must have seemed to the circle of Afghan men, who tried very hard not to ogle her, like one more Western aggressive weapon as potent as a Stinger missile or a mine. They didn't know what to make of her, much less what she was trying to teach them. "So this guy is arrested for stealing the carpet. What's the first question you want to ask about the crime?" The men mumbled and cast their eyes down, absorbed in the papers before them that laid out the hypothetical crime. She badgered them: "Come on. What's the first thing you need to know?" She singled out a student to answer. He said, "Does the man *need* a carpet?"

"No, no, no. Analysis. Analysis. Do we care whether he needs a carpet or not? No, we don't. What do we care?" Exasperated, she scanned the circle of men, all now thoroughly disgraced by the wrong answer.

"Okay, okay. First question: Is it a witnessed crime? Or is it not a witnessed crime?"

Whether anybody saw the crime being committed helps

determine whether police can search a place without a warrant, which in turn helps determine whether a clever defense attorney can get incriminating evidence excluded on a technicality—and the technicality, I soon learn, is what this kind of criminal defense is all about. ("We're teaching argument, not law," says the instructor. And to her students she says, "You see what a very small, small argument it is.") It occurs to me to wonder whether the students are confused because they are still naively searching for something like justice. But now they have a goal as they peruse again the dog-eared papers outlining the hypothetical case, and within five minutes someone has guessed the correct answer.

"Very good! Excellent!"

The teacher is gratified, the students relieved. She's set up a dichotomy—is it *this* kind of crime or *that*?—to begin an analysis that will take the prospective defense attorneys through a long series of either/or steps in the official penal code so that they can see at last how to argue a case on the basis of the law—the written-down word, with all its convenient technicalities—rather than tangle with the teachings of the Prophet or wander aimlessly in the fog of human motivation and kinship and circumstance and undiscoverable fact. Could the knotted clump of Afghan laws really be disentangled in this way, I wondered: one tiny thread of Western logic at a time? As far as I could see, the Afghan mind doesn't run to dichotomies, at least not much beyond the monumental opposition between men and women, or between good women and bad; and even that latter opposition seems a psychological defense, the same one we commonly use in the US to distinguish good people (us) from evil ones (them), that quickly dissolves in the complicated heart of a good Afghan Muslim, like Zulal. But never mind. I should pay attention.

"Okay, now you've determined it's a witnessed crime. What's the next question you need to ask?"

Bafflement again. But the dynamo teacher is undaunted. She begins to dress each day in a new handmade Afghan outfit, as if to show the students that she is just like them, so how hard can it be? Relentlessly, day after day, she pulls the answers from the lawyers' dazzled minds by sheer force of will. If anyone can transform the defense process in Kabul courts, she will do it. But I wonder what the transformation—if it comes—will do for women. I'm attending the training because I've been told it holds immense potential for women charged with crimes, but having been encouraged to search out dichotomies, I'm stuck in the fundamental one: who says that the male lawyer who's learned to defend the carpet thief—without uselessly inquiring whether he *needs* a carpet—will defend the carpet thief's wife?

One year later I attend a conference on women's rights conducted for members of the judiciary at the Supreme Court. There the Minister of Women's Affairs Massouda Jalal complains to Afghanistan's most eminent jurists that despite changes in the politics and governance of the country, women still have no rights. The eminent jurists themselves enunciate opinions about this state of affairs and about the laws that govern the fate of women. Perhaps because few of them have much legal education, they say nothing of witnessed crimes or nonwitnessed crimes or the exclusionary rule or designated limits on periods of detention or any other matters broached in the intensive training for criminal defense attorneys. Instead the weighty justices pronounce verses of the Quran, in Arabic. None of them really seems to know Arabic, apart from the few favorite Quranic verses he has learned by heart to shore up his own opinions, so the resultant exchange is a series of unchallenged monologues rather than a discussion that might reach a consensus through a process of give and take. The jurists are not interested in the fine points of the penal code. That is the concern of international consultants who conduct trainings on the texts and technicalities of the written laws. The jurists are interested in God, and in his Prophet, and—though they do not say so—in their own cushy places in the pockets of local commanders like Abdul Rasul Sayyaf and former president Burhanuddin

Rabbani, who shape the Supreme Court's policies and decisions behind the scenes.[6] These men are rumored to be the architects of recent illegal seizures of choice Kabul land, and collaborators with President Karzai's former minister of defense Mohammed Fahim, who engineered the particularly lucrative seizure of the Sher Pur area. The land seizures are "legitimized" by decisions of the court and the chief justice himself and supported by systematized corruption in the Ministry of Justice and—it is widely assumed—in the higher reaches of government.[7] In the Sher Pur deal, which removed residents from public land and transferred lots valued at up to $170,000 to government and army insiders, only four cabinet ministers declined to participate.[8]

The chief justice, a tall imposing figure in brown robes, might pass for God himself in his long white beard and fine white turban. A muslim cleric, he taught Sharia law in a Pakistani madrassa for decades before the Islamist interim government named him in 2002 to head the Supreme Court. He strides to the podium attended by ranks of black-garbed bodyguards armed with automatic weapons, a display of power that reveals the political nature of his judicial position. He tells the conference participants that women under Islam have all the rights they need, and special privileges as well, not accorded to men. Those privileges are three. First, women have the privilege of praying, except when they're polluted by menstruation. (He doesn't need to remind them to exercise that privilege at home; mosques are reserved for men.) Second, women have the privilege of obeying their husbands. And third, women have the privilege of restraining themselves from committing bad acts. He adds as another "extra" special privilege of women the well-known fact that Afghan men will undertake jihad to protect them, as if women should be grateful for the gift of twenty-three years of war. There's a lot more to his long speech, mainly warnings to women in the audience not to be drawn into the corrupt ways of the infidel Western world, where women are exploited as sexual objects. But about Afghan law and how it may relate to the rights of women under Islam or to their three perfect privileges, he says not a word. Subsequent speakers voice variations on the theme. One discusses the extent to which a woman should exercise her right to pray, and the heavenly rewards likely to come her way. Some advance the view that the Prophet permits women to be educated, but others take issue. Another promises that women will receive their rights "in the next life."

It's not that these doggedly misogynist jurists have never heard the views of more liberal Islamic scholars far better qualified than themselves. International organizations have occasionally imported Islamic experts from places like Malaysia, India, Iran, and Bangladesh to update the Afghan justice system's resident Taliban. At a National Conference on Women's Rights, Law and Justice in Afghanistan hosted in May 2003 by the International Human Rights Law Group and sponsored by UNIFEM (United Nations Development Fund for Women) and the governments of Germany and Italy, and attended by many of the same conservative Afghan justices, one Islamic scholar after another explained with painstaking references to the Quran exactly when, where, and how throughout history Islam had been distorted by "vestiges of Arabian custom and tradition," "indiscriminate reliance on apocryphal and weak *hadith*"(sayings of the Prophet) that depict women as intellectually and morally deficient," "tribal practices," "entrenched patriarchal values," an obsessive tendency to "over-emphasize sexuality," and a "medievalist" conception of women that "became the dominant pattern in clear contrast with the praxis and model that was set during the time of the Prophet."[9] Dr. Mohammad Hashim Kamali, professor of Islamic Law Jurisprudence at the International Islamic University of Malaysia, told the audience of Afghan Islamists that Islam had been distorted too by "the rise of modern conservatism in the twentieth century, and the current wave of Islamism which continues to evoke the medieval theme of women's innate physical and mental deficiency in support of their jaundiced outlook." As a result, the scholar said, "patriarchal attitudes come in the way of women's rights to equality" in clear contradiction to "the evidence of the Koran"; and "cultural mediation and prejudicial practices erode women's rights even in cases where legislation and official policy dictate otherwise."[10] All the other imported Islamic scholars seemed to agree with Professor Kamali's indictment of jaundiced Islamism, and even the jaundiced Islamists themselves in the audience politely applauded. Yet at every subsequent legal conference I attended, the speechifying went on in the same old-fashioned jaundiced vein. Every meeting begins and ends with popular notions of Islam—or rather pseudo-Islam hijacked by patriarchal pontificators—interspersed with medieval reminders of the biological difference that gives women the very special right to be protected by men. No one ever gets to the specificities of the law because the generalities of "Islam" must first be exhausted, and Islam is by nature inexhaustible.

At last a woman professor of law from Kabul University rises to her feet in the audience to say: "The pen that records the rights of women is always held in the hand of a man." The men laugh. She says: "The pen that recorded the Holy Quran was held in the hand of a man." The men stop laughing, and in the chastising silence that follows, the woman sinks into her chair. Then the men go on speaking. As uncontestable proof that women are lesser creatures, unworthy of human rights, one of them cites woman's monthly "three-day sickness." So many others repeat the argument that I take an Afghan colleague aside and ask her, "Do you really menstruate for only three days?" She laughs. "Of course not, but if they knew the true number of days we are 'polluted,' they would bury us alive." By the time the conference ends two days later, it's clear that a lot of other information eludes the most eminent jurists in the country. One group, after two days' discussion, still puzzles over the question of whether people charged with crimes have the right to defend themselves in court. The judges can't agree about the law because they don't seem to know what it is.

THE INTERNATIONAL "EXPERTS" WHO "TRAIN" AFGHANS IN LEGAL theory and practice do little better. What exactly is the nature of Afghan law? Countless workshops and trainings and conferences and manuals and research studies are devoted to pinning it down. The best exegesis I heard was offered at another training for defense lawyers by an eminent Arab scholar of Islamic law who works on human rights for the UN. He had the advantage over Quran-quoting Afghan jurists in that the holy book is written in his native language. But unlike them, he didn't begin with Islam. Rather, he explained that the Afghan Constitution of 2004 takes precedence over every other kind of law in the country, including Sharia, and that it specifically upholds the principles of the major documents of international human rights—that is, the Universal Declaration of Human Rights, the International Treaty of Civil and Political Rights, and CEDAW: the Convention on the Elimination of All Forms of Discrimination Against Women—and it specifically assigns all sorts of duties to the State (including affirmative action) to make sure that women attain rights equal to those of men. The Constitution also specifies that "no law can be contrary to the beliefs and provisions of the sacred religion of Islam."[11] But the very inclusion of this article, the Arab scholar said, demonstrates the Constitutional assumption that the principles of human rights, the principles of Islam, and the Constitution itself coincide in perfectly equitable and harmonious agreement. Various schools of Islamic jurisprudence prescribe various rights and restrictions for women, he said; but taken all together as "Islam"—the word the Constitution uses—they name rights of women equal to those of men. "Brilliant," I thought. "You can't argue with that." But the men being "trained" did argue with that, loudly and for a long time. "No, women can't divorce." "No, women can't travel without a male escort." "No, women can't be mullahs. Or imams. Or presidents. No. No. No."

Later I repeated the Arab scholar's analysis to a German legal expert who advises German agencies in Kabul and an American legal scholar who advises the Afghan government. The German said, "No, sorry. He's wrong." He began a painful dissection of the Arab scholar's theory but was soon interrupted by the American who agreed that the Arab scholar was wrong but disagreed with the German about precisely where and why he was wrong, and I put my head in my hands and prayed that no Italian would join the discussion. The Italians, alone among all the donor nations supposedly aiding the recovery of Afghanistan, were chosen to sort out and reconstruct the Afghan justice system. The *Italians*. Many UN and INGO officials recommend that the Italians be given some help. Privately they joke that Italian jurisprudence is perfect for the emerging Afghan narco-mafioso state.

FORGET THE LAW. EVEN IF AN APPLICABLE LAW CAN BE IDENTIFIED, it can't be adjudicated in most of the country because most of the country has no functioning courts belonging to the central government's judicial system. In a great many provinces the court buildings have been destroyed. Those that remain or have been rebuilt are not staffed because the judges assigned to them prefer to remain safe in Kabul. (District courts should have three judges; those in Kabul have six or seven, while many in the provinces have none at all.) The central government and its judicial system simply have no authority in most of the country, which remains "insecure." The judges at the Supreme Court conference concluded that "[t]he government must establish throughout the country the rule of law in accordance with Islam through the Afghan Constitution, other national laws and regulations, and international documents. . . ."[12] That's a necessary plan, and overdue, but how to accomplish it can scarcely be imagined.

So what really happens, even in Kabul, to restore the social balance when a "crime" has been committed is this: the family of the accuser and the family of the accused get together and make a deal. Latifa's second husband (or his brother) pays off the first husband. Husband number one drops his complaint against husband number two, and he goes free. Maybe husband number two cares enough about Latifa to bargain for her freedom as well, or maybe not.

When bribes fail, there may be threats, between families or between a family and the authorities. A woman professor of law told me about her brief career as a judge, more than twenty years ago. Her first case (in Kabul) was that of a young man who had murdered his teacher in a particularly vicious and brutal crime. She sentenced the killer to fifteen years. The next day, men went to her home and offered her husband a lot of money to make her discharge the case. She sent the money back. That night the men returned and told her husband that if she came to court again, she would be killed. "That was the start and the finish of my career as a judge," she said. She taught high school for fifteen years before she dared return to the law as a university professor. "These things still happen," she said. "Being a judge or even a lawyer—it is not a safe job."

Under customary and tribal laws such as the Pashtunwali code of the Pashtuns, family bargains are codified. Murder a favored wife and you owe her family (her husband) four new copies of the Quran, four women, and one fat sheep. If you don't pay up, the husband is perfectly justified in killing you. That act may seem like simple vengeance, and it may in fact be motivated by revenge—the desire for revenge can simmer for years in the Pashtun heart—but the payback murder looks to the Afghan like appropriate retribution: an equivalency that sets the scales of social justice back in balance. Lesser crimes also carry prescribed compensations, or blood money; and for injuries inflicted in incessant Pashtun quarreling, equivalencies have been elaborated. The wound that causes a man to lose an eye or an ear counts as half a murder. A cut to a man's genitals is equal to two murders and must be compensated by even greater gifts of sheep and women and copies of the Holy Quran.[13] The problem for women in the Welayat—for Afghan women generally—is that few have the worth of a favored wife and none is half so valuable as the genitals of the lowliest man. Worthless as a woman is, who will strike a deal on her behalf?

HOMA WAS A FAVORITE AMONG THE GUARDS AND THE OTHER prisoners of the Welayat; her cheerfulness seemed so rare a gift in this place. Smiles brightened her pretty face. She looked healthier too: a chubby little figure among ranks of emaciated, undernourished women. She seemed to have led a happier, more comfortable life, until her imprisonment. "I think it is because she has no husband," Zulal said.

She'd had a husband once, when she was about sixteen, but he had been killed in the wars, leaving her with a baby boy. Although other men asked for her, she chose to remain a widow, living with her parents, her brothers, and her unmarried younger sisters, and raising her son. She had a happy life for ten years, she said, until a cousin whose marriage offer she had rejected found her at home alone one day and raped her. She didn't report the assault because despite Afghanistan's surfeit of law, there is no specific law against rape. Rather, rape is covered in a subsection of the law against adultery; a woman who reports rape is arrested, charged with adultery, and imprisoned while investigators decide whether or not she consented to the act.[14] (She had sex, didn't she?) But after the rape Homa lived in fear that her cousin might return and try to rape her again, which is exactly what he did. This time she was ready for him. She threw kerosene at him and struck a match. He ran screaming from the house and quickly was taken by others to the hospital.

Homa said that when she explained to her cousin's father what had happened, he recognized the truth of her story right away. He was deeply shamed by his son's actions and offered to compensate her father with sheep and other goods, but before they reached a final agreement word came from the hospital—some three days after the incident—that the man had died. After that the father accused Homa of murder and demanded that she be put to death. She claimed she had acted in self-defense, and that she'd meant only to drive off her cousin, not to kill him. She thought he had not been badly burned, and she wondered if he might have died of other causes or simple medical negligence—a reasonable question given the sorry state of Kabul hospitals since the reign of the Taliban, but one that was not explored. When we talked to Homa, she had been imprisoned in the Welayat for several months while her case was investigated, but recently the investigator had reached a conclusion: that she was guilty of premeditated murder. After all, she hadn't killed her cousin during the act of rape. Instead she'd waited for him to try again, and she'd "made a plan." The investigator suggested there was another possible scenario as well, although he had no evidence to prove it except what he knew of the true nature of women. Perhaps there'd been no rape at all. Perhaps Homa had seduced her cousin, then murdered him in cold blood to cover it up.

Things looked worse and worse for Homa, and the dead man's father saw the opportunity to receive compensation. He offered to resolve the whole matter in exchange for several fat sheep (the number was negotiable) and Homa's two younger sisters. It's an old custom—called *bad* or *bad-la*—that offers women or girls as recompense. Usually the women or girls are married to men within the family of the "victim." Often they become second (or third or fourth) wives, providing household labor as well as sexual service, while the perpetrator of the original crime goes free. Binding the two families of aggressor and victim through these multiple marriages is thought to be a particularly effective way of stitching things back together. But because women have no real say in the transaction and no safe way to initiate divorce, a woman forced into marriage as compensation is in effect enslaved. In the West such a deal would itself be a criminal offense, but under Afghan customary law it's a handy patch that is thought to make whole again the exquisite fabric of society. One problem is that it seems to make whole again a society exclusively of men—a society in which women serve, like sheep, as bargaining chips.

Another problem, revealed by recent research, is that the *bad* system does not actually make social relations whole at all, but rather more often makes them worse for everyone concerned; and in addition it probably causes crime to increase by letting violent perpetrators off the hook. A study of the practice of *bad* in ten provinces, including fifty cases within the city of Kabul, concluded that "the entire family system is disintegrated in the aftermath."[15] Some men suffer from being forced to hand over women and girls they might have been able to sell, while other men and boys may be saddled with wives they don't want but are obliged to support. The principal victims are girls and women. The report is full of cases like that of Miss Z who was given as *bad* to the family of a man her brother had killed, and who managed to escape after three years only to be hunted down and killed by her father-in-law. Crimes like that are covered up, says the report, because although "we are witnessing women's slavery in the 21st century . . . nobody cares for the hardship and suffering of the person who has been used as a conflict resolution tool."[16]

The Afghan judiciary doesn't seem to care. For the record the court inveighs against the practice of *bad,* as in this recommendation produced in 2005 by justices attending the Supreme Court conference: "The government should take action to eradicate harmful and discriminatory customs incompatible with Islam and the laws of the country, such as giving women in compensation which is forbidden by Article 517 of the Criminal Code."[17] Yet judges persist in the belief that the *bad* system works very well to restore harmony among men—the only people, after all, who really count—and they commonly defer to such informal settlements rather than go to all the trouble of finding an applicable law and conducting a trial to uphold it. The head of the Kabul District Court himself, even as he contemplated the death penalty for Homa, let it be known that the court would accept such an agreement and let her go free. But Homa refused to allow her sisters to be given away, even to save her own life. That decision confirmed Afghan opinion that she was a bad woman—so bad that she refused to submit to the will of men for the good of "society." Still, the judge was politic enough to realize that executing a widow carried a whiff of the Taliban. It would not go down well with the international donors who prop up the country. He spared Homa's life and sentenced her to fifteen years.

ONE DAY, AS WE TALKED WITH HOMA, WE WERE DISTURBED BY A commotion in the corridor and the sound of men shouting orders. The blanket in the doorway was thrown back and we were struck by blinding light. All at once we were surrounded by barking men. One of them shoved a TV camera in Zulal's face, while another— an Afghan translator—asked her in Dari what crime she had committed. It was an Italian television crew, come like dozens of Western journalists before them, to film Afghanistan's most popular human-interest news story: the women in "Kabul jail." The on-camera reporter was a young Italian woman who asked me to leave so my Western presence wouldn't spoil their footage. There was no use trying to continue our work or explain how the onslaught of aggressive men and machines terrified and humiliated the prisoners. The crew had a job to do, and they'd bribed the guards handsomely to let them do it. "Don't worry," the reporter said. "We'll create a lot of sympathy for these women. This place is so terrible. It's a super story." She turned to the cameraman who was still filming Zulal as she struggled to get to her feet. "That's stupendous. She's so upset. She's so thin."

That story and many others like it that winter—even one in the *New York Times* that managed to use the words *toasty* and *bright* in reference to the women's jail—probably did create a lot of sympathy around the world for Afghan women and the medieval prison of law that confines their lives.[18] It was an important story too, counteracting self-congratulatory blurbs from the Bush administration about Afghanistan's newly freed female citizens. But it didn't do much for Afghan women. It encouraged internationals like me to come and "study" them, to undertake "needs assessments" and "vulnerability studies" (in the jargon of the aid business) and file reports and hope that somebody else—somebody with more power, more money, more pull—would do something.

When Beck issued her report on the girls and women of the Kabul Welayat in March 2003, she attached two pages of recommendations. Number one had nothing to do with the law. It read: "Funds should be made available and an implementing agency should be selected to renovate the detention house where women and their children are currently held."[19] First things first. But even Beck's recommendation was couched in the form universally prescribed for official reports everywhere: the passive voice. It lends itself splendidly to moral indignation without actually ascribing blame or assigning responsibility. Right-thinking recipients of the report could read it, discuss it, even rant about it, and above all agree with it that something should be done by someone. And then they could file it under F for Frauen die Helfen or W for Welayat or someplace they never would find it again, after first noting its title on their own quarterly work report as an item to which they had devoted some time. The efforts are sincere—

writing, reading, ranting, filing. The circulation of reports in the passive voice, like the circulation of white Land Cruisers through the streets of Kabul, is what makes the aid business go round and round. Beck had worked hard for months to gather all the facts, make all the contacts, arrange all the appointments, conduct all the interviews, attend all the meetings, compile all the statistics, consult all the legal experts, and organize all the information that was to go into her report. Then she wrote it. She edited it. She issued it. After that, for many months, nothing happened.

Then Rosemary Stasek came to Kabul. Rosemary was not in the aid business. She had risen through the ranks of Silicon Valley to run her own Web development business in Mountain View, California; but at heart she was a politician. She had a young woman's energy and an old-fashioned idea that the purpose of government is to advance the interests of the common people. In the area around Mountain View, where Rosemary served on the city council before moving into the mayor's office, many of the common people were Afghan-Americans. Since the 1970s, when politically persecuted Afghans began to flee their country in large numbers, thousands had found their way to California and to the region that included Rosemary's town. As a good politician caring for her constituents, Rosemary visited their neighborhoods, listened to their concerns, attended their fund-raisers, ate in their restaurants, and bought crafts and carpets from shops sending profits back to widows in Kabul. In 2002, she signed up for a two-week educational tour of Afghanistan to learn more about their country. In Kabul she wangled appointments with cabinet ministers and sat down with President Karzai himself to talk things over, as one politician to another. She asked him in her charming way, "What about the rights of women?" and he answered in his charming way, "Yes. Exactly. What about the rights of women?" She told him that what his administration did for women would determine in the end what Americans thought of him.

Rosemary returned to California wearing a new embroidered Afghan shirt and began to give speeches and slide shows. She spoke on the radio and on TV. She wrote articles for the newspaper. She was a popular figure in her district. People liked her fresh, open face, her cheerfulness, her can-do attitude, and her homemade Web site where she told her constituents what she was doing. She was a small local miracle of American politics: a hard-working, high-achieving, principled, popular, perfectly transparent public servant. In the old-fashioned movie that is her political life, she'd be played by Jimmy Stewart, moving fast. Her constituents sent donations, and in June 2003, Rosemary returned to Kabul with five thousand dollars and an obligation to spend it for Afghan women. She checked in with women's rights activists she'd met on her earlier visit, and Beck Bradshaw said, "Why don't you fix up the prison?"

The pocket notebook Rosemary kept during that visit is full of numbers: the measurements of rooms and door frames and electrical lines, and the cell phone numbers of men and women whose cousins or uncles are carpenters or plumbers or know a little something about wiring. Other entries record her progress. Not wanting to send men into the women's prison, she first searches Kabul for skilled women workers. There are rumors of women working construction for Mercy Corps, but when she visits the jobsite, she finds that "all they do is hand the hammers to the men." She confers again with the warden. Men it must be. But finding the right men is also a problem. "Mr. Habibi: cousin Najib—has bro in freelance construction, maybe." "Soraya's husband: knows painter????" And the phone numbers. Her entry for June 12 reads: "awful day when the builders showed up, went to the jail, they measured & stuff and then came back later w/a price of 25K. NOT!" But she's undaunted. She has a "yummy lunch" and makes more phone calls. Then there are pages of diagrams and more measurements and at last a small list that will be the basis of a contract:

        5 Rooms
            Replaster
            Paint
            + ceiling
            w/ wiring
            $3,500
            + <u>840</u> (paint, 280m^2)
            $4,340

That leaves money to spare. The next pages are full of lists of things it might buy: sheets, medications, sanitary towels, underwear, cigarettes, soap. The rest of the journal records a frenzy of trips: to the bazaar to buy opaque fabric for window curtains, to the seamstress with fabric and window measurements, and almost daily to the prison to check the progress of plasterers, painters, and electricians. She praises the work, insists that some things done carelessly be redone, calls for more cousins to make the work go faster.

In the end, the five main rooms of the prison have been wired for electricity, plastered, painted a pretty pale yellow, carpeted with thin industrial carpeting, and hung with blue curtains. The ceilings have been finished with white paneling. There are sheets on the beds. Rosemary makes another list at the back of her notebook—a list of things still to be done at the prison:

1. reconstruct the corridor
2. build a^2 bathroom
3. septic
4. repair 6th room
5. kitchen???

During the next year INGOs finally will get to work on some of the items on Rosemary's list. ("You shamed them," Beck says later.) But even as she surveys the five glistening rooms at the heart of the dismal Welayat, Rosemary is happy enough. "You can't do everything," she says. She has twenty dollars left over. She spends it on a tiny bottle of Christian Dior perfume—a gift for Beck for having given her such a good idea and so much support. Then she flies back to California to report to her constituents. She has been in Kabul two weeks.

AFTER THAT WE COULD BEGIN TO THINK ABOUT THE PRISONERS' other needs, and their rights. FDH sent a big motherly psychologist named Zorha to the prison once a week to talk with the prisoners. It brought volunteer Afghan-German doctors—all women—to the prison (and the local hospitals) to care for women and their children. It started a legal aid program, led by an Australian criminologist, to train women defense attorneys to help the women get out of jail. The guards began to grumble that the prisoners lived better than they did, so the legal aid staff started a project, headed by young Marzia, to bring the guards and the prison up to the Minimum Standard Rules for the Treatment of Prisoners prescribed by the UN. They trained them in management, bought them notebooks and pens, designed forms for them to keep records of visitors and medical problems and appointments with lawyers. They taught them the basic rights of prisoners and the professional duties of prison staff. They taught them to inform the defense attorney when a prisoner was summoned to court. They brought in a cabinet and a real desk.

One morning in February 2005, when it was snowing hard in Kabul, Zulal and I went with Rosemary to visit the prison again. Twenty months had passed since Rosemary first went to work on the prison, sixteen months since the legal aid program started its work, two years since Zulal and I spent all those long afternoons in the guards' room, shivering in our winter coats as women told their tales. In that time it seemed that everything had changed. The old wooden door had been replaced by a modern one of steel, painted green. Next to it stood a newly built gatehouse bearing a sign: WELCOME TO THE WOMEN'S PRISON. But the guard wouldn't let us in. Who did we think we were anyway, showing up without an appointment? "Good!" Rosemary said. "You can't just walk in anymore, or bribe somebody. This is a big improvement." Then we saw Zarmina, the warden, approaching through the snow—a big, round woman wrapped in black shawls, materializing in the white air. She recognized Rosemary from a long way off and hurried to embrace her. She enfolded us all in her voluminous shawls and hurried us through the new green door.

Inside we walked down a bright corridor. The walls were painted white. Electric lights beamed from the ceiling. A gray carpet lay underfoot. We entered her office—once a ruined cell. Two FDH defense lawyers sat by the woodstove sipping tea, waiting to talk with newly admitted prisoners. Zarmina, beaming, produced a packet of biscuits from the drawer of a desk laden with record books. I said, "It's good to see you in a proper office at a proper desk."

Rosemary protested. "I liked it better when we sat together on the bed in the guards' room and talked about what color to paint the walls."

"I never go there anymore," Zarmina said. "That's a prisoners' room now. I have this office." She was a well-educated woman, with a master's degree in criminology, who had spent years sitting on an iron bed in a cell making tea on a propane burner. She still earned less than seventy dollars a month and counted herself lucky if the salary was paid on time. But she was a professional now. She threw back her shawl and made a sweeping gesture, taking in the desk, the chairs, the cupboard, the little table where tea cups were being filled by a young inmate. She said again, "I never go there."

"It's a nice office," Zulal said.

Later we walked through the prison together, entering each room, greeting the women, wishing them well. I scanned the faces, hoping the women I knew had gone free. Rosemary was looking at the walls, the curtains, the floor. Each room had electric lights now, and an electric fan bolted to the ceiling, and a woodstove radiating heat. The five rooms Rosemary's crew had reconstructed still looked good, though the walls were soot-darkened from the smoke of the stoves. "You can wash them in the spring," Rosemary said happily. The two prisoners' rooms and the tiny, one-hole bathroom reconstructed later by big INGOs were already shabby. "They spent tens of thousands of dollars," Zarmina said, "but they didn't pay attention. Someone took the money and left us with this. What do they care? It's not their money. It's not their prison. But you see, it should be done again." Outside in the yard two men with picks were attacking the cement pavement that had been installed during the past summer and paid for by another big INGO. The water pipes lay on the ground just beneath, frozen solid. "Oh, dear," Rosemary said. "Somebody else not paying attention."

We entered the far wing of the building, the wing reconstructed a year earlier by an agency of the UN. Already the roof was leaking and the paint flaking from crumbling walls. One big room was set aside for sewing classes given by an INGO whose colorful banner hung on the wall. Twenty Chinese-made Butterfly sewing machines were piled in a corner, the cases askew. "The trainers came only for two months last summer," Zarmina said. "The women wanted to make clothes for their children and other things to sell, but the trainers brought only enough materials to teach them to make doll clothes. They don't have dolls. The women stopped coming to the class. Then the trainers stopped coming too. They said the women were ungrateful and showed no initiative." She shrugged. "They can't sew in winter anyway. As you see, there is no heat." Farther down the hall was a small, cold room where a visiting doctor held clinic hours twice a week, and another room where prisoners could be interviewed in chilly privacy by investigators or lawyers. "These are big improvements," Rosemary said, smiling, but I could see her methodically taking inventory, making mental lists.

"What about the legal status of women now?" she asked. "What charges bring them here?"

"It is as before. Running away. Elopement. Zina. Stealing sometimes. Or kidnapping. And drugs. There are more drugs now."

And more prisoners. There were forty women in the Welayat now, and sixteen children. There was a seventh room for prisoners, in addition to the former six, a room furnished with traditional Afghan cushions because it was too small to hold enough beds. Eleven women and four children slept on the tushaks on the floor. There was a new women's prison too, outside the city within the walls of Pul-i Charkhi where so many thousands of political prisoners in the past had been tortured and killed. (Pul-i Charkhi was a place, like any gulag, that should have been preserved only as a caution of history or blown to smithereens, not reopened for business.) But the Welayat was overcrowded. In nine months, FDH's defense lawyers had cut down the time prisoners were detained awaiting trial; they'd gone to court with prisoners and got forty-two of them released. They'd succeeded in getting many morals charges dismissed altogether. Yet more and more women were being arrested for moral offenses, in clear contradiction of international women's rights and the Afghan Constitution. It was as if the Taliban still patrolled the streets, working overtime to fill the Welayat faster than the legal aid program could empty it. But opening another prison was not likely to solve the problem of overcrowding; it's a truism of penology that convict populations expand to fill the space allotted for their accommodation. (If you build it, they will come.) What if police just stopped arresting women for moral offenses? What if judges threw these moral noncrimes out of court? You wouldn't need another prison then.

"Pul-i Charkhi is so far from the city," Zarmina said. "It's difficult for the prisoners' families to visit them. And their lawyers, too. It takes so much time."

"How do you decide who to send there?" I asked.

"We send the women who will be in prison for a long time."

Zulal looked at me. Was she too thinking of the long-termers we knew? The "prostitutes" and "murderers"? The well-remembered faces we had not seen today? Perhaps Najela, or Ejar? Or Homa?

EVEN WHEN PRISONERS GET OUT OF PRISON, THEY'RE NOT FREE. They're not safe. The shame of a woman's alleged offense hangs over her and over her family. Sometimes a woman is cleared in court and released from prison only to be found dead a few days later, murdered by her father and brothers, wiping the family slate. The legal aid program took on a new obligation: assuring the safety of prisoners released through the efforts of their defense attorneys. Norinne Fafoe, the criminologist who headed the program, formed a mediation team—herself, her translator, the Afghan defense lawyer—to meet with the woman's family before she was released and to call again after she had rejoined them at home. Where emotions ran high, the team enlisted village elders or mullahs to help with mediation and protect the woman. They tried to keep the mediation team small, so as not to attract unwanted attention to the family already parched by public shame, but in one case they agreed to take me along.

Amina had lived happily enough with her husband and children in a household that included her husband's five brothers and their wives and a multitude of children. Then one day Amina's father found her husband having sex with her sister, and he killed them both. The father was arrested for murdering Amina's husband though not for murdering his own daughter, a justifiable act any good father might commit under the circumstances. Amina too was arrested for the murder of her husband on the peculiar grounds that she should have reported his adultery to the police. With the help of a defense attorney, she pleaded successfully in court that she knew nothing of her husband's relationship with her sister; and she was released to go home to her children. But she was scared to death. Even though she knew a woman's life is not the equal of a man's, she was afraid her husband's brothers would kill her in partial retribution for the murder of their brother. The mediators and the mullah descended upon the household to negotiate. The brothers were persuaded not to kill Amina, the mother of their brother's children. They decided they would lock her up in the house instead. She was never to go out, never to visit her own mother. More negotiation produced a modified written agreement: Amina would be allowed to go out to visit her parents' home, but only if she informed all five of her brothers-in-law in advance. After two weeks the contract remained in place, the household in tenuous balance. Then Amina's father succeeded in bribing his way out of prison and went to his home. Amina wanted to visit him and her mother. The brothers-in-law would not allow it. That's where things stood when we visited the home of the brothers-in-law three weeks after Amina's release.

The house was a mud box, one of a stack that mounted the lower slope of a Kabul mountain. We climbed the slippery path and were let into a bare yard and then the house itself. It had no door, only a blanket slung across the entrance of a small, dark room full of women: Amina's sisters-in-law. They were beating the family tushaks in preparation for slipping them into fresh covers. They greeted us perfunctorily and went on with their work. The subject of their sister-in-law seemed to fill them with such belligerent energy that I thought the cushions might fly apart under their fists. Only Amina sat apart in a corner, a squat figure sitting cross-legged, slumped in dejection. We seated ourselves on the floor, and Laila the lawyer asked Amina how she was.

"*Khub astum.*" I'm fine. She didn't look it.

The lawyer asked to speak with Amina alone, but the women wouldn't hear of it. "Our husbands are not home," said one, a feisty little woman who spoke loudly for the group. Her face was streaked with dirt, and her bare feet were cracked and blackened.

"If you talk to her, the children will tell our husbands, and they will beat us." All the women were angry with Amina. "She is nothing but trouble," another said.

"Why should she visit her father?" asked another. "Who is she?"

"Does she think of who will have to take care of her children?"

"The children will cry and our husbands will beat us because she is not here to take care of them."

"Does she think about that?"

"She is nothing but trouble."

They were all talking at once now—a shrill chorus, their voices hard, their faces mean.

"You cannot stay here. You must come when our husbands are here."

Laila the lawyer set a time, and we returned a week later to find four of the five brothers-in-law sitting in a row on the newly covered tushaks. Dressed alike in baggy cotton pants, long tunics, and woolen vests, and wearing identical turbans and beards, they seemed to have been mass-produced, as I suppose in a sense they were. The room had been tidied. The women had washed their faces and put on clean skirts. They sat on the floor, all in a row opposite their husbands, their arms around snotty-nosed toddlers who stood staring at us blankly. Again Amina sat apart in a corner, but she sat straight-backed as if to show that she hadn't yet been defeated. Addressing the oldest brother, the lawyer expressed our concern that Amina be allowed to visit her family, in keeping with the original agreement the brothers had accepted by making their marks. She reminded the brothers that Amina was obliged only to let them know where she meant to go. "No," the oldest brother said. She was obliged not just to notify the five brothers but to get their permission, and they in turn were free to withhold it, in which case Amina was going nowhere.

The atmosphere was brittle with tension. The women smirked and said nothing. The lawyer collected her thoughts. Norinne's translator riffled the buttons on her cell phone, looking, I supposed, for the mullah's phone number. We seemed to be on the verge of another big and bitter renegotiation when the eldest brother spoke again. "In any case, we are not opposed to our sister-in-law's visit to her family. It is only our young brother who opposes this. It is only he you must persuade. But as you see, he is not here."

The moment passed. There would be no fight. But the decision would remain the same. Amina would not be allowed to visit her family.

"When shall we come again to talk with your young brother?" the lawyer asked.

"That I do not know," said the oldest brother. The other brothers didn't stir to enlighten him. The atmosphere grew tight again. The oldest brother addressed his remarks to the air above the lawyer's head. "Actually," he continued after a long silence, "we are planning to move to a new house. We are looking now for a house with cheaper rent. As soon as we find such a house, we will organize a gathering. We will invite the father of our sister-in-law. We will invite you." The brothers nodded. The wives smirked.

"That is a generous and wise idea," the lawyer said. She paused. "It is time you all sit down together and work things out."

"Yes," the oldest brother said. "Some things need to be worked out—or another person can get hurt."

When the mediators returned a week later, the family, and Amina, were gone. The lawyer was not surprised. "Did you notice," she asked, "that they never gave us tea?"

But that's what happened in nearly every case the lawyers sought to mediate. They'd be filled with optimism at first, only to be out-foxed. Norinne thought the mediation team was too conspicuous; she believed that by unintentionally attracting more attention to the families they visited, the team hastened their move to a new neighborhood. Norinne herself was a tall, slim beauty with spiked hair and a flamboyant, idiosyncratic style of dress that turned heads; and once under political pressure she'd taken along a Deutsche Welle television crew. She hoped that a trimmed down mediation team might have more success, but families kept moving, just out of reach. Was it shame they eluded, or the foreigners' unwelcome intrusion? The foreigners' ideas of justice? The foreigners' peculiar notion that attention must be paid to a woman?

SOME TIME LATER I LEARNED THAT HOMA, THE WOMAN WHO HAD set her rapist-cousin on fire, had been set free and received happily in her parents' home. I was pleased to hear the news. But hadn't she been sentenced to fifteen years? How did she get out? I went to see Marzia, who was still running the training program at the Welayat, to find out.

"When her case went up to Secondary Court for more investigation, the sentence was knocked down to six years, and then the Supreme Court cut it down to three."

"It sounds like the defense lawyers did a great job."

"Oh, no," Marzia said. "This was before we started the lawyers' program. She didn't have a defense lawyer. Nobody did then."

"So why was the sentence reduced?"

"Oh, the courts always do that. They always give big sentences at the Primary Court because they know the higher courts will cut them down. They don't have to give a reason." I was surprised at the offhand way Marzia described the legal process.

"That sounds more like poker than justice," I said.

"Like what?"

"Like a kind of game."

"Yes. You are right. But it was another game that got her out. It was Eid."

Every year, on the first day of the month following *Ramazan*, Muslims celebrate the Eid al-Fitr. After the month of fasting and discipline, the Eid al-Fitr is a celebration of thanksgiving and new beginnings. President Karzai celebrates by pardoning prisoners; and a disproportionate number of those he pardons are women. In theory only certain people are eligible for presidential pardon: petty offenders, the old or infirm, parents leaving children unattended, and prisoners who've served a big chunk of time—one-third of the sentence for a man, or (in another instance of legal disparity) one-half the sentence for a woman. But in practice Eid offers one more opportunity to tender a bribe and strike a deal with the system. Among the women pardoned at Eid 2003 was one released after serving five months of a three-year sentence for illegal marriage. Another had served ten months of a four-year sentence for the same offense. Another sentenced to twelve years for elopement was released after serving only eight months. And another—Homa—who had once been threatened with execution, was released after a year and three months. Since every woman prisoner I interviewed, like Homa, had been thrust into "crime" by poverty, coercion, or violence and convicted on circumstantial evidence or none at all, I was happy to see them released. But what are the implications for justice? How much easier is it for police and prosecutors to put a woman away if they think she'll be pardoned anyway? How much more tempting to turn a profitable deal on some trumped-up moral crime if nobody takes it seriously? How much more comfortable to ignore forced marriage, rape, wife beating, and forced prostitution if the girls and women arrested for running away from such violence won't really have to stay in prison very long? And what then is the point of the justice system and all those layers of law if a woman's fate is still to depend upon the whim of some man who, in this case, happens to be the president?

Norinne took her objections to the deputy chief justice of the Supreme Court. She told him the erratic application of "justice" raised problems among the prisoners as some were treated too severely and some with inexplicable leniency. She said it teaches disrespect for law and encourages prisoners to revert to the traditional system of bribery. Many prisoners and their families had thought of the defense lawyers all along as deal makers for hire. They'd grown surly and threatening when the defense lawyers

IN THE PRISONS 139

declined to take or offer bribes. What incentive would they have now to appeal to lawyers and the rule of law at all? The deputy chief justice agreed with Norinne's analysis, but he said that pressure to release the women en masse came from "the international community." Maybe it was all those newspaper and TV stories about the wretched prison that did it. Maybe it was all the stories about the Taliban. Now the world wants to see the "new Afghanistan" be nice to its women. So the deputy chief justice "feels pressured," he said, to choose spectacle over substance, the grand gesture at the expense of justice and genuine change. Making nice to women makes Hamid Karzai look presidential, and George W. Bush positively imperial. But it made Norinne write in her semiannual report—that other human rights workers at other organizations will file under F for Frauen die Helfen or L for legal—"the question to be asked is why follow the legal procedures and why have defense counsels if ultimately the prisoner will be released at Eid."[20] What's the point?

When Rosemary and Zulal and I walked out of the prison into the snow, Rosemary was up and I was down. She had accomplished a lot. The prison had been improved "200 percent," as Norinne also wrote in her report, and the prisoners' standard of living had surpassed that of the average Afghan citizen. Some prisoners were winning their cases in court. It was a start. Yet there were far more prisoners than before, and more prisons. And what would happen in a few years, I wondered, when the UN and the INGOs were gone and Afghanistan was on its own again? Who would pay the defense lawyers then, when everyone knows it's far more efficient to spend the money on a bribe or a deal. Think how many copies of the Quran you can buy for the price of a lawyer. How many big fat sheep. Still, it is a start. An idea. A glimmer. This is what aid workers say to themselves nearly every day, working both sides of the argument in their heads, driving themselves crazy. Sometimes all the work seems pointless, and sometimes it seems to do little but help pull the wool over American eyes and bring credit to the very politicians who've made a mess of things, but sometimes it seems like a start. Afghans have a saying: *Qatra qatra darya mesha.* Drop by drop a river is made. Some days you believe it. Some days you don't.

I WAS THINKING TOO ABOUT AMINA—A WOMAN WHO WAS FREE and not free. Amina, who had been released from the prison of the Welayat into the confines of everyday life as a woman in Afghanistan. How do you secure the future for women who have no history? Where *do* you start?

King Amanullah made a beginning nearly a hundred years ago when he peeled off his queen's veil in public as if to say, "Look here! What a surprise! Underneath all this cloth. It's a person!" Until that time, as history books record, the story of human life in Afghanistan was the story of men. Then, as now, women lived somewhere behind the scenes, behind the walls, hauling water and firewood, serving food and sex. Some men collected them in harems, like Amanullah's grandfather Abdur Rahman who was said to have 199 wives. At some point in history, men began to cover women up. They required women to hide their bodies, and often their faces as well, in the equivalent of a plain brown wrapper. The practice, euphemistically known as veiling, is common in one form or another throughout the Muslim world and is said to be "Islamic," although, as liberal Islamic scholars tirelessly point out, the Quran recommends veiling, if at all, chiefly for the wives and daughters of the Prophet; and even that suggestion seems to have been made abruptly at a time when the Prophet was particularly peeved by the rude behavior of male guests who hung around after dinner to gape at his women. (It is accompanied by another suggestion: that male guests eat their dinner and go home.)[21]

Historians who busily recorded the doings of men down through the ages took remarkably little interest in the lives and the wardrobes of women; so it's difficult to say with certainty just when and why Afghan women came to be clad in pleated polyester body bags. Some say that veiling reached Afghanistan with nomadic Arabs who copied the fashions of wealthy city-dwelling Byzantine Christians and Sasanian (Persian) Zoroastrians. Others say it came to Afghanistan from India, where Muslims adapted the styles of wealthy Hindus.[22] If such theories are correct—and who knows?—veiling seems originally to háve been an affectation of the urban leisure class by which rich men publicly advertised the fact that their wives did not have to work. (Who could work in such a getup?) Nineteenth-century tycoons in America did the same thing, packaging their ladies in hoops and corsets and bustles, draping them in jewels and furs, and parading them about like ambulatory display cases, flashing the owner's financial status.

A more common explanation of veiling is that it is necessary for "protection." But protection of whom? From what? That is where opinions differ. Many male commentators report that Allah endowed Muslim men with awesome sexual prowess and desire. Any man is likely to be aroused by the mere glimpse of an ankle or a wisp of hair escaping from beneath a scarf. Can he be responsible for what he then feels compelled to do? Of course not. So to protect women from the uncontrollable God-given sexual appetites of men, women must keep themselves under wraps. This argument also has a long history in non-Islamic societies, such as the United States, where it is most often used to shift the blame for rape, incest, and the sexual abuse of children to the victim; but in Islamic countries it takes on a self-fulfilling logic. Predictably, the effect of hiding the faces and bodies of women is to make them seem to men even more mysterious and alluring (and even less like real human beings), so that the woman who is not entirely enveloped—the one who even inadvertently shows a bit of hair or skin—may be in real danger from some aroused and predatory male who believes that Allah, in a remarkable oversight, has failed to give him the ability to control himself. The young Afghan women who work for Madar, and who go about their business in Kabul wearing simple head scarves or shawls, went last March on a pilgrimage to the Shrine of Ali in Mazar-i Sharif where thousands gather to celebrate the New Year. When they returned they were oddly depressed and silent. It took them several days to confess what had happened. "We had to wear burqas," Lema said, while the other women looked at the floor. "The men stood by the doors of the shrine. Very many men. We must pass the men to get in. They all look at us. They push us. They touch us. They say very bad things. It is terrible. Nadia is crying. What can we do? We go to bazaar and we buy burqas and we put on. Even when Taliban went away I say I never wear burqa again. But what can we do?"

The same belief in supermale sexual appetite is also used in Muslim societies today—in another self-serving twist of the Prophet's apparent intentions—to justify polygamy. After many of his male followers were killed in warfare, Muhammad suggested that Muslim men of sufficient means take poor war widows as additional wives to provide for their welfare; and some Afghans will argue that similar postwar conditions in Afghanistan today make polygamy almost mandatory. But the average Muslim shopping for additional wives—like his Western non-Islamic counterpart looking for a new girlfriend—is not eyeing indigent widows or thinking charitably about the welfare of women. Instead, he is likely to cite his God-given sexual superpower to justify the acquisition of yet another (younger) wife.[23] After all, how is he to satisfy his holy lust when his first wife is "polluted" with her monthly "sickness" or bearing a child? Better another wife—even a temporary one—than the sin of fornication. In Afghanistan men say that first wives always "freely" consent to the coming of a second or third or fourth wife. Since first wives have no other place to go, what else can they do?[24]

Some commentators on Islamic society, on the other hand, argue that veiling is prescribed to protect men from women. In this view, it's women, not men, who are thought to be endowed with an insatiable sexuality that makes them immensely powerful and potentially overwhelming. (This was the vision advanced by ear-lier Western travelers and "Orientalists" who popularized tales of the harem and lush oil paintings of languid odalisques.) Women must be kept under wraps then to safeguard the whole commu-nity from the disruptive potency of their whopping erotic capaci-ties. Scary visions of the *vagina dentata* spring to mind and we know we're slogging through the swamp of unassimilated psy-choanalytic material, deep in the jungles of primal fear. But the theory helps to explain the extraordinary exertions of conserv-ative Islamists to control not just the packaging of women but every aspect of women's lives. Like an avalanche that slips free of the mountain, the woman who escapes control may rain destruc-tion on men and their houses and their whole bloody village. The fear of social debacle often seeps through casual observations of Afghan culture, like this remark from a 1962 study by a group of American scholars: "Water ranks with property and women as a source of dispute in Afghanistan."[25] Afghans themselves have a saying that names the three sources of social discord as *"zan, zar o zamin"*—women, money (gold), and land. When Afghans cite threats to the social order, they name women first.

A century ago Amir Habibullah, son of the much-married Abdur Rahman, lost favor with his gossiping subjects when his wives were seen in public riding horses and wearing "short veils." According to Afghan women friends who remember what their grandmothers told them, the usual veil of upper-class urban Afghan women at the time was a voluminous ankle-length affair very much like a burqa. (One historian describes the standard long veil as "tent-like.")[26] The short veil adopted by the cream of society was a kind of hip-length burqa worn over big, baggy accordion-pleated trousers, meant to be pulled up over a dress—an arrangement that fully covered the woman but enabled her to engage in activ-ities, like horse riding, impossible in the full-length tent. This cos-tume, and the extraordinary behavior it permitted the women who wore it, caused Afghans to question the amir's ability to rule not just his family but his country. If a man can't control his women, they asked, how can he control his subjects? But Amir Habibullah was drawn to things modern. He is credited with having started "several processes of Afgan modernization which continue today" in Afghanistan—though even today modernization in Afghanistan is not what you would call a trend.[27] He loved cars and built a road or two. He hired an American engineer to build the country's first power station and install electric lights in the palace. He took up photography and posed himself in Western haberdashery among his four wives and thirty-five consorts, all of them unveiled and in Western dress. Given this kind of carrying on, Afghans seem to have been neither surprised nor especially sorrowful when one night as Amir Habibullah slept, someone put a bullet through his head.

Men covered up women's history too. Perhaps the absence of women from history books was deliberate, a question again of control, depriving women of a context for achievement and possibility. Perhaps it was simple unscholarly neglect, a failure of effort and imagination. Perhaps it was a reflection of how little women mattered, not just in the amply chronicled adventures of rulers and warriors, but how little they mattered at all. Perhaps an androcentric and misogynist literature is simply the inevitable outgrowth of an androcentric and misogynist society. Even the Quran is addressed largely to men and men's concerns. The Prophet's wives complained about that, calling his attention to his many female followers. After that he dictated some *suras* for women as well, but it seems at best a halfhearted effort. Can we expect historians to do any better than the Prophet himself?

The conscientious inclusion of women's lives and activities in history began in the United States only in the 1970s as a consequence (and a part) of the feminist movement. In the Islamic world, women entered the history books much earlier, in the nineteenth century, as the topic of discussion among Muslim male intellectuals, particularly in Egypt and Turkey, about their treatment under Islamic law and custom. The issue was raised by the encroachment into Muslim lands of European colonial powers, bringing European products, politics, and ideas that called into question such common practices as purdah (the confinement of women), sex segregation, polygamy, and easy divorce (for men). As the debates continued, the treatment of women became entwined with other critical social issues, including nationalism, national advancement (later "modernization"), political and social reform, and cultural change. Some argued that the status of women in the Islamic world could be raised only by abandoning the cultures of Muslim countries altogether and adopting the cultural traditions of more "advanced" European nations. It was a peculiarly colonial argument. Western feminists in equally misogynist Judeo-Christian societies were not scrapping their heritage for a foreign model but were fighting for their rights on their own ground. Why couldn't Muslim women, too, challenge their own culture? According to Islamic scholar Leila Ahmed, it was in this context of colonial domination "that the links between the issue of women and the issues of nationalism and culture were permanently forged."[28] In the cultural debates, politics, culture, class, religion, nationhood, law, custom, governance, Muslim male privilege, and the status of Muslim women get wrapped up together in a single flag that looks for all the world like a veil.

Ever since Europe and the Middle East first collided, Muslim nations have alternately battled Western imperialism and selectively welcomed Western modernization. They have condemned Western moral corruption while denying its pleasurable attractions mainly to their women. They have denounced Western materialism—rightly, in my opinion—while buying Western materials. In Afghanistan King Amanullah installed running water and telephones in the palace as fast as he could, and no Afghan man has ever been known to turn down Western weapons. But let Muslim women remove their veils—or try to wear them to a public school in France—and the result may be a public stoning or a legislative ban. What a

Muslim woman wears is not just a matter of gender. She wears the whole weight of the Islamic world.

During the last century Islamic nations one by one succumbed to the universal masculine fascination with the gadgets of modern technology: cell phones, cars, computers, and a full range of weapons of war. They bought into Western moral corruption: alcohol, prostitution, rock and roll, Havana cigars. Influential minorities advocated modern Western ideas: democracy, equal rights, freedom of speech and the press, secularism. But the more men modernize, the more they rely on the traditional dress and behavior of their women to maintain the "culture" and "Islam." (Just as ruthless Victorian capitalists counted on the purity and stuffy high-mindedness of their ladies to maintain a certain moral tone in the avaricious classes.) Imposing "conservatism" and "honor" on women frees men to live as they please. But it puts them in fear of losing control. And fear makes them cruel.

When Amir Amanullah inherited the throne in 1919 he was a young man with some modern ideas. He'd been influenced by his father-in-law, the liberal intellectual and nationalist Mahmud Tarzi, who had long published a bimonthly newspaper in Kabul—*Seraj-ul Akbar* (The Light of the News)—critical of both European imperialism and Afghan factionalism and resistance to change. Amir Amanullah gained immense popularity by winning a quick Anglo-Afghan War (the third) and prising the country at last from under the British thumb. Then he announced a new Constitution and a long list of policies to modernize foreign affairs and domestic institutions. The national assembly he established rubber-stamped some reforms, but balked at intrusions into family life. Amanullah's new marriage code called for taxing polygamous marriages. His education program established a school for girls. What was at stake was not "tradition"; his ban on traditional slavery was easily accepted. The sticking point was the status of women. Tribesmen rebelled against many of the amir's innovations, but historians say that what angered them most were those intended "to emancipate women from the absolute power held over them by their male relatives."[29]

In 1926 Amanullah assumed the title of king, and the following year he announced plans for a royal visit to Europe. It wasn't just a junket—he had serious foreign policy objectives—but the royal progress through the capitals of the Western world was to change the future of king and country. King Amanullah and Queen Suraya set out in December 1927 with a large retinue. When they returned six months later, the king was at the wheel of a snazzy new car he'd driven all the way from Tehran. He'd paid official visits to France, Belgium, Switzerland, Poland, and the Soviet Union; he'd met King Fuad in Egypt, Mussolini in Italy, President Paul von Hindenburg in Germany, King George V and Prime Minister Stanley Baldwin in England, Kemal Ataturk in Turkey, and Reza Shah in Persia. Along the way, Queen Suraya had doffed her veil. She'd been photographed in public wearing European dresses with no sleeves and notable décolletage. (The dresses look a little too small, as if she didn't know just how they were supposed to fit.) She'd even visited the shrine of Mashhad, one of the holiest Islamic sites in Persia, without a veil. Anybody could see there'd be hell to pay when the royal couple got home.

But apparently not King Amanullah. He'd barely crossed the border when he announced that Afghanistan needed widespread reforms that could be brought about only with the emancipation of women. Two months later he summoned 1,001 tribal chiefs, mullahs, and khans to a five-day *loya jirga* at Paghman, presented them with new clothes—morning coats, white shirts, and black ties—and ordered them to dress up like a European parliament. Then he introduced them to a series of changes. The most popular was a plan to buy a lot of guns for the army. The most controversial (and arguably the most prescient) was a requirement that mullahs who wanted to teach or preach be examined and licensed, and that mullahs from the ultraconservative Deoband seminary in India be banned from Afghanistan altogether because they might be "bad and evil persons" spreading treacherous foreign propaganda.[30] The most unpopular reform was an attempt to raise the legal minimum age for marriage to twenty-two for men and eighteen for women. That proposal, which would have interfered with child marriage and the practice of giving girls as compensation for crime, got exactly nowhere. Angry delegates said it ran contrary to Islam.

King Amanullah was relentless. He convened another audience of government ministers, civic officials, prominent citizens, and foreign diplomats and commenced a four-day series of speeches, still plugging his exciting new European ideas. On day one he described his trip as a triumph of foreign relations. On day two he revealed that all those fine new guns for the army would be paid for by docking the soldiers' pay, a move of dazzling stupidity for a man who was about to need an army. On day three he marched oratorically onto unfamiliar ground, seemingly unaware of landmines that lay underfoot. He announced new rules for the veil. The "Afghan veil"—the full-length, tentlike, face-covering burqa—would be banned. (It was a safety hazard for women walking in the streets of Kabul, he said—and it still is.) In its place women would have the option of wearing a small "Turkish veil" covering the lower half of the face—or no veil at all. Then the king turned to his queen and asked her to remove the veil she was wearing. Historians tell us that women in the audience applauded, but how the men responded, they do not say. Anticipating how the mullahs would react, King Amanullah went on to attack them as a bunch of ignorant fanatics. On day four of his speechifying, the king had to confess that his appointed prime minister had been unable to persuade anyone to serve in the new cabinet. Undeterred, the king said that he himself would carry out his proposed reforms. "I am a revolutionary king and desire to cause a revolution in every phase of life in the country," he said.[31] A revolution is exactly what he got.

The leaders of the Shinwari Pashtuns, who headed the rebellion, drew up a manifesto denouncing the king's policies. Of the ten charges they laid against him, six had to do directly with the status of women. First, the rebels claimed, the king was guilty of "framing of his own codes and disregarding Shariat." (Although the rebels cite no specific codes, the charge clearly covers such "un-Islamic" intrusions into traditional family practice as Amanullah's effort to raise the legal age for marriage.) Second, the king limited men to only one wife, while the Quran allows four. Third, he ordered all government officials to divorce any surplus wives. Fourth, he banned the chador (the veil) and would allow women not only to cut their hair but to keep "naked their arms and breasts." Fifth, he banned purdah, the confinement of women. And finally, he planned to send "grown-up girls to Europe." (The king meant to send them for higher education.) Another of the rebels' grievances—that the king would require documentary, rather than oral, evidence in court—also bears on the status of women; the rule would make it harder for a man to dispense with an unwanted wife by accusing her of a crime, and harder for bribed judges to collude in convicting women as scapegoats in crimes committed by men. Another grievance—that the king would open "theatres and cinemas and other places of amusement"—also bears upon women, for the new policy invites Western entertainments in the age of the flapper, the suffragette, and the New Woman. The rebels also condemned King Amanullah for encouraging "corruption," as if this were something new, and for changing the day of prayer from Friday to Saturday; but these charges—numbers eight and nine on the list—seem mere afterthoughts.[32] It's clear that what set the Shinwari on the warpath was the king's interference with "their" women.

The first act of the new claimant to the throne—another Amir

Habibullah, an ex-bandit known as Bacha-i Saqqua—was to abolish all taxes, and more importantly, all schools. When he was overthrown only nine months later, the new King Nadir Shah reopened the schools and established new ones, but only for boys and men. He too issued a ten-point list: the policies of his new, conservative Islamic government. Point one declared "all Afghans . . . equal in Islamic brotherhood."[33] It also required all women—who clearly were not meant to be included among "all Afghans" in the "brotherhood"—to be veiled. Nadir Shah revoked the ban on purdah at once and thereby immediately returned women to the custody of men. In 1931 his government adopted a new constitution that did not mention women at all.

Nearly thirty years passed before women were allowed to remove the veil again. In 1959, during the reign of Nadir Shah's son King Zahir Shah, Prime Minister Daoud and other members of the cabinet and the royal family appeared on the reviewing stand at independence week celebrations with their wives and daughters unveiled. Daoud had quietly tested public opinion first by sending unveiled women to work as announcers for Radio Afghanistan and as receptionists and flight attendants for Afghan Ariana Airlines; and the public had quietly accepted them. When the mullahs protested the independence week unveiling, Daoud was ready for them. He challenged them to find a single passage in the Quran or the hadith that specifically requires veiling. (The prime minister's own band of scholars had assured him that no such passage exists.) He had the mullahs jailed until they thought better of opposing him.[34]

In the sixties and seventies, Kabuli women came out from under the chador and into the world of work. "Western dresses, nylon stockings, and lipstick" became "signs of social distinction" for women, according to observations of American anthropologists published in 1962. (Men achieved comparable social distinction by donning Western suits and ties.)[35] Many women wore miniskirts on the job and on the campus at Kabul University, where some ultraconservative mullahs and young Gulbuddin Hekmatyar threw acid at them. Many Kabulis—men and women—say the very best years were the 1980s, during the Soviet occupation, when the communist government guaranteed equal access to education and work, and massive Soviet aid brought the capital a period of relative plenty. The good times meant that women could enjoy more freedom, and men could afford not to mind. Then the Islamist mujahidin took Kabul, and President Burhanuddin Rabbani ordered women to cover themselves up. They dropped their hemlines to the ankle, their sleeves to the wrist, covered their heads with a shawl and crept about the city while the mujahidin destroyed it. Then came the Taliban, and security, and the burqa.

I tell you this long story so you'll know that the burqa didn't come from nowhere. That it has a history as hidden and as real as the history of the women who from time to time are forced to wear it. A history that has nothing and everything to do with Islam and with the ambiguous relationship between Western imperialism and the Muslim world. In the West the history of the centuries-long struggle for women's rights has about it the same flow and ebb, the same pattern of progress and backlash that leads feminists to describe the recurrent historical periods of our greatest achievement as waves. But in the West the struggle has been waged almost entirely by women, thousands of whom devoted their lifetimes to it. To list only the foremost leaders in North America and Europe would take many pages; and a list of the rights that Western women now exercise would be as long as, and mostly the same as, a list of the rights of men, though misogyny in the United States has never really gone into remission. In Afghanistan, on the other hand, the rights that women can claim are few, and in many ways different from those of men, for even those that exist under the law or under Islam are in fact contingent upon the approval of a father or husband. The right to leave the house without wearing a body bag. The right to attend school. The right to work outside the home. And the list of women leaders in the struggle for women's rights is short. Feminist ideas have been voiced in Afghanistan for a hundred years, but mostly by members of the intelligentsia on their way out of the country, so the battle still takes place one woman at a time, one day at a time, behind the walls of men's houses.

What goes on in those houses is complicated by the psychic devastation of war. While men fought, the house was women's place. Then the men came home, themselves traumatized by what they'd seen and done, and the domestic space closed in on them, reproaching them with glimpses of what might have been a peaceable life. All the accusatory weight of women's resentment fell upon them too, for they were jobless now, with no work as soldiers or traders (there was nothing to trade) or farmers (the land mines saw to that). What good were they after all, these freedom fighters who had laid waste their own country? So they beat their wives, and raped them, and used them like animals, and they lusted after the pretty dancing boys as they had in the time of soldiering. The beaten women beat the children, and the children tied up the dogs and clubbed them until they fell apart.

Any beaten woman, forced to submit, may recede into depression and passivity. She may slide into somatic complaint. She may suffer crippling backaches or headaches or excruciating pelvic pain. Parts of her body may grow numb, or she may lose the feel of it altogether. She may split off from her emotional feelings too and live somewhere outside her body, spying on herself. She may throw her body down the well to get rid of it, or she may bang her head against the wall to get back in touch with her mind. In the city, she makes endless trips to the doctor for sympathy and medication. (The standard handout to patients is a mix of five or six antibiotics, pain killers, and tranquilizers. The chemical pollution of overmedication is now suspected in the rising numbers of Kabuli babies born with congenital heart defects.)[36] It's a rare Kabuli woman who doesn't have a "problem" and a purse full of pills.

Complaining only of low blood pressure or blinding headaches, she "rests" when she can and waits vaguely for someone to give her the rights some women remember, the rights they've been hearing about lately once again. The UN maybe. Or some international NGO. Women gain some rights, or they lose them, or they gain them again at the whim of some man who happens to be a husband or father or brother or president—a few scraps cast into the yard to quiet the hens, like a pardon from prison in honor of Eid.

But many women understand that rights must be claimed. An Afghan colleague comes to the office bruised because her Talib brother hit her last night with the teapot and forbade her going to work. She came to work anyway, and tonight her brother will hit her over the head with the portable radio so hard that the plastic case shatters and flies apart, and tomorrow she will come to work again because she believes she has a right to be here and that her brother has no right to take her right away. We who love her fear for her life because we can see that she means to win this fight. We try to think of ways to save her. ("Where are the mujahidin gunmen when you really need them?" asks her European boss. It's a dark joke born of our helplessness.) But it's at this point that this Afghan woman chooses to make her stand. She risks her life to claim her right to work. There must be thousands like her all across the country, resisting alone and in silence. Some will win.

IT'S POSSIBLE TO READ THE PREWAR AFGHAN HISTORY I'VE recounted as a history of progress for women in Afghanistan. Just as in the West, each wave of reform washes a little farther up the beach, until the tide ebbs and the rocky patches emerge again, only to be overwhelmed by the next advance of the flood. That's the way women claimed their rights in the Western world, little by little, over a long period of time marked by many setbacks. But in Afghanistan this history is turned upside down and read backward as a cautionary tale for those who would hold power. The historical fates of Amanullah and Daoud and a succession of communist presidents who advanced women's rights (along with many other controversial modern innovations) merge into a single great admonition to the current government—and all the international "stakeholders"—to avoid the issue of women's rights altogether. President Karzai and his cronies seem to make it a rule never to speak up for women's rights, though Karzai has occasionally told the mullahs to do it. One of Karzai's close advisers says, "He's learned the lesson of history very well."[37] Another Karzai pal offers another wimpy excuse, but this one is in truth a threat. "If women get equal rights, they will lose their aura of sanctity," he says, "and then they will be raped." But Karzai and his men probably wouldn't speak up for women in any case, even without the lesson of twisted history. He keeps his wife more closely secluded than any other Afghan ruler since the nineteenth century.

On the other hand, some international agencies are meant to speak up for women's rights. Ever since I first came to Afghanistan I've been going to their meetings. There are small strategy sessions with other activists, just two or three of us trying to figure out what to do about a young woman sentenced to eight years because she's been raped by four policemen, or how to rescue a woman locked up in a "shelter" because she's run away from a brutal husband, or how to forestall the forced marriage of a gifted Afghan colleague who wants to finish medical school and become a pediatrician. (In all these cases and many, many more, there is nothing we can do.) There are also large public meetings sponsored by various government ministries, or UN agencies, or INGOs. By 2004, almost every agency and ministry has a gender adviser— *gender advice* sounds less threatening than *women's rights*—and gender advisers seem to be a gregarious lot. Their job is to get the various offices and institutions of government to "mainstream" gender issues—or in other words, to build in to their plans and policies a bit of concern for women; and because considering women is a revolutionary concept in a culture as intensely patriarchal as the Afghans', gender advisers often seem to go wrong.

Take for example a conference offered early in 2005 by the Ministry of Justice and planned by the ministry's gender adviser in cooperation with the embassy of Iran. It featured three closely veiled Iranian women discussing the Islamic implications of CEDAW, the United Nations Convention to End All Forms of Discrimination Against Women, an international human rights document about which they knew little because their country had refused to sign it.[38] They were followed by three (male) Quranic scholars chosen in the interests of diversity from three different Islamic countries. They discussed at length the question of whether the world's predominant religions consider women to be fully human and hence eligible for human rights, but unfortunately they were unable to reach a definitive conclusion.

Once a month UNIFEM, the agency of the UN whose job it is to advance the cause of women, holds a meeting to talk about violence against women. It's called a "multistakeholder meeting" because it's open to everybody from every "sector": the UN, various branches of the Afghan government, the World Bank, international and local NGOs, and Afghans from civil society organizations and associations. Everybody comes and everybody agrees that many forms of violence against women are commonplace, widespread, and terrible, and that we should do something about it. But during the run up to the presidential elections, an American UNIFEM leader warns us with exquisite tact to lie low lest the election be lost by Hamid Karzai or, more important, George W. Bush. Maybe we should form some subcommittees, or maybe even (after the meetings have been going on for two years) think about possibly drawing up a preliminary plan of action. The presidential elections are over, but *gradual* is still the operative word. It's not that advocates of women's rights are trying to impose some radical Western program on innocent Afghans. Our "consultative body" is made up mainly of Afghans; and the dreadful customary practices we oppose, like selling nine-year-old girls to horny old men or delivering women to make amends for murder, have already been outlawed by the Afghan Constitution. But international bodies and Afghan women are alike in their trepidations. Their survival depends upon performing service without giving offense.

At the same time, Bush the Lesser has made much of the mythical "liberation" of Afghan women, so lip service must be paid. Occasions must be found to publicly praise women. Like March 8— International Women's Day. For two or three years running the Ministry of Women's Affairs and UNIFEM, the UN Agency that advises the minister, open the big loya jirga tent on the grounds of Education University to hordes of women. The women, swathed in long coats and big, dark shawls sit silently on folding chairs and listen to speakers. First the mullah reading the Quran. Then a man representing President Karzai. Then a man representing the Ministry of Foreign Affairs. Then a man representing the Ministry of Justice. Each one says we should be happy to be celebrating International Women's Day because it is a special day set aside for us. Lest we underestimate the privilege, they point out in aggrieved tones that no comparable special day has been set aside for men. Then, when all the men have finished, they hoist themselves from the easy chairs in the front row, where they've been sipping tea while their cronies orate; and they exit in a pack on their way to more important things. Then it's the turn of designated women to speak. Shouting into the unfamiliar microphone, they read long, mumbling speeches—the minister for women's affairs, the head of this and that, and finally the timid American from UNIFEM who begins in English, "Dear ladies." Each one says we should be happy to be celebrating International Women's Day because it is a special day set aside for us. Then it is over and all the women quietly file out and go home to their housework. The second year is the same. The third year I skip the event, but a friend who attends describes a break with tradition. President Karzai appears briefly to deliver his speech in person, telling the women to be happy about celebrating International Women's Day because it's a special day set aside to remind them to vote for him in the upcoming presidential election. One woman rises in the audience and actually speaks. "My husband will not let me register to vote," she says. "What should I do?" Karzai treats this serious question as his mentor, George W. Bush, would—as a joke. "Don't you worry," he says. "I'm going to call him up and tell him to let you vote." The remark seems to affirm the husband's notion that the franchise is a favor, not a Constitutional right. But of course Mr. Karzai doesn't have the phone number, or the phone numbers of any of the other husbands who have put the same strictures on other women in the audience. My informant says: "You know, Afghan women are deferential, but they're not stupid. After that, they just stopped listening to the speakers. They started chatting with their neighbors, and by the time the UNIFEM lady got up to dismiss them, the buzz of conversation completely drowned her out."

Perhaps that's the reason the Ministry of Women's Affairs turns the 2005 celebration into an exclusive event. The mass gathering under the loya jirga tent is abandoned for a deluxe luncheon by invitation only at the Intercontinental Hotel, Kabul's finest. In keeping with Afghan custom, the invitations go to the relatives and friends of senior officials in the ministry who can be counted on to display gratitude for lunch by listening politely to speakers. International donors foot the bill—enough money to fund my small teachers' education project for the next thirty years—but only a handful are invited to the table. The German ambassador, whose government puts up 10,000 euros for the occasion and who wants a little public recognition, is given a speaking slot near the bottom of the list. Meanwhile, back at our office, we do what Afghan women and their international colleagues are doing all over town:

we eat yellow cake and we dance. Housekeepers drum on their upended plastic washtubs while the rest of us whirl and twirl and laugh like women who truly have something to celebrate.

THE AFGHAN WOMEN I KNOW AND LOVE ARE WORTH CELEBRATING. They are strong women, as resilient as any on earth. Every one of my coworkers has suffered harrowing hardships and sorrows during the last quarter century, and most wear depression like a second skin; but they arrive at the office each morning looking good. Many have no electricity at home, and some have no water, but they manage to be perfectly groomed. They wear long straight skirts or knee-length tunics over trousers topped by a blouse or jersey and a smart jacket. Black leather is popular. They tread the treacherous potholed streets in strappy high heels, a fashion one Afghan friend describes as "thumbing my toes at the Taliban." They cover their heads with soft shawls or scarves that often fall away as they work. They greet each other with smiles and a full recitation of ritualized inquiries about one another's health, well-being, family, and previous night's sleep, all delivered quickly and in chorus together with three kisses on the cheeks: left, right, left. Internationals may settle for a wave or a speedy hello, but not these Afghans. From the boss to the part-time housekeeper, each woman is saluted before any work can begin. When I move from a house full of Afghans to a house full of internationals, I feel suddenly alone. No one kisses me. No one asks how I slept. I am invisible. I go to the office—to the Afghans—to feel recognized again. This is what some women have done for each other, I think, through all the long years of war. This is how they survive.

Yet in the interests of survival, they can turn heartlessly on women whose unconventional behavior challenges the definition of womanhood on which their own safety seems to depend. Good women try to preserve themselves by bludgeoning the "bad." I'm thinking of the reaction of my Afghan colleagues to the murder in Kabul of a popular TV presenter, a young woman who hosted a ho-hum music and chat show that seemed daringly modern by Afghan standards. Her murder—commonly attributed to her father and brother—was the talk of the town, and of our office, too, where the European head of mission called a meeting to discuss it. New to Afghanistan, she thought the staff would want to organize a demonstration or issue a protest. But to Afghan women Shaima's death was only what she deserved. They said it was bad enough that she appeared on TV. And there were other things. She smoked. She talked to men. She went to parties. She drank alcohol. Probably she was pregnant. Yes, definitely they'd heard that—that she was pregnant. So she'd probably just committed suicide, which would have been the smart thing to do, but anyway it was a very good thing she was dead. To international women at FDH, Shaima's execution was a terrible violation of basic human rights, but our Afghan colleagues wouldn't—couldn't—be persuaded to see it that way.

In the streets, women go about their business, walking to their jobs, shopping in the bazaar, taking their children to school. Many women are still encased in burqas, though many are not. Most wear the burqa for safety, some for anonymity, some from habit, and perhaps a few for the status they think they gain from a garment once associated with a higher class. Whether a woman wears it or not has something to do with when she came of age, and where. My friend Moska is forty; she grew up in Kabul during the rule of Daoud and the communists. As a student at Kabul University, she wore miniskirts and sleeveless dresses and never felt the need to cover her head. When the mujahidin came to power, she lowered her hemlines and donned a scarf under duress; but that was just a warm-up for the reign of the real fundamentalists. When the Taliban took over, she bought a burqa and wore it on three occasions to walk the short distance to the house of relatives. "It's supposed to protect you," she says, "but it turns you into a thing. You lose who you are—your personhood, your humanity—and you lose whatever prestige you had with men. Even young boys feel free to tell you what to do. 'Don't walk here.' 'Wait over there.' 'What are you doing here?' 'Go to your home.' As if you were a dog." After those three short trips, she put away the burqa and stayed inside the house for five years. Another friend, Selmin, is only about twenty-five, but she still wears the burqa wherever she goes. She can't see through the latticework of the face panel, so she suffers from terrible headaches and she often falls down. In the heat of summer, packaged in polyester, she faints. She feels angry and ashamed to wear it, but her mother-in-law says she must, and her husband backs up his mother. The mother-in-law is an illiterate woman who grew up in purdah in a small village, adopted the burqa during the Taliban time when she came to Kabul as a refugee, and still awaits orders to take it off.

Burqa or no, the women I know in Kabul lead what look like normal lives, though most of them are poor. They think about getting the laundry done and the house swept and the dinner cooked, though dinner is likely to be bread and rice with a bit of sauce, perhaps, made of potatoes or carrots. (Much of the Afghan malaise is malnourishment and anemia.) They worry about keeping their children safe and their husbands happy, and they may never think about their rights at all. Why should they? Either they have enough "rights" to be content, or they don't—many young women don't remember or understand what "rights" are—and there's not much they can do about it. Many women are happy in their marriages, proud of their children, enamored of their kind husbands, pleased to have interesting jobs. Others lead lives of quiet misery. A Swiss doctor teaching Afghan midwives techniques to relax their patients during delivery has them practice gentle neck massage on one another; some of the midwives, unfamiliar with the caressing touch of a gentle hand, begin to weep. At the New Year, a friend makes me a present of a large black, suitably Islamic shawl that can only be meant to envelope my head and shoulders. Another gives me a bright red lipstick. The gifts reveal nothing about me—I'd never use either of them—but they say a great deal about the variety of Afghan women, and the incipient schizophrenia of their moment in history.

One cold winter afternoon some of the women on the staff of Madar come upstairs to my little room with the teapot and a plate of cookies. They crowd around the woodstove, chattering happily. Madar has moved to a different neighborhood where rents are less expensive, and my new window looks out over a devastated hillside in Karte Char, District Four. Here and there among the ruined houses a man sweeps snow from a rooftop, a woman fetches frozen laundry from a clothesline, a boy with a shovel beats a yellow dog. Snow falls over the scene that spreads before us like a Breughel painting—a panorama of domestic life in Kabul in winter. In the foreground just across the road stands a tiny shop, no bigger than a closet, owned by an old man who appeared in the movie *Osama*. He played the lecherous old mullah who takes the little girl called Osama as his bride. At the end of the film he lowers himself into a cleansing bath after raping the child. There he sits now in his tiny kiosk, his long white beard and turban just visible amid the clutter of candies and sundries he sells. Lema says, "Maybe you could marry him, Nadia. He's a film star." That's how I learn, amid peals of laughter, that Nadia thinks she must find a husband.

For two years Nadia and Lema have told me they will never marry. They are both in their early thirties, but unconcerned about the ticking of the biological clock. (Given the Afghan woman's innocence of sexuality, high rate of childbearing—7.7 children is the national average—and life expectancy of 46 years, they may not know about the biological clock or that it ticks for them.) They like their jobs. They like the very act of leaving home every day, the importance of having appointments and duties and records that must be kept. Their older colleagues are widows whose husbands died long ago—one tortured and killed by communists, the other blown apart by an American rocket fired by mujahidin. The widows look back on marriages that were brief but very happy. One of them had married a fellow university student for love. But their present lives as working widows are agreeable enough to prove that a woman can live fairly well without a husband or father, as long as a brother or uncle will take her in. Now Lema too confesses that a husband is not out of the question. But why? It seems that both Nadia and Lema, whose fathers died in the fighting, have been told by their brothers that they will not be "kept" indefinitely. ("Kept" is the word the brothers use, although it's the women's salaries that support the households.) The women must now find other homes—other men. Both are afraid of the power and violence of men, the loss of friends, the dissolution of pleasant lives. They speak of the lethality of childbirth. (In Afghanistan, which has one of the worst maternal mortality rates in the world, a woman dies in childbirth every thirty minutes.) But they see no other choice.

"I don't want to marry with a mujahid or a Talib," Lema says.

"All men Taliban," Nadia says.

Lema says, "What can I do?"

I tell them that in my country they wouldn't have to marry if they didn't want to. "You enjoy working for a living," I say. "You could rent a house and live together, like sisters." Lema's eyes widen in astonishment. "But we have no money," she says. Unmarried working women like Lema have no economic independence because they feel obliged to hand over their salary to their family. Like nineteenth-century American mill girls whose wages bought their brothers' Harvard education, Nadia and Lema work for what the men of the family choose to buy, and not for themselves. That may be one reason they take so much pleasure in the work itself; they're not in it for the money. But this economic servitude—just as much as the customary practices wrongly called "Islam"—keeps Afghan women in their place. And that place is always in some man's home, under some man's control.[39]

Nadia says, "Can't live Afghanistan women, no men."

"People would think they are prostitutes," explains the widow Moska. "Even as widow woman I must live with my brother." Those are the rules. If a woman likes her family or her husband and is treated well, she may find her life happy and rewarding. But her real economic and social status is that of a slave. And if they don't like her, or they don't treat her with kindness—well, that's another story.

For many women the problems start in childhood, as the children of mothers who are still children themselves—child brides sold into marriage and traumatized by wedding-night rape. What can they know of what we call "mothering"? "This is a nation of mothers who are rape survivors," says a German psychoanalyst. "In Germany people are in therapy for twenty years for such a family history." A UN specialist in counter-trafficking says, "How can I do my job in this place? The whole society is trafficked."

Take the case of the Herati shelter girls. One of them told me later, when I talked to her in the prison where she was serving time for prostitution, "All our difficulties begin with parents who don't give love and respect to their children." She'd never read the work of eminent psychologists who advance that view. By age nineteen, she'd learned it from life. The twenty-eight Herati shelter girls first came to the attention of human rights workers in January 2003 when a man reported to the UN High Commission for Refugees (UNHCR) that girls were being held in "protective custody" by Ismail Khan, then the autocratic governor (or warlord) of Herat. The women proved to be double refugees. Most had fled Afghanistan with their families during the civil wars and traveled to Iran. Growing up there, they'd enjoyed more freedom than they would have known in Afghanistan; they were used to walking freely in the streets, going by themselves to the bazaar or to the houses of their friends. But then each of them had fallen victim to violence—not in the streets but at home, in the family. L was sold in marriage at age thirteen to an old man who raped and beat her until she ran away. M ran away from home after her Iranian stepfather sexually assaulted her when she was about fourteen. Others were beaten and put out of the house by stepfathers who refused, as Afghan men often do, to support another man's child.

One by one, the runaways made their way to Mashhad, to the shrine of Imam Reza, where they found temporary refuge in pilgrims' hostels. There some of them fell in with the pimps, traffickers, and drug smugglers who haunt the place, and they were put to work. Some who were repeatedly spotted by security cameras were picked up by the police. Officially—or semiofficially, for reports of this affair remain "internal" and incomplete—the girls were classed as "unaccompanied females." Some of them say they were taken to court in Iran for cursory deportation hearings, but in the absence of documentation, it seems possible that many of them were simply handed over to an Afghan border official, a nephew of Ismail Khan, and subsequently to the Herati governor himself. Several of the girls told UNHCR investigators that one day "some men who worked for Ismail Khan" picked them up and drove them across the border to "shelter" in nearby Herat.

What happened there is unclear, and the women refused to speak of it. Unlike Western women, who may report victimization, Afghan women know they'll be blamed for anything "bad." In the guesthouse where they were confined, the women lived in very close quarters, guarded by men. Some of the younger girls reported that a dominant group of five or six older girls had "relationships" with the guards, and that this group often went off on "picnics" with men. The UNHCR investigator found evidence of beatings by the guards, fights among the women, self-mutilations, repeated suicide attempts, and profound psychological disturbance. S feared her family would kill her because she had had sex. N tried to kill herself with an injection. K tried to jump down the well. F tried to hang herself. M doused herself with kerosene and was saved from self-immolation only by the intervention of other women. The list went on, recording physical illnesses and mental "vagueness" and "handicaps" that probably indicated post-traumatic stress. Some women were unable to speak at all.

After the investigation, UNHCR officially classed the women as "refugees" and persuaded Ismail Khan to turn them over to Shuhada, an Afghan NGO founded by Dr. Sima Samar, former minister of women's affairs and head of the Afghan Independent Human Rights Commission. Shuhada quickly set up a "shelter" for the women in Kabul, promising them literacy and vocational training. Though none were charged with wrongdoing, the women were again confined—"for their own protection"—this time in closer quarters, and again with male guards. The promised vocational training turned out to be carpet weaving, a grueling profit-making venture meant to defray the cost of keeping them. The women refused to do it. They began to act out. They made themselves up. They dressed provocatively. They played loud music. They flirted with the guards. They smoked. They danced.

UNHCR called in international psychologists and doctors who diagnosed the women as deeply traumatized by physical and sexual violence, and by great loss—the loss of home and family and in some cases children they'd had to leave behind. One German psychologist who worked with the girls for several months during their Kabul captivity, said: "They were defiant, like a gang of street kids—but not aggressive, not malicious. They were a bunch of young girls who drew their fantasies from Indian Bollywood movies. They wanted to be film stars. They had spirit. They were survivors."[40] The psychologist reported that most of the girls were not depressed. They were angry at being locked up.

A few managed to escape, but Kabul police caught two of them walking "unaccompanied" and sent them to prison. At least one, with her young daughter, was sent to a mental asylum where she spends the days in a rage, obsessively scrubbing the child's genitalia. Dr. Samar sent half a dozen of the brightest girls to a

Shuhada-sponsored clinic in the central mountains to train as nurses. But what to do with the rest of them? Dr. Samar was stymied by the problem that faces every organization that tries to give shelter to women victims of violence. You can get them into shelter, but how do you get them out? In the West women victims of violence who take refuge in shelters are never locked in; and when they want to move on, they get a job, find transitional housing, rent an apartment, or move in with friends or relatives. But this is Afghanistan where a woman's one and only refuge is the family. That she might need a refuge *from* the family is well known and universally denied. In Afghanistan a woman who falls out of the family can't climb back in, and a woman on her own is as good as dead.

Dr. Samar applied an Afghan exit strategy. She put the girls up for sale. That is, she let it be known that marriageable young women were available, and men stopped by to inquire. When a match was made, Dr. Samar asked the prospective bride for her consent. She could agree to the match or stay locked up. Only two women refused to marry. As brides go, these women went cheap: a necklace, a few bracelets, a small pile of cash. That put them within reach of men who couldn't afford or expect much—men who had nothing really, except their gender, to recommend them. The weddings took place, one by one; and some time later Shuhada gave me the newlyweds' addresses so I could see for myself how happy they were. I found one young woman, badly bruised, who said her husband and his brother often beat her. She said they'd bought her as a servant, though they used her for sex too, and she hoped to run away. I heard that another new bride had already escaped. But the other addresses on the list came up empty. They were good addresses, nice houses, but the women didn't live there.

To Western human rights workers, these transactions look a lot like trafficking. But an Afghan representative of UNHCR praised Dr. Samar and Shuhada for coming up with such a creative answer—a cut-rate bride sale—to the otherwise insoluble problem of independent women. Dr. Samar herself maintains that she did the women a big favor by vouching for them, selling them off, and restoring them to a legitimate place in Afghan society. "It was only my recommendation that got them husbands," she says. "And what else could we do? We couldn't keep them forever."[41] You might ask by what legal right she kept them at all, but that cogent question is trumped by the other question—the Afghan woman's question: What else can I do?

AT MADAR, WE ALWAYS START THE DAY WITH AN ENGLISH LESSON for the staff women. Even on March 8.

"Today we have a party," I say. "Why do we have a party?"

"Because today International Woman Day!" one woman says, stumbling over the clutter of "international."

"What do we do at the party?"

They call out answers in a swift, imperfect review of simple verbs: "We dance. We sing. We happy. We eat. We drink tea. We beautiful. We talk."

"What do we talk about?"

"We talk about women's rights," Moska says.

"What are women's rights?" I ask. Silence. Everyone but Moska looks blank until Nilofar the dressmaker ventures, "What we want? Go to job?"

"Yes," says Hosai. "Go to office."

I write on the chalkboard: *The right to work.*

"*Maktab,*" says the widow Meryam. "Stoody Inglesh."

"School," says Taiba. She helps Meryam write the English word for maktab in her notebook. I write on the board: *The right to go to school. The right to education.*

Happily married Hosai offers, "Right to husband cook."

"Right to husband clean," crows Taiba, who escaped from a violent marriage to a powerful mujahidin commander. "Right to husband sweep."

There's no need to tell them about Western feminists' renegotiation of housework nearly half a century ago; they've come up with the idea themselves. Besides, I see that in Hosai's household, headed by a gentle man, ideas of fairness already arise.

Nadia says, "Right to no husband," and everyone laughs. She points to the chalkboard, and I write: *The right to choose your husband.* A discussion in Dari ensues about the meaning of the unknown word "choose," and heads begin to nod seriously. Here's the crux of the issue for them: who picks? Of all the women in the room only the widow Meryam selected her own husband. Hosai's parents arranged her engagement when she was five and married her at age thirteen to her twenty-two year-old fiancé. Later, after she'd given birth to three children, she went through a period of hating her husband for stealing her youth. Like many Afghan women she'd been living "*shir ba shir*" (from milk to milk)—from lactation to pregnancy to lactation and pregnancy again, with no menses in between. But later still, after three more children, and the death of two, she somehow grew to love her husband and think herself a lucky woman. They had become companions.

I write on the board: *The right to vote.* This is 2004. All faces turn to me eagerly, anticipating something new, and Homaira asks, "What means vote?" I pantomime writing on a piece of paper, folding it, and handing it over, saying, "Karzai. No Karzai. Vote. Choose the president." There's that word "choose" again. "Karzai. No Karzai." Light crosses their faces. "Oh, vote. *Baly.* Yes. Vote." They've got the word, and the concept, but I see they're not impressed. What can choosing a president mean to women who cannot choose a husband? Other things are more important. The right to survive, and the thing nobody mentions: the right to their own bodies—the right to safety, security, freedom from violence, peace.

"Choose," Meryam says. Taiba helps her write the word in her notebook. "Right to choose."

IN 2003 REPORTERS NOTICED THAT WOMEN IN HERAT WERE setting themselves on fire. Stories appeared around the world about the many cases of self-immolation in Herat. UNIFEM estimated 190 self-immolations in a single year, but nobody ever came up with definite statistics. Hospital records are incomplete and inconsistent, and police acknowledge that successful suicides are never reported at all. Better to bury the burned girl in the yard and spare the family shame. But reporters used words like *epidemic*. Most of the burned girls who wound up in the hospital were teenagers who had set themselves on fire to elude a forced marriage. There was a whiff of romantic protest in the stories, although they had nothing to do with love. Forced marriages are business deals; a man buys a girl from her father. They are common in this impoverished country where often a daughter is the only commodity a man has to sell. Other girls burned themselves because they'd been seduced and abandoned in classic Afghan fashion: the boy persuades the girl that if they have sex, their parents will have to let them marry, but afterward he refuses to marry a "whore." Now she's damaged property, unsaleable to anyone else, a shame to her family, as good as dead. But the news stories focused less on the girls' reasons for setting themselves on fire than on the curious question: Why Herat? My Afghan colleague Salma thought the question was laughably obtuse. "It's not Herat," she said. "They found suicide in Herat because Herat is where they looked. Herat is a famous city. The journalists wanted to go there. So they went to Herat and looked and that is what they found. But you can look anywhere. You will find the same." To prove her point, she took me looking in Kabul.

We went from hospital to hospital to stand by the bedside of girls and women who'd eaten rat poison or swallowed caustic cleaners or unidentified drugs, hoping to die. This one had been sold to an old man. That one had a husband who beat her and made her do what women do in the pornographic movies on satellite TV. Another was despondent because her husband threw her out after taking a new wife, and she was afraid her brothers would kill her if she returned to her parental home. Another wanted to marry her school friend, but her father planned to sell her to somebody else. One by one each woman told a version of what seemed to be contradictory stories: some had men forced upon them that they didn't want, while others wanted men they couldn't have. But all the stories were the same in the end, and there was nothing romantic about them. Violence ran through them like a dark vein. They were all about choice denied. They were all about the familiar question: What else can I do?

The answer was more violence. Inflicted on the self. Later, human rights investigators surveyed Herati men and women at random about acts of violence against women—women who were beaten, locked up, raped, forced into marriage or thrown out of it. In every case they asked, "What advice would you give a woman in this situation?" The most common answer, from men and women of all ages, was: "She should suicide."[42]

Karte Se Hospital is the central burn hospital for the country. Once it may have been a comforting place, set under broad-leafed trees beside the Paghman River, but the trees have been cut and the river diminished to a reeking sewer. The dingy hospital buildings need paint and disinfectant. One of three wings, with seventy beds, is set aside exclusively for burn victims. Many people are burned in Kabul, especially in winter when the propane tanks so often used indoors for lighting and cooking explode. The hospital receives these victims from Kabul, and the most serious cases—burned over 50 percent of the body—from other cities connected to the capital by air. (In the countryside seriously injured people haven't a chance.) The most critical cases of self-immolation in Herat are sent to this hospital. This is where many of them die.

"How many?" I ask the hospital director, a fierce-looking black-bearded Pashtun. But he can't say. The hospital hasn't tallied the patients or their specific complaints. He says instead that between 3 and 6 percent of burn victims are cases of self-immolation. (How he calculates percentages without data remains a mystery, and later a woman doctor on the women's ward ups that percentage to 10.) I ask how many of these cases of self-immolation are girls, and he stares in dismay. "All girls," he says. "Men do not set themselves on fire."

"And the girls? Why do they do it?"

He shrugs. Motives lie beyond his view. He says, "You can ask them."

In the dirty emergency room, in the far corner, out of the way, lies a young girl. Perhaps sixteen. She lies on her back, wrapped to her chin in a filthy blanket. Above her, strands of soot droop from the blackened ceiling. Her arms lie on top of the blanket, wrapped in thick layers of oozing gauze. An IV tube snakes into the bandages at her wrist. The girl moans and chokes on her tears. She catches her breath and screams, a long low wail, and then begins again to moan. Beside her bed a younger sister weeps, stabbing at her tears with the hem of her scarf. The head nurse stands at the foot of the bed and outlines the case dispassionately, as if the patient were not there. This girl was made to marry an old man, she says. Then he accused her of adultery because a friend of his saw her talking to a boy in the street; he told her to return to her father's house. She hadn't wanted to marry this husband, but to go back was to spread shame upon her family, like a stain. She was afraid her father would kill her to wash it away. In this crisis, she went for advice to her neighbor, who said: Why don't you burn yourself? So she did. She drenched her body in diesel fuel and set herself alight. The flames burned 90 percent of her skin and spared only her head, which lies now on a tear-drenched pillow in a kind of separate agony of consciousness and pain, apart from the wrapped and ruined body, already as good as dead. I go to her and stroke her dirty face. She quiets at once and turns her wet brown eyes to mine. What I see there is too much for me. I glance away to her dark hair. It is dry and dirty, and gray with the dust of the streets. At its roots a layer of scruff seems to lift away from her scalp, or perhaps it is the skin itself peeling from her skull. I cannot tell. She screams again and cries out distinctly, "I want to die." The nurse says, "You will." The next day, she does.

She is only one. Two or three girls and women who have tried to kill themselves are received every week at Kabul's Khair Khana and Wazir Akbar Khan hospitals. Ten women and girls classed as victims of *khoshoonat hlai zanan*—violence against women—are received each week at Rabia Balkhi hospital, and among them is at least one who has attempted suicide. Rabia Balkhi is supposed to be a maternity hospital. A doctor at Kabul's other maternity hospital, Malalai, tells me, "We get not many suicides, but we get many, many girl babies every day, on the steps. Women have too many babies. They can't feed them. When they have already two or three girls and they come here to get another, they leave it with us. On the steps. Nobody wants girls."

Boys are their parents' future. They're the ones who stick around and take care of their mothers, while girls are soon traded off to serve others. So nobody wants them much, and nobody treats them very well. Girls are transients, so it doesn't pay to take too much notice of them, or to grow attached. Empathy is unknown. Even in warm and loving families, girls occupy a peculiar and precarious psychic space, and even that is dependent upon their good behavior. Beloved as they may be, they live on sufferance, like lodgers. In an op-ed piece in the *New York Times,* the French writer Bernard-Henri Levy told the story of twenty-one-year-old Homa Safi, a talented reporter with *Nouvelles de Kaboul,* the French-Afghan monthly magazine that he started in Kabul. She fell in love with a perfectly respectable young man, but her father wouldn't let them marry because "the young man was a Shiite, not a Sunni, and . . . anyway she was promised to the son of his friends, a man [she] had never met." Homa Safi bought a lot of "medicine" and took her own life. The grieving father, "mad with despair," swore that "if God returned his beloved child, he would give her to the young man she loved." Levy concludes that Homa Safi is dead "not because of cruelty but because of the infinite folly that fundamentalism brings."[43] But to pin this domestic tragedy on conservative Islam is to miss the point, and worse, to drown the dead woman's clear voice in the static of politics. Homa Safi is dead because her father knew her desire, her choice, and he denied it. This is cruelty. It is also common. What was she after all, this "beloved daughter," but a girl? A friend tells me happily that her cousin has come from a village to give birth to her first child in a Kabul maternity hospital. The next day comes news of a daughter. My friend reports that mother and baby are doing well, although the mother is of course very sad. "Why?" I ask. "Her husband is not speak to her. He say this is shame for him." A week later my friend reports that the mother is learning to accept her unwelcome daughter. The baby's father has spoken to his wife only long enough to say, "If you do this to me again, I will kill you."

The way girls are welcomed into life helps explain why so many are willing to leave it. That and khoshoonat hlai zanan—violence against women. The doctor in charge at Rabia Balkhi is a short sturdy little woman who looks very professional in an immaculate white smock and cap. She is very angry. She says, "You come here and ask me about violence and suicide, but you do nothing about it. And you are not the first ones to come. I tell you in Farsi. I tell you in Pashtu. I tell you in English. They are dying every day, these girls. These women. They are beaten. Raped. Mutilated. What is needed is a central hospital for women victims of violence of all kinds. Because there is no end to it. Then we say to all the hospitals, please do not admit these women but send them to the central hospital. Then we care for them. We give them psychological help, legal help. We help them find a way to live. Otherwise, what can I do? I fix them up and send them back to the same husband or father or mother-in-law who beats them and rapes them and burns them again. Maybe next time they go to another hospital. No one keeps a record. There are many, many cases, but they are lost. You must do something."

Salma explains that we can only offer advice to the government; but mention of the government sets the doctor off again.

"This is not politics," she says. "This is not one regime— Karzai, Taliban, Rabbani. This is patriarchy."

This was the first time I heard an Afghan woman speak aloud the forbidden word "patriarchy" that came so often to my mind. What she described was patriarchy as it was in the West less than a century ago, and as it still must be in some quarters. Human rights investigators estimate that 95 percent of Afghan women are subject to violence—the comparable figure for American women has fallen below 35 percent—and Afghan women experience violence more frequently, many of them many times a day. But the greatest difference between Afghan and American women lies in what we believe about ourselves, and about our rights and wrongs. In Afghanistan most women believe that husbands by right will determine their sex life. They believe that husbands and mothers-in-law by right will dictate what they wear, where they go, and what they do with their lives. They believe that husbands and mothers-in-law by right can beat them at any time, and that fathers by right can kill them if they bring shame upon the family. Even young educated women who might be expected to dispute this allotment of rights ask instead, "What else can I do?" Young well-educated Marzia, who is such a kind friend to the women of the Welayat, opposes my view that women should not be arrested for sexual offenses. (Like Christian fundamentalists in America, and the late Pope, Afghans mistake sexuality for the moral life.) "We must have laws against zina," Marzia says. "Otherwise men will not feel safe in allowing their wives and daughters to go out to work." She can't even imagine a world in which decisions are held in the hands of women.

Another difference between Afghan and American women arises

from what their respective societies believe and teach through the law. Almost all Americans believe that wife beating is wrong. Although decades of feminist political agitation were required to persuade the public to this opinion, it is now reflected in laws that criminalize domestic violence, rape, marital rape, stalking, trafficking, forced prostitution, and enslavement, and in other laws that mandate social supports for women victims of violence. Almost all Afghans seem to believe that men are superior creatures who have every right to do exactly as they please.

In this culture, marriage itself can become a kind of violence. It may begin with the forced marriage of a child bride—like that of the girl Osama in the movie—and a forced consummation that leaves the girl torn and permanently incapacitated. Many young Kabuli brides are brought to hospitals for repairs the morning after their wedding night, and some of them die. Then there's the emotional trauma: the little girl of nine or ten who knows nothing of life except helping her mother is handed over to total strangers, one of whom—her "husband"—pins her down and rapes her so she rips apart and bleeds. Since nobody keeps track of birth dates or marriages, there can be no statistics on child marriage, but in the countryside it seems to be the rule. Poor families counting on a bride price do well to sell a girl off early, before she's old enough to soil the merchandise. Afghan law now requires boys to be eighteen and girls sixteen to marry, and Sharia calls for girls to be at least fifteen. But fundamentalists who believe in emulating the Prophet point out that he married one of his wives when she was nine. (She was playing on a swing when summoned to her wedding.) In the countryside they take wives of seven or eight. In the cities too. In Herat, researchers found child brides among women they surveyed; almost a third of them had married at ages younger than sixteen, some as young as seven. In Kabul, midwives who serve the poorest neighborhoods sometimes find child brides locked up or chained to prevent their running away. ("We must not encourage women to escape from home," the woman judge said, "because we must have a good moral society.") We found them in the Welayat, where most of the prisoners had been married young. We found them in the maternity hospitals, where they were giving birth.

At Malalai Hospital seventy women or so give birth every night, and in the morning the doctors give them a brief talk about "family planning" and send them home with their new babies. (Only about 5 percent of husbands permit contraception, the chief doctor says; so most women ask for injections or undetectable IUDs.) In a recovery ward at Malalai Hospital we find eleven child brides unconscious or asleep. They lie on their backs. Their hospital gowns are tucked up on their ribs so that their naked bellies are exposed. Around each pale sunken belly runs a track of clumsy black stitches. "Caesarian sections," the doctor says. These girls, at eleven or twelve, are still children, their bodies still too undeveloped to give birth. In the countryside, without surgical intervention, they would die. As it is, the doctor says, such young girls are likely to bear malnourished, defective, or retarded babies, babies that can not thrive. The doctor says she's noticed another curious thing about the child brides, such as those who lie before us laced up like tattered lampshades. "They do not bond with their babies," she says. "It is as if they feel nothing."

Yet she thinks these girls are lucky. "We can help them," she says. "They don't die." The doctor is a tiny woman, little bigger than a child herself, but she is brisk and efficient. She keeps a very clean hospital. Groups of women in dark blue smocks are washing the walls and floors with disinfectant, and as she leads us from ward to ward, she pauses here and there to encourage them in a kindly way. "The girls who burn themselves are the worst," she says. "We could prevent it with proper education. It happens only because they don't bleed."

"Excuse me?"

"Yes, that's why they kill themselves. You didn't know? They get married, you see, and on their wedding night they must bleed or people will say they are bad girls and beat them and put them out of the house. They are afraid to go back to their father's house, you see. So they burn themselves." We reach her office, and she seats herself behind a big desk under a framed certificate from Kabul University Faculty of Medicine. "There are other reasons, of course, but this is the most common. Virginity is very important in our culture, you see, so we must educate all people about the seven different kinds of virgins."

"Seven?"

"Yes, seven."

"Please excuse me," I say, "but I believe that in my country we have only one kind."

"There, you see. Education is very important."

She tears a piece of pale green paper from a tablet on her desk and draws with a blue ballpoint pen a series of seven tiny meticulous sketches of the cervix. Each one proves upon examination to be very slightly different from the others in shape or in some minute detail suggested by delicate cross-hatching. "You see that there are seven kinds of cervix," she says. "Seven different kinds of virgins. The important point is that only five of them bleed. These two here . . ." she says, making circles with her pen around two of her tiny drawings, "These two kinds of virgins don't bleed."

"Really?"

"Yes. You see what a problem they have. They do not bleed. People think they are bad girls. They beat them and put them out. So they burn themselves. They die. It is very sad." She stares thoughtfully at the sketches she has made. "If our people knew that some virgins do not bleed, they could send girls for testing. In Kabul many educated fathers bring their girls to us for testing before the wedding. Many times, you see, we can fix them if it is needed. Sew them up a little. But unfortunately most of our people are not educated." She passes the green paper with the little blue sketches to me. "You must help us educate them about science."

Salma and I go back to talk again with patients in the burn hospital, and we learn that passing the bleeding virgin test is no talisman against the long, hard violence of marriage. This time we make our way to the general women's ward, a broad gallery with a low, soot-blackened ceiling slung between supporting arches, like a crypt. In the bays between the arches are iron beds where burn victims lie under blankets propped up like tents so as not to touch the drying wounds. A nurse conducts us through the gallery and stops beside the bed of a withered ageless woman who ignores our greetings. The nurse pulls back the bed tent to display the woman's right leg, seared on the front from knee to ankle. The skin has been burned away from the knee, exposing the patella and the sinews of the joint. The wound is a deep, dusty maroon color, shading to purplish green, and dry like an old side of bacon. The edges of the wound are livid. The nurse says that this woman had a fight with her husband, and being upset, she accidentally spilled hot cooking oil on her leg. As the nurse speaks, the woman turns her face to the wall. "All the women in this ward suffered accidental burns," says the nurse. Then seeing my skepticism, she says that it's often impossible to learn what really happened to a burned woman. The women are afraid to tell, she says, because eventually they must return to the same family where the "accident" happened, and where it could happen again. Sometimes hospital officials report suspicious cases to the police, she says, as they are required to do, but the police don't take much interest in these "kitchen victims." This one has lain on her back in this bed, with her leg propped under the tent, for eight months. No one knows whether she will walk again, and helping her to do so is not the job of this hospital. Her husband has not visited her, but in two or three months' time she'll return to her work in his house, less serviceable, and perhaps more sullen, but having learned some secret lesson shared by the women lying in this room, under the dirty tents, staring at the blue ceiling.

This is the secret: the subjugation of women by violence. It is subjugation softened by family tradition and the consolations of Islam, and sometimes transformed by love; but it is subjugation nonetheless. It is so well concealed, or so universally ignored, as to pass for a short-lived shortcoming of the Taliban; but it is so complete that even women never subjected to physical violence know the code. Their resignation is the mantra that passes for a question: What else can I do? Women of the Afghan diaspora—Afghan-Americans and -Canadians, Afghan-Germans, -Swiss, and -French—who have returned to help their "fatherland," and refugee women returned from years in Pakistan or Iran speak with frustration of Afghan women who never left the country. "Brainwashed" is a word they use a lot. "Patriarchy begins at home," says an outspoken Afghan-Canadian named Rajiba. "Today's women learned as children to do as men say. They learned to think that men are better than women. They really believe it. Deep down, they think it's really true."

"It's not that women don't have their tricks," says Afghan-German Tamina. "They're very tricky. They have to manipulate to get through the day. They have their little illnesses and their little rivalries and their little gossip. They can throw knives around a corner." But these are the subversive tactics of people who know they have no real power. "Basically," says Tamina, "they accept whatever men say, and they do as they're told."

"Afghan women are brainwashed from childhood," says Professor Nahid Rahimi, who teaches at the university. "When men are in the room, the women students don't speak up. They don't answer questions. You'd think they were completely stupid. I encourage them, but I can't blame them. I do the same myself. If I am in a meeting or discussion with male colleagues, I am always careful not to say too much; and even when I know the answer to a question, I am careful to keep it to myself."

THIS IS A WILLING SELF-EFFACEMENT, A WILLING SUBSERVIENCE, A voluntary dumbing down of half the population that takes place even among educated, professional women who would appear to

be the exception to the rule. Perhaps such self-abnegation is symp-
tomatic of the trauma of war. Perhaps it arises from the intense
peer pressures of tribal culture. (Afghans wear the same clothes,
eat the same food, sell the same products in the same side-by-side
shops, pray the same prayers five times a day, and worry all the
same that they may stray away from the norm.) Or perhaps this
routine everyday self-demolition of women is, as so many Afghan
women seem to think, the consequence of childhood condition-
ing, a customary brainwashing indelibly inscribed by the occasional use of force. Researchers report that one of the greatest
"constraints on women's participation" in life beyond the household in the mythical new Afghan democracy is that "violence
against women is used as a way of reinforcing women's adherence
to local *purdah* norms."[44] But after all the personal and political
violence Afghan women have undergone, there's usually no need
for heavy-handedness. A small reminder puts a woman in her
place. When Professor Rahimi lectures to a class of conservative
male students at the university, they turn their bodies ever so
slightly away, and they never look at her. Her father, her husband,
and her male bosses at the university have all given permission for
her to teach, but now she comes up against the next phalanx of
men: her students and her male colleagues.

Living like this, always at men's pleasure, women must learn to
anticipate men's wishes, and to do so they must learn to see things
as men see them. Many adopt the male perspective so completely
that they cannot seem to feel the suffering of other women.
Instead, of necessity, they compete with one another. Captives of
patriarchy, they look out for themselves with an intensity that
eclipses empathy and loyalty and collaboration. "That's another
thing they learn as children at home," says Tamina. In a big family
with scarce resources always allotted first to men and boys, girls
learn to scramble for the scraps. Later, after marriage, they compete with sisters-in-law and vie with a mother-in-law for a husband's allegiance. How can they support each other? Professor

IN THE PRISONS   181

Rahimi says she gets no backing from women colleagues in the university. Rather they discourage her from "making trouble," and they strongly advise her not to speak so much of her special interest: the human rights of women. Outstanding women students in the university complain of being treated distantly by other students; they say that professors who ought to encourage them warn them instead that they don't "fit in." The competition to be accepted shuts them up. Let one woman speak up in a mixed discussion and no other woman will back her, even if she has voiced a common complaint. They don't trust one another. They don't support one another. Even when they dance, they do it one at a time.

Much of this is not peculiar to Afghan culture. Girls of my generation growing up in the US learned the rules too, less draconian certainly, but mean enough. Doors were closed to us, and ways of being. ("Don't be smart." "Don't be mad.") Christianity taught subservience, self-effacement, precious chastity. In my case too, repression was enforced by violence at home and by the threat of violence from men in the street. The subjugation of women in Afghanistan is extreme, but it's nothing new, and those of us who deplore the Bush administration's milking the issue for political gain must be forgiven our jaded feminist disgust. The subjugation of women in Afghanistan is not a consequence of their being Afghan. It's not a consequence of their being Muslim. It's a consequence of their being women. It's merely made worse by poverty, war, illiteracy, isolation, fundamentalism, imperialism, and the operative conditions of the current fourteenth century.

ON LONG WINTER EVENINGS, WHEN IT WAS TOO COLD TO STRAY far from the woodstove, the women of FDH used to sit together on the tushaks in the living room and talk. We were internationals from six different countries, but the work was hardest for Nooria, the only hyphenated Afghan among us at the time. An

Afghan-German, Nooria is a gynecologist who volunteered to spend a month at a Kabul hospital. Her father had been a leader in a centrist democratic party during the struggle between the communists and the radical Islamists. Like former president Rabbani, he'd received an Islamic education at al-Azhar University in Cairo, but he'd gone on to Germany for a doctorate in history and taught Islamic studies there for many years before he returned to Afghanistan. Nooria said, "He was a man with a mind for both worlds, Islam and a kind of grassroots Western democracy that accords with Islamic principles of social justice. That's what he was working for here when he was assassinated." Nooria's mother took her children back to Germany where Nooria got her education. Now, twenty years later, she'd come back to Afghanistan with her mother to visit her father's grave and the relatives they'd left behind, and to do what she could to help. Nooria shared her father's hope of reconciling disparate cultures, but like many other hyphenated Afghans who return, she found little in common with her former countrywomen. She speaks of them with a kind of despair.

Nooria says that her mother remembers Afghans being rather indifferent to one another before the war, but now after such conflict, after witnessing such unspeakable things, they've become hard. She says the women she works with at the hospital seem to be always talking about their own grievances, about their female problems and their inadequate pay and their aching backs. They are always calculating, she says, always thinking about money. If their pay is two thousand Afghanis, they work only what they imagine to be two-thousand-Afghanis' worth. They believe that if they were paid five thousand Afghanis they would work much harder, but since they are not paid the mythical salary that would require exertion to their imagined full capacity, none of them works very hard at all.

The senior doctor strolls in, well dressed, heavily made up, nose in the air, and announces that she is not on duty in the delivery room today. The next says that she has forgotten to bring a gown so she cannot perform deliveries today. Another one, summoned to an imminent birth, cuts the episiotomy, delivers the baby, hands it to the nurse, and leaves. She doesn't stick around to see if mother and child are all right or to repair the cut she has made in the woman's tissues; she leaves those tasks to junior doctors, not as important as she. Most births fall to the most junior of all, the midwives. A labor is long and three midwives try to speed things up by beating the woman. They slap her face and pound on her belly and shout at her: "Push, you shit-faced dog!" From the next bed a woman is crying out, but none of the doctors or midwives pays the slightest attention. "Help me, please," she says. At last a nurse lifts the sheet to reveal a pond of soupy shit between the woman's legs. The nurse walks out. Minutes later the woman cries again for help, and a baby slides on its own from the birth canal into the puddle, and there it lies while the woman cries and cries for help and the nurses and doctors stand watching from afar.

"What kind of women are they," a Spanish lawyer asks, "with no empathy for other women?"

"What kind of women?" says Nooria. "They are Afghan women. How would they learn to have empathy for other women? What they believe is what men tell them and what all their experience confirms: that women are worth nothing. Not as much as a car or a cow or a television set. Nothing. And childbirth is just another task, maybe more painful and dangerous than some others, but still just routine."

I tell Nooria a story my Afghan colleague Salma told me, about a time when she was a girl fleeing down the road from her village under attack by the mujahidin. A woman just ahead suddenly sank to her knees. Groaning, she clutched her burqa closely. Salma's mother and father stopped to offer help. After a few minutes the woman pulled a bloody newborn from under the burqa, wiped it off with the hem of her skirt, got up, and ran on. Another task.

"Yes," says Nooria. "I see how they learned."

She repeats a story that her mother heard from a relative: the story of a man who was killed by mujahidin, chopped up, and thrown piece by piece into a pot of boiling water while his wife and children were forced to look on. Then the mujahidin did the same one by one to the children. Nooria says, "Of course it's really a story about the woman who was made to watch." That was during wartime. I remember, though I do not speak of it then, what one of our counselors told me about a client of hers. She is the widow of a mujahidin commander, one of Gulbuddin's lieutenants, who used to pour boiling water on her abdomen and thighs and genitalia to "clean her up" before raping her. He would celebrate his climax by biting hunks of flesh from her breasts and arms and legs and face. Her limbs and body are pitted now and scarred, according to the counselor who accompanied the woman to a medical exam; and the flesh of her belly is so shrunken by scarring that she can no longer stand upright. The counselor said, "She used to be beautiful and tall, but now she is short. He is dead, but she is still afraid. She is really very short." That happened after the wars, in peacetime. It is these things, experiencing these things, witnessing these things, hearing about these things, even when like the counselor you are paid to listen, that make you hard. There are enough stories like that in Afghanistan to turn a whole country hard as rock.

Not long after I arrived in Kabul in 2002, I attended a big UN-sponsored women's conference that gathered women from all the neighboring provinces. It was held at the Intercontinental Hotel, which at the time was Kabul's rundown finest. While we listened to speeches in the conference room, the hotel staff laid out a grand buffet in the hall. When the speeches ended, I headed for lunch with my translator, a university medical student from a prominent Kabul family. At the head of the buffet tables, I reached for a plate, but a woman came from behind me and snatched it from my hand. I reached again, but another woman laid a block into my shoulder that spun me around the end of the table and into the wall. My translator caught me as I bounced off and led me aside. "I think we must wait," she said apologetically. Women who'd seized the plates were moving fast to fill them, snatching chunks of meat and sopping handfuls of potatoes and cabbage. Some didn't bother with plates but stood at the buffet table eating fast with both hands. One woman picked up a platter of chicken legs and tipped it into her handbag. Others carried off bowls of boiled meat or rice pilau. Two women struggled over a tray of sliced cake while a third woman picked it clean. It was like the old cartoons of women fighting over the sales tables in Macy's basement, but this scene unfolded in silence. Wordlessly, the women worked over the food with the systematic voraciousness of locusts, and when they finished, there was no morsel left. The frenzy of their desperate, solitary eating had brought me close to tears.

"I can get you something from the restaurant," the translator said.

"No, thank you," I said. "It's not important." But she was apologetic and deeply embarrassed.

"These people don't know to behave in a good way," she said. "I think it's only that they are very hungry."

"No," she said. "This is the way we live."

Paradoxically, the same single-mindedness that drove such frenzied feeding can be the engine of self-restraint in situations where a woman's actions or speech might be troublesome enough to "make things worse." Afghan women possess a kind of unassuming fortitude, indistinguishable from "passivity," that enables them to survive hard times and hard people. Take the women who work at Madar. The little NGO always teeters on the edge of insolvency, and Caroline lives in hope that one day one of the foreign "experts" who come from time to time to help her will possess a financial brain the equal of her own good heart. Hope leads her to give them the benefit of the doubt, so that even though she's very nearly Afghan herself, she entrusts Madar to one foreign expert after another who knows nothing about Afghanistan at all. The Afghan women of her staff, who have been with her from the beginning, have no choice but to tack with the winds of dubious expertise. One visitor wants to teach Afghan farmers how to farm. Another wants to train mothers to care for their babies. Several, including me, try to teach teachers how to teach. One is determined to solve Madar's fiscal problems by turning its popular handicraft shop into an upmarket boutique. She switches the team of dressmakers, whose traditional embroidered Afghan garments have sold well for years, to manufacture of her own dowdy frocks. Afghan staff women dutifully file the appropriate plans and take the appropriate permissions, shifting without a word of complaint or confusion from the Ministry of Agriculture to the Ministry of Health to the Ministry of Education to the Ministry of Commerce. Through it all they speak softly among themselves and keep their own counsel. Even when I know they are dismayed, their faces remain as changeless as that of the broken clock on the wall of the makeshift office that is always undergoing rearrangement. Toward the end, under the noisy autocratic reign of Mary Lou, the fashion expert, some of the dressmakers go home after work and weep in secret.

"She makes us cut up the beautiful silk," the head dressmaker tells me in a whisper.

"Have you complained to Caroline?"

"No, no. We will discuss when Mary Lou is gone back to America."

"But that could be months away. Why don't you speak to Caroline?"

"No, no. Never mind. There will be time."

The women sense the appalling ugliness of the stuff they are forced to make, but they assume that some people somewhere must like such things, for Mary Lou keeps going on about "the market." What bothers them is having to cut the silk they've always saved for very special orders. They know the women who wove it. They know how hard it was to do the weaving and how long it took. And the fabric is so beautiful. Nevertheless, they cut and stitch and press as required until all the silk is gone and so too is the American expert, leaving behind piles and piles of costly Mary Lou Modes that nobody wants to buy. In the end, the expert has made money for her services and Madar has lost by them; but the women still have their jobs, and not a single word of unpleasantness or complaint has been voiced by the Afghans, except quietly, occasionally, in a whisper, to me. (It is not that I am their special friend, though it serves them to encourage me to think so. They must have whispered complaints about me too, to others they wished to mollify, like the dread Mary Lou herself.) That's how they deal with their families. That's how they faced the Taliban. That's how they survive now the onslaught of foreign "help."

Is this behavior heroic endurance, cowardly inaction, enlightened self-interest, or post-traumatic stress? Or is it some complex survival strategy designed for waging life in zones unknown to our tidy pseudo-psychoanalytic diagnostic dictionaries? Quite a few inspirational books have been written in the past few years about the heroism of Afghan women, about their courage and fortitude and resilience. Most of the books describe the Afghan woman's strength as "hidden" or "veiled," as indeed it had to be under the Taliban when so many women risked death to carry out the task of teaching children. Heroism sometimes consists in lying low, so Afghanistan, like every patriarchal society, is short of outspoken, upfront women heroes. I can think of only two, and one of them is dead.

Her name was Meena. As a middle-class girl growing up in Kabul in the 1970s, she studied history and literature with progressive teachers at Malalai Girls' High School and Kabul University, then simmering with radical opinions. In 1977, as a twenty-year-old student, she founded the Revolutionary Association of the

Women of Afghanistan (RAWA). It began as an intimate group of young women who exchanged ideas about women's rights and equality, and went on to spread those ideas through literacy courses for poor women. Unlike political groups of men on the university campus at that time—groups like the Maoists and Professor Rabbani's incipient Jamiat-i Islami—RAWA rejected both ethnic sectarianism and Islamism as the basis of the state. Alone among Afghan political parties to this day, RAWA calls for separation of mosque and state in a secular republic and denounces the Islamist mujahidin—all those heroic "freedom fighters"—as "terrorists" and "bandits" and "fundamentalist criminal gangs." That explains why Meena had to flee from Afghanistan, and why RAWA has never been invited to the postwar "nation-building" table. In the early 1980s, she moved RAWA's operations to Quetta, Pakistan, to serve Afghan refugees; and there she was murdered in 1987, probably by agents of the ever-present Gulbuddin Hekmatyar. By that time, Meena and RAWA were well known in Europe. Meena was a charismatic speaker, and RAWA had always been savvy about public relations. In the Taliban time, when the world began to notice Afghanistan, RAWA was the only organization of Afghan women to be found on the Internet. American feminists discovered them there and adopted them. Rallying to support "the women of Afghanistan," they sent money and moral support to RAWA, still operating in the refugee camps of Pakistan, while thousands of unknown women risked their necks to run home schools and health services in Afghanistan in defiance of the Taliban. With Meena gone, there seemed to be no one to lead RAWA back home, and in the new oppressively conservative Islamic times, few women—or men—to follow the secular cause. Prominent Western feminists still import RAWA members to speak about Afghan women, yet the organization idolized in America is almost invisible at home.[45] There the real hero Meena has been eclipsed by another radical charismatic leader who is her exact contemporary, Osama bin Laden.

Another real-life female hero, as brave and outspoken as Meena, appeared at the constitutional loya jirga in 2003. Twenty-five-year-old delegate Malalai Joya rose to ask why the warlords and mujahidin commanders sitting in the front rows should not be tried by an international court for their war crimes against "barefoot Afghans." Ordinary Afghans troubled by the same question applauded her courage, but the warlords and commanders who sit in the Karzai cabinet took offense at such free speech. The chairman tried to expel her from the constitutional convention, and she had to be placed under UN protection to save her life.[46] It may be a mark of change that in 2005, Malalai Joya was elected to the new Parliament.

But Meena and Malalai Joya are nothing like the traditional heroines held up as role models, though ironically Malalai Joya must have been named after one of them: a Pashtun girl who served at a decisive moment in history as a kind of cheerleader for militant men. In 1880, during the Second Anglo-Afghan War, the legendary Malalai rallied failing Pashtun troops by singing out this inspiring couplet, or Pashtu words to this effect:

Young love, if you do not fall in the battle of Maiwand,
By God, someone is saving you as a token of shame.[47]

The shamefaced men returned to the fight and won, but Malalai was shot dead on the battlefield to round out a story that is both an inspiration to fighting men and a cautionary tale to women who might actually want to follow her example. Afghanistan's other traditional "tragic heroine" is the accomplished tenth-century Arabic and Farsi poet Rabi'a Balkhi, whose brother, the ruler of Balkh, had her wrists slashed in the *hamam* when he learned she was in love with a Turkish slave. Her tale, too, is meant to caution willful women, but she is much admired for having written one last poem to her lover—in blood—as she died, a feat generally ascribed both to the transcendent power of poetry and the terrible disruptive power of female sexuality. To honor the tragic heroines Afghans name their daughters after them, and public buildings too: Kabul's two big maternity hospitals and the girls' high school from which Meena graduated. So far nothing has been named for her.

Now, though, there's a new fantasy female hero, also named Rabia. She's the lead character in an action film dreamed up by a Kabul policewoman, Saba Sahar. Because the Afghan police are trained and supported by Germany, Saba Sahar went to the German technical assistance office in Kabul to ask for 8,000 euros to make a movie about a policewoman; and because the German technical assistance office is headed by a creative German woman who likes movies—and 8,000 euros is chicken feed—Saba Sahar got the cash. *Quanoon* the film is called—*The Law*. And the law is represented by the dedicated policewoman Rabia. Cagney or Lacy she's not, but she does look very smart in her uniform and wrap-around shades. The film opens on Rabia, at her desk, recalling the recent graduation ceremony at Kabul Police Academy where she—Rabia, daughter of Abdullah—proudly swore to serve the people of Afghanistan. She's called out to confront some drug dealers who offer her two million Afghanis (about $40,000) to walk away, but Rabia is incorruptible. They warn her that even if she arrests them, they'll be free in a matter of hours—a realistic reflection of the current operations of Kabul justice—but she does her duty nonetheless.

Rabia is called next to the scene of a family argument. A man has gambled away his ten-year-old daughter in a card game, and the winner is trying to tear the child away from her mother. Rabia sets things straight by arresting both men. Next she rescues a child from a male trafficker disguised in a burqa. (It's something about the way he walks.) Then she cuffs an arrogant young man who's been harassing a girl in the street. We're only minutes into the film, and the newly graduated policewoman is cleaning up Kabul and striking fear—well, maybe not fear, but consternation—in the hearts of Kabul's narco-mafiosi. (The bad guys are the ones in Western

clothes drinking Western booze from Western bottles and worship-
ping Western riches. The big bad guy, who looks American, explains
himself—I'm quoting from the filmmaker's own English translation
of the Dari script—"I am a killer, I am a bad man, I am a human
assassin, and without wine I do not eat and drink other things.
Without killing and destroying I do not have other jobs. . . . Now I
want to be a rich man and money has captured all the world.") But
what can these bad guys do with a policewoman who is not suscep-
tible to the usual bribes? "With every breath," says one flummoxed
criminal, Rabia "is saying 'Qanoon is my father, Qanoon is my
mother, Qanoon is my life, Qanoon is my everything.'" She says she
will starve before she takes a bribe. If she were a man, the master
criminal Sultan would have her killed; but since she is a woman, he
need only have her married. He dispatches one of the gang, a sleazy
guy with a skinny mustache, to offer Rabia's father a bride price he
can't refuse; and the next thing we know our heroic Rabia is suck-
ing up to her new husband and asking his permission to return to
her job.

Rabia is taken in for a while, even unwittingly transporting
drugs for Zahir, her husband, in a car he bought her. But before
long the honeymoon ends in confrontation. "Yes, I was thinking
that my husband is a businessman," Rabia says, "but now I got
to know that you are the businessman of drugs, parts of children's
body, kidnapping the small innocent children and then killing
them and doing business by their kidneys. . . . I am a policewoman. . . . I have sworn that I will serve my people and my
country. The government has spent on me and made me a police
now I will perform the law on you." But first, she tries to make
him see the error of his ways: "Those children who you kidnapped and take there, you take out their kidneys, take out their
eyes. Doesn't he have mother? Doesn't he have father? You smuggle
narcotics, that hopeless mothers, by how much difficulty they
have grown up their children and you get them in use with narcotics, instead of serving their old mothers, they come to serve

you bloody people." Then she cuts loose all the persuasive powers of a good woman: "Look Zahir, look Zahir, I am your wife. . . . I shed tears for you, not for this that you have defeated me, I shed tears to you for our people, for my destroyed country." And then the peroration: "Come Zahir help me, come Zahir, save this hopeless peoples' lives from these bloodies and killers. Come, come. Join hands with me. Join hands with me. Join hands with me. Join hands with me. You will assist the police. You will cooperate with the people; we will join hands together, join together, we will submit those bloody to the law. The law will help you."

She wins him over, of course, but his gang rubs him out, whereupon Rabia, in a peculiar display of love for her criminal husband who's boasted of having used her all along, vows to drink their blood. There's much more. Rabia rescues the kidnapped children. She rides across some spectacular desert scenery on a big Jin Hao motorcycle—slowly, so her chador doesn't blow away. And she gets shot a few times. But in the end Rabia and the movie are saved by the good guys riding hard out of the west: scores of German-trained Afghan Police in German-donated four-wheel-drive Afghan Police vehicles. Once they've put the gang away, they join a horde of grateful citizens in the hospital room where Rabia is recovering from bullet wounds. One officer tells her, "I am proud of your presence in here. The police is proud of you and the people of Afghanistan are proud of these kind of police." Rabia responds at the fadeout: "Thank you, officer. Be a life, this is the duty of a police to serve the people and to serve their country. Thank you."[48]

The posters are better than the film. Rabia in uniform with red braid around her hat. Rabia with her gun. Rabia on her motorcycle. Rabia wearing a lot of eye makeup. But Rabia as action hero is a disappointment because at heart she's such a "good" submissive Afghan woman. She marries a man she's never seen because her father says she must. She asks this man's permission to live her life. She "loves" him even when she learns that he's in the business of killing children and selling their body parts on the black market and that he married her only to get her out of the way. She goes after the whole gang by herself, as if she learned nothing from the German training program, and has to be rescued by the largest mobilization of (male) police in the history of Afghanistan. Maybe that's why the film is entitled *The Law* instead of *Rabia*. Behind the fantasy lie truths about the thriving narco-mafiosi (outside and inside the law) and about the life of Afghan women—and the stunning fact that any woman, no matter how mature and dedicated and thoroughly trained and highly placed in a position of value to herself and her country, can be bought and sold.

AT EID, AFGHANS DRESS UP AND VISIT THEIR FRIENDS. I WAS never able to decode the signals that told Kabulis which families were to circulate and which to stay at home and receive, but Caroline was always a circulator. In 2005 I traipsed around the city with her to call on the families of Madar staff members. We went first to a fourth floor walk-up apartment in one of the old, wartorn Soviet apartment blocks that make the district called Third Macrorayon resemble certain desolate parts of Vladivostok or Murmansk. It took Caroline's driver, Hasan, a long time to find the right building in the ranks of identical unnumbered clones; he had to run into one entrance after another to inquire. At last we made our way through the trash-strewn doorway and up the littered concrete steps, hurried along as in a wind tunnel by a rush of icy air streaming through the broken windows of the stairwell. These are the most coveted apartments in Kabul because they were originally equipped in the 1970s with flush toilets, hot water heaters, and electric lights that may—who knows?—one day work again. Local gossip holds that one such apartment recently sold to a foreigner for $70,000. The fact that Nadia's poor family of schoolteachers had recently moved here was another bit of Kabuli logistics I couldn't decode; but there was Nadia at the top of the stairs, smiling happily, and singing out a welcome to her new home—as if none of us knew that this was the home her brother was asking her to leave. Inside, an oil-cloth was spread on the floor of Nadia's narrow room—a room her brother coveted—and there we sat cross-legged on the tushak that was her bed and ate the pilau she placed before us. Caroline was the kind of dedicated eater who doesn't like to be distracted, but that day she kept looking up at the hole in the room's outer wall where once a shell had struck the building. The gap above the skewed window frame had been stuffed with rags and covered with plastic, but still the cold wind came through. "Are you going to fix that?" Caroline asked. Nadia shrugged. "Yes," she said. "Maybe. Maybe my brother. He fix it."

Nadia came with us to drive across town to the house Lema and her family rented in Taimoni. It was a typical old wide-windowed Kabuli house of unfinished mud brick set at the top of a little garden, bare now but holding the promise of spring greenery. In April the slim sticks that stood against the garden wall would become flowering trees. Lema and her two unmarried sisters greeted us at the gate and led us to the *gulkhana,* the sun parlor, where their beautiful, always-ailing mother rested on cushions under the sun-warmed windows. This was a house of women, and soon the wives of two of Lema's brothers joined us. Three little boys, the children of one of the sisters-in-law, sat in a row against the wall near the door, as though they had just dropped in and didn't mean to stay. They sat quietly, saying nothing, listening to the conversation of women. Three pretty little girls, the children of the other sister-in-law, sat on the floor around her as she put her new baby to her breast. Her first boy. Their brother had been with them only a week, and already the girls could see his power. Their mother's smile was radiant.

"*Mubarak, mubarak,*" Caroline said. "Congratulations on the birth of your son."

"I am very happy," the young mother said. "And my husband, and my mother-in-law too. We are all happy." The mother-in-law managed a wan smile from the cushions where she lay. "Before I got only girls. I was so sad I said, 'Let me have no more children.' But now I got this boy I want to get many, many more children. Maybe now, *ensh'allah,* many, many boys."

The new mother's younger sister was also visiting, and though she was not yet married, she too said she hoped to get many, many boys. In the meantime, she said, she would drop out of school and come to help her sister. Was it the addition of this girl to the household of Lema's brother that made him push Lema to marry?

"I love to clean the house," she said. "And do washing. This is very good work, and I can practice. Also I can help take care of the boy."

"But you must finish your studies," said Lema, the career woman. "You do not need to practice to clean the house. There is always a house to clean, and any person can do this. But if you finish your studies you can do other things." The girl kept a respectful silence, but I could see that she was skeptical. "Look at me," Lema said, offering herself as the role model few girls have in their own families. "I finished my high school. I take English courses. I take computer courses. Now I have a good job. I work in a good office. Every day I can leave this house and go about the city and do my work. I can give money to my family. And my work also is good. It helps many women. This also makes me feel very good."

"But you have no husband," the girl said.

"If I want a husband, I can get a husband, but now I do not want one. I do not want to give my life to clean the house. Believe me, it is best to finish your studies."

The new mother's eldest daughter replenished the teacups of the guests and the row of listening boys while the second little girl passed the plate of yellow cake. The new mother herself spoke up to defend her sister, the potential house cleaner. "Dear Lema," she said, "when you come from your work, you are tired. You do not help us cook the dinner or clean the dishes or make up the beds. You do not do the things that are good for a woman to do."

"I pay for the food," Lema said. "That is something for you too. Your husband is jobless."

"That is very true, Lema dear, but it is not a proper work for a woman. The first thing is to get a husband, and the most important thing is to get a boy."

Lema laughed. "Maybe so," she said, "but I would not be a happy woman without a job."

"But Lema dear," said the young mother, "without a boy, you are not a woman at all."

Caroline invited Lema to come with us to call on the widow Meryam, who lived far away on the ground floor of another anonymous Soviet-built apartment block. The concrete walls seemed to radiate cold like a refrigerator, and the bare living room was cold as ice. Meryam brought two propane heaters and an armload of blankets. We wrapped ourselves up like spectators at some wintry football game and huddled together on the tushaks drinking green tea that grew chilled the moment Meryam poured it into the cups. Meryam, who tended toward depression, looked as radiant as the new young mother we'd left nursing her baby at Lema's house; and the reason once again was a boy. Her fourteen-year-old son Hamid had come home for the day from the military boarding school he attended far outside the city. Hamid was an only child and a posthumous one, born months after his young father was killed on a Kabul street by a mujahidin rocket. The government paid for the education that would train the boy to be an officer in the Afghan National Army. (The US had chosen to pour money into the army, which might catch Osama bin Laden, rather than the police force, which might have brought some measure of security to the people of Kabul.) Hamid was thrilled to be in the air force program, Meryam said. He planned to be a pilot.

Meryam left the room and reappeared with the boy. He was good looking in the soft way of boys riding the wave of adolescence, and he was already taller than his mother. He wore a dark shirt and a well-cut Western suit. He stepped into the room and sank onto a cushion near the door in the provisional posture of the little listening boys at Lema's house. Like them, he listened in silence to our women's conversation until I made the mistake of directing to him a question about his air force ambitions. Without answering, he rose and hurled himself from the room. He was too old to sit in the women's room, and too young to have learned to leave it with authority and nonchalance. Meryam soon followed to serve him tea and cake in a room of his own; and later, when we invited her to join us on our round of visits, she declined. "*Man bacha*," she said. My boy. She couldn't leave him. He was the home of all her love, and the source of all her joy. In the years ahead, he will come home on school holidays, like Eid, to let her wait on him. When she grows too old to work, she will stay at home, perhaps here in this same icy room, and wait for those occasions. If he is a good Afghan boy, he will continue to care for her, more even than for the wife or wives he will surely have some day. He will support her, and he will come when he can. But he will be away, flying.

THREE YEARS AFTER OUR FIRST TRIP TOGETHER TO THE WOMEN'S prison in the Welayat, Beck and I drove out the Jalalabad road past the big ISAF camps hemmed by sandbags and razor wire, and turned south across the Kabul River toward Pul-i Charkhi prison. Zulal came with us to translate. From a long way off we could see the stone walls rising out of the empty plain, and because the road was so bad, we moved toward them as if in slow motion through a haze of dust and trepidation. President Daoud built Pul-i Charkhi to "reform" or remove those who might oppose his republic, and Afghan rulers of one stripe or another have used it ever since to rid themselves of their enemies. It is the place where my friend Orzala was held as a child with all her family until the International Red Crescent managed to get the women and children out. It is where my friend Sharif was crippled by torture, where my friend Moska's husband was shot, where my friend Acquela waited before the gates month after month for the day that never came, when her sons would be released. It is where my friend Obidullah's father was tortured because he was a communist, and where Obidullah, many years later, was tortured because he was not. Almost everyone in Kabul has a history here.

We handed our letter of permission to gray-bearded police commanders at the gate, and then we were inside the walls crossing a littered yard where a dozen male prisoners stopped their volleyball game to gawk at carrot-haired unveiled women passing by. Before us loomed the cell blocs with their long barred windows set high enough so that prisoners couldn't look out. We passed more iron gates, more armed policemen, and crossed the big desolate field, still strewn with broken boards, that was the yard of the newly reconstructed women's section. The yard seemed empty but for a single straight-backed chair that stood all alone in the center of this vacancy. Then we noticed at the far end a woman marching up and down in high-heeled boots. She hadn't done up the zippers, so the boot tops flapped around her ankles like manacles. We recognized her as one of five Chinese women arrested when police swept through brothels that had been slow to pay their baksheesh. The city was now full of brothels and a small army of sex workers—six thousand was the rumored figure in 2005—including many Chinese and Filipino girls trafficked in to sate the exotic appetites of the men of the international community, the embassy staffs and the American contractors. (Afghanistan is a "non-family" post, too dangerous for Western wives.) The illegal market in female flesh, catering exclusively to foreign men (chiefly Americans), made it hard for us Western women to speak convincingly to Afghans about women's rights.

A bus pulled in behind us and brown-shirted policemen appeared from nowhere to push us aside. The door of the bus swung open and blue burqas emerged one by one: a small parade of new prisoners transferred from the Welayat. I watched their feet, wrapped in strappy high heels and platform shoes, step gingerly to the ground. And their hands: one snatching up the hem of the burqa, the other clutching a plastic shopping bag or the hand of a tiny child. The policemen had brought out a table and several chairs, and they sat down, seven of them, to argue about the proper procedure for registering the new prisoners. Two policemen pushed the women toward the table. One picked up a board and brought it down on a woman's back. "Hey!" I shouted. It was an automatic reaction, not a smart one, and Beck touched my arm. The guard slumped away as if he hadn't heard.

We stepped into the long dark corridor of the prison. Like parts of the Welayat, the refurbished building was already beginning to revert to ruin. Dampness seeped through the yellow-painted walls, and mildew bloomed like blue flowers. The cement floor of the corridor was awash with water oozing from the toilet. Iron bunk beds stood two deep along the walls of the big cells, each housing fifteen or twenty women. Each cell had a chattering TV set—the humanitarian touch of international donors—but most of the women ignored it. They lay on their bunks with their faces to the wall, losing themselves in some kind of solitude or sleep. A guard we knew, a wiry little policewoman with dramatically dyed black hair, came to greet us with a toothless smile. She'd been transferred here from the Welayat against her will, along with nine other female guards; and if she missed the staff bus in the morning, she was out a lot of money for a taxi to drive all the long way to work. Like everyone else in the place, she wanted our help. She was overworked too, she said. There were only ten women guards with eighty-seven prisoners to look after—and now the bus had brought more. "We never had so many prisoners before," she said. "More every day."

She let us into a meeting room at the end of the hall and returned a few minutes later with Serena, the prisoner we'd come to see. We drew some of the uncomfortable straight metal chairs into an intimate circle and sat down. Beside us on the wall hung an antiviolence poster that showed mean-looking men hitting their wives with sticks. We tried to feel at ease. The prisoner Serena was one of the Herati shelter girls, one I hadn't met before because she was good at making escapes. But Beck knew her, and from Beck I'd learned scraps of her story. Beck held Serena's hand while I led her through a revisionist version of her life, heavily censored and abridged—her imaginative re-creation of herself. Here's what I already knew: she'd survived rape, imprisonment, prostitution, suicide attempts, and a gang rape by four men—a local commander and his body guards— so brutal it caused her to abort a pregnancy. She was about nineteen years old, all alone in the world, and ten months into a five-and-a-half-year sentence for alcohol use and prostitution. Here's what she told me: a fairy tale in which brutal memories of the Herati shelter vanished in a poof of picnics. No mention of prostitution or sex or fights with other shelter girls or suicide attempts or the despair that caused her to take a blade to her arms again and again, leaving the scars I traced with my fingertips to let her know that I was with her and read on her body a different text. It was the shelter in Kabul that was horrible, she said—dirty and cramped. No respite. No picnics. Serena escaped. The police picked her up and brought her back. A month later she escaped again. The police arrested her again for alcohol use and she spent more time in the Welayat. A legal aid lawyer got her released, and she was sent to another lockup that called itself a shelter. She broke a window and escaped again, sliding down a rope of bedsheets. Life is a movie. She was in and out of jail for drunkenness, which she admitted with a laugh, and prostitution, which she didn't.

Then, she said, she went to live with a woman friend—someone she met in jail. She said that for three months she didn't get her period. Then there was a morning when she went to the *hamam* and someone noticed she was bleeding badly and got her to a hospital. I nibbled at the gaps between these events with delicate questions and it came out that there were "two cops" who picked her up and raped her and did some other things to her and threw her into the street, and that is why there was a lot of blood. I asked if she might have lost a child, and Zulal put the question gently in Dari. There was a pause. "Probably," Serena said. But she couldn't speak of it, and I wouldn't push her. She was creating a new self: not a girl who was beaten and raped and left for dead, but a woman who would like to learn English and some day get a job. Sometimes, she said, when she was swept with regret that she had left her father's house, she remembered how tired she was of her life. But she tried not to think about that. When I asked if I could write about her in this book, she agreed without hesitation. "You can use my name," she said. "It's not my name. None of this is about myself."

She was a smart girl. It was Serena who told me that all of women's difficulties in life come from their parents' failure to love and respect them. She had gone as far as class eight before her father stopped her education at age thirteen ("enough for a girl") and tried to force her to marry a cousin she disliked. She wanted books to read because being in prison was so boring; and when we asked what kind, she said, "physics." She said, "Not children's books, please. Physics." Through it all she was so well mannered, so gentle and polite, so soft spoken, so courteous, asking if she might be excused for a few minutes to smoke a cigarette, that Beck said, "In England she'd be considered a very good girl."

"She is a very good girl," Zulal said. "It is Afghanistan that is not good."

Not long after we returned from Pul-i Charkhi, a report came in from Badakshan Province in the north that a young woman and her alleged lover had been charged with adultery and sentenced to punishments approved by a local commander. Afghan radio said that the accused man was given one hundred lashes. The woman was dragged from her house, with the help of her husband, and put to death by stoning. Amnesty International reported that this was the first such execution since the rule of the Taliban. My friend Ingrid was part of a delegation sent to Badakshan by the European Commission to investigate. They spoke to the district governor and the police and to the warlord and the elders and mullahs who approved the sentence, and to the woman's family and the young man's family who lived next door; and they returned to Kabul convinced only that they would never know the truth. They had been told that the young man wasn't really her lover. That her husband wasn't even there. Nor any other men of the town. That she wasn't stoned really, but maybe beaten by her family or just strangled. (Town officials had dug up her body so the local doctor could take a look.) Everyone said this was a family matter, of no concern to the public, or the law. And in any case, the commander and the mullahs behind it were so well connected that there wasn't any point really in trying to blame them. Anyway, it wasn't the first time they'd done something like this in Badakshan, so what was the fuss about? Ingrid asked the Afghan question: "What else can we do?" She said, "Everybody knows exactly what to tell us. They all know the jargon of women's rights. Could you imagine that there are so many feminist warlords and mullahs in Badakshan? There, where women are not even allowed out of doors? They are all in favor of education for girls and women, all in favor of women going to work and voting and running for parliament. The international men settle for that. They say, 'Well, it's just a family matter after all.' They're so excessively careful, you know, to respect the Afghan family, the Afghan culture. I tried to argue. I said, 'This woman was murdered.' The head of the delegation said, 'You know, you really mustn't be so Eurocentric. We're speaking of local customs.'"

Just about that time, I learned from the newspaper that Kabul would soon have another women's prison. Schools were needed and health clinics and refuges for women and street children. Housing too. In Kabul in winter people were still living and dying in tents. But the UN agreed to put up $300,000 to build another prison for women. The deputy minister of justice, Mohammad Qasem Hashemzai, proudly announced that this one would be built "to meet international standards."[49]

It's a joke among international women that when men are in charge of an aid program they think first of concrete. They like to build things; and they argue with some justification, that large concrete objects in the landscape remind local citizens that we are actually "rebuilding" their country. But why another prison for women? A prison that predictably will quickly be filled with more prisoners. What kind of "reminder" is this? Then comes the hard question for me: what have I been doing here all this time? Through the work of internationals and Afghans, laws have been changed, defense attorneys trained and provided to women, judges taught to administer the law; and the result is that men—international and Afghan—have decided to build yet another prison for women. There's talk of building jails for women in the provinces too, where before now there have been none. I had thought all along that I was "helping" women in prison. But it is undeniable that in the aftermath of America's regime change and the "liberation" from the Taliban more Afghan women than ever before now languish in Afghan prisons—for the same old "crimes." I thought again about the woman judge's explanation: "We must not encourage women to escape from home because we must have a good moral society." Even women believe this. Even women prisoners believe this. I thought again of the Afghan proverb that on so many bleak days had kept me going: *Qatra qatra darya mesha.* Drop by drop a river is made. Some days you believe it. Some days you don't. Then comes a day when you look at the river and you see which way it runs.

PART III

IN THE SCHOOLS

"You look at the map and you see all these small shapes with heavy black lines around them. Some are colored green, some yellow, some pink. Each one has a label: Afghanistan, Pakistan, Kyrgyzstan, and so on. You look at all these different colored countries, and you think they're real."

My European friend pauses to refill our cups with green tea. We're sitting together in the garden of his home in Kabul on a morning in late winter when the sun is so piercing that we've had to move into the shade of an ancient evergreen. Around us lie rows of sunken flower beds and hedges stretching away to the walls that protect the garden from the busy street beyond. At the top of the garden sprawls the old house, long and low, warmed by many windows and skirted by terraces that spill gently toward the trees. This was Kabul before the wars—a serene and gracious life sequestered behind walls, maintained by another class of cooks and cleaners, gardeners and guards, and men who shoveled human shit and hauled it away. There is something surpassingly comfortable in sitting here now in the sun, nibbling almonds and mulberries, sipping bitter tea, and listening to my friend talk of the old days, before the wars, in this country he knows so well. But it is unreal, this coddled moment of seeming safety here in the geometric garden where nothing now blooms. The people who once lived here amid such gardens—the "better" families, the intelligentsia—were persecuted in one regime or another, and those who survived fled long ago to Europe or North America, leaving behind those who had labored to sustain the class that couldn't sustain the country. Most of them will never come back.

"Afghanistan was never a real country," says my friend. "Like Pakistan, it was always a political fiction. Always the invention of other countries—real ones—that had some use for the space it occupies on the maps they drew." He lapses into silence as an American combat helicopter roars overhead, and I think of Afghans far away who might even now be recalling this garden, this city, this country as real.

"And today?" I prompt when the chopper has passed.

"The government wants to rebuild some kind of nation-state, such as what was gradually developing before 1978, before the Soviet invasion. But the Americans have other agendas. The real one has to do with permanent military bases and pipelines and some significant remodeling of this part of the world to suit Washington's imperial design, but the advertised plan is instant democracy—unfortunately imposed just like communism from the top down—and a so-called free market economy."

"As if Afghans needed Americans to teach them how to trade!"

My friend laughs. "Yes, they've been at it for, what, a couple of thousand years? But now, in the so-called free market, they're required to buy American exports. It's not trade actually. Rather more like compulsory shopping." He pauses to raise to his lips a pottery teacup inscribed with designs that must go back a thousand years. "Of course, the big rush was just to get Bush returned to office," he says, "so maybe they'll back off now and go on to the next crusade. If they were smart, or kind, they'd let the Afghans get on with it. But of course they're not smart, and kindness never comes into it."

"But Afghans say they don't want America to abandon them. Surely you don't think the US should walk away again."

"Afghans want peace," he says. "Let them keep government by B-52. Let the planes keep flying. You don't see them way up there, but everyone can hear them. Everyone knows they're there. And let the Afghans get on with finding their own way."

The cook approaches with a fresh pot of tea and a plate of yellow cake; and we while away another hour, sitting in some absent Afghan's garden, discussing theoretically the fate of the long-lost country that seems never to have been a real country at all. Then I walk home through the filthy streets and look again at the map that hangs on the wall of my room. Afghanistan is green.

I CAME TO AFGHANISTAN IN THE FIRST PLACE NOT TO THEORIZE but to do something practical to help put it back together. But there's not much I know how to do. I'm good at sitting in gardens, even pretty good at maintaining them, but I don't know how to remove a land mine or build a road or repair an irrigation system. One thing I can do well is teach, and it seemed to me that after the damage done to the school system by the Taliban, Afghanistan was going to need teachers. Then I learned that there was more to it than the Taliban. Afghanistan has always needed teachers and schools. On paper Afghanistan has had free primary education since 1915 and free *compulsory* primary education since 1931 when the idea was inscribed in the Constitution.[1] But it's no use having compulsory education if you don't have money to build schools or train teachers or print books; so in fact, hardly anybody ever went to school. By the time I got there in 2002, Afghanistan had an education system described by the United Nations Development Program as "the worst in the world."[2]

Islam enjoins all Muslims, men and women, to seek knowledge and education so that they can advance social justice in the Islamic community. But since knowledge is most easily pursued by those with time on their hands, education long ago became the art of an elite class, practiced at the Islamic courts of the Samanids in Balkh in the ninth century, the Ghaznavids in Ghazni in the tenth and eleventh centuries, the Timurids in Herat in the fifteenth century, and in Kandahar in the eighteenth century. By the nineteenth century, this elite scholarship had become the basis of a traditional education intended to transmit Islamic doctrine and little else. Teaching went on in private madrassas attached to mosques and supported by communities and wealthy patrons. The curriculum, a mélange of Quranic dicta, classical Persian poetry, and customary tribal practices and beliefs, varied from one madrassa to the next, and because the content was thought to come from Allah by way of the Quran, it was not subject to critical inquiry and discussion. Many of the teachers were poorly educated mullahs, barely literate themselves, whose "methodology" was learning by rote—repetition and memorization stimulated by the "long stick" still used in Afghan classrooms today.[3] Students learned to recite the Quran in Arabic, but not to read and write in their own languages. Nevertheless, thanks to the Prophet's advice to his followers to seek knowledge, even the halfway educated man received respect.

Amir Abdur Rahman—he of 199 wives—is usually credited with initiating educational reform, though even now it's hard to see that much has changed. History has it that when he came to power in 1880, bent on establishing a centralized nation-state, he searched for thirty clerks who could read and write, and he found only three. He built schools to educate the civil servants his ambitions required, and he reined in the mullahs, thus launching the continuing contest between "modern" and traditional education. Presumably Abdur Rahman schooled some literate clerks, but traditional teachers went on teaching the Quran and the *Panj Ganj*

(Five Treasures), the most popular textbook of proper Islamic behavior, inculcating such eternal truths as the natural superiority of the Muslim male.[4]

The next "turning point" in Afghan education is said to have been the result of a trip to India undertaken by Abdur Rahman's son Amir Habibullah in 1907. After seeing young Muslims learning law and modern commerce at Aligarh College near Delhi, he returned to Kabul to establish Habibiya High School for boys where a faculty of Indian Muslims taught both modern European school subjects and traditional madrassa classes. It was Habibiya High School that educated the generation of men who staffed the government and ran the country during much of the long hazy reign of King Zahir Shah. Amir Habibullah's son, the "revolutionary" King Amanullah, accelerated the move from traditional to modern education, from the mosque to the modern high school. In 1921 he opened the first high school for girls—with a female faculty of French, German, Indian, and Turkish teachers—and in the following years he opened two more. He also founded three additional boys' high schools where classes were taught by foreigners in a foreign language: the French Istaqlal (where Ahmad Shah Massoud studied), the German Nejat, and the English-language Ghazi where classes were led first by Anglo-Indians and later by British teachers. Establishing these high schools was the biggest leap in the history of Afghan education, yet it was a baby step. The schools were few, the enrollments small, and the whole system cloistered in Kabul. At the end of Amanullah's reign, in 1930, the entire modern education system of Afghanistan consisted of thirteen primary and secondary schools, and the total number of students enrolled was 1,590. This new government-sponsored modern education became the pursuit of the elite, and these few foreign-language high schools the path of the next generations to power. During the war years, almost all the important political leaders were graduates of one or another of the state high schools.[5]

Many of the leaders also attended Kabul University, which got its start in 1932 as a Faculty of Medicine affiliated with the University of Lyon in France. A Faculty of Law affiliated with the University of Paris was added in 1938, then Science, then Letters. Women were admitted in 1957 to separate all-female faculties that were abandoned four years later in favor of coeducation. The university continued to add faculties into the 1960s, each with a foreign affiliate, including several American institutions. The Faculty of Agriculture partnered with the University of Wyoming, the Faculty of Education with Columbia University Teachers College, and the Faculty of Engineering with the US Engineering Team, a consortium of nine American universities and institutes of technology.[6] More significant for the future of Afghanistan was a partnership established in 1951 between the Faculty of Theology (Sharia) and Egypt's al-Azhar University, and another partnership established in 1967 between the Polytechnic Institute and the Soviet Union.

At the time, during the Cold War, men were sitting in stuffy offices in Washington and Moscow, examining maps of the world cluttered with little pink and green and yellow countries. The men in Washington sent aid to little Afghanistan to thwart the men in Moscow and their communist ambitions. Much of that aid went into education, with the result that English became the most important non-Afghan language in the country and the one prescribed by Afghan regulation for secondary use in all foreign embassies. Louis Dupree points out that language "spreads ideology . . . simply by the way it expresses ideas, both concrete and abstract," but the American ideology didn't quite come across. Even when USAID put up the money in 1964 to consolidate the disparate faculties of Kabul University in a single American-style campus, the West German company that built it got the credit.[7] But by that time, close to two thousand Afghan college students—mostly men—were going abroad each year to study on scholarships provided by the host countries: the USSR, Egypt, and the USA. They returned with new ideas.

Until then, despite the interference of more powerful, more real, countries, Afghanistan had managed over centuries to protect itself from unwelcome ideas. The landscape alone discouraged interference. Non-literacy put much information out of reach of 95 percent of the population. So until fairly recently, Afghanistan was something of an ideological tabula rasa on which the effects of modern education were inscribed by the political acts of a minuscule educated elite. Send a generation of impressionable Afghan male students to the Soviet Union and some ten to twenty years later, you get a communist coup—as deposed King Zahir Shah realized too late—and then another, and another. (These are Afghans, after all, who can't agree.) Send another generation to study in Egypt, the home of both the Muslim Brotherhood and a repressive military regime, and you get various parties of radical Islamists who are prepared, like the communists before them, to fight it out with one another, if not for social justice then certainly for power. Take another much, much larger group—not the elite this time with their modern international education, but impoverished non-literate boys with little hope, many of them orphaned by war—and entice them into the neglected precincts of traditional education, into the radical fundamentalist madrassas of Pashtunistan, and you get the Taliban. Now America is back in Afghanistan again, and USAID is pouring millions of taxpayer dollars into Afghan education, so it seems pertinent to ask: What next?

But that's a big question. I have to admit that at the start, that first time in Kabul, I focused only on little things because it was on those little things that survival seemed to depend. Like *barq*. Electricity. It's the first word Westerners learn in Dari. The first question, and the biggest, is *Barq darem?* (Do we have electricity?) The first sentence is *Barq nes.* (There is no electricity.) Nearly four years after the American bombing stopped and the American-led recovery began, barq remained a big issue unless you lived in the city center and forked over big time baksheesh. Even the Ministry of Energy and Water admitted that only 6 percent of Afghans have even intermittent electricity.[8] But when I first came to Kabul there was almost no electricity at all. People said President Karzai had issued an ultimatum to the relevant minister: provide electricity to the capital or . . . or what? Still the barq did not come. It had vanished with the rivers, dried to random puddles by the long, long drought that brought the giant turbines of Sarobi hydroelectric plant to rest. People spoke too of a new generator of monumental size that would provide barq to the whole city, if only the diesel fuel could be found to feed it. By 2005 the heavy winter snows and spring rains had nearly filled the river, the Sarobi turbines were turning again, the former minister of energy had been replaced by the formidable ex-mujahidin commander and ex-governor of Herat Ismail Khan, who promised to end corruption, the power still came and went, the big man at the neighborhood energy office still collected baksheesh, and I had learned to make longer sentences in Dari about other things.

But back then, as I gazed from the window of my darkened room at night, I could see arising from the heart of Kabul, the area where Karzai himself lived, a distinct electric glow. I figured that important people must have generators, or perhaps—given the congregation of government ministers in central Kabul—electricity itself, while we in less influential neighborhoods remained in the dark. One day in the English class I was teaching, a student who lived on the far side of town reported that she had watched television the night before until some time after nine o'clock when the power went out again in the middle of a program about auto repair. "How did you get electricity?" I asked, envious of a mere three hours. The randomness was inexplicable and maddening to me as a spoiled American still unused to the daily vagaries of life in Kabul. But to the other Afghan students, the woman's report was heartening. "Maybe tonight my house get," said one. "Maybe tomorrow night we have," said another. "It is possible," said a third. "Anything is possible," said Nasir, the class philosopher. No one bothered to ask about the television program their classmate had seen, or what she might have learned about auto repair. Afghans don't waste time with inessential stuff that's over and done. Instead, they seem ever expectant and hopeful, waiting for barq as once they waited for Ahmad Shah Massoud.

That class, those students, powerfully focused my attention. The first long cold winter, they became my means of survival. My own energizing barq. They were English teachers themselves who worked in the Kabul high schools left standing after the civil wars and the American bombs. (The most venerable—Habibiya, Malalai, Ghazi—were in ruins.) At that time, as students returned to school after the terrible interruption of the Taliban, English was still acknowledged to be the international language of choice, and all students were required to study it from class seven to class twelve. But this requirement presented many problems. With so many school buildings destroyed, the remaining schools were overcrowded and the classes too large—say, maybe sixty or seventy youngsters. Many of the best-educated English teachers had fled the country. Women teachers had been shut up in their houses for five or six years; and although many secretly taught children at home, most had no chance at all during the Taliban time to practice their English or their teaching.

Worse yet, very few of them had ever learned the language in the first place. They could make out bits of meaning in a simple English text, but they couldn't pronounce the words. They couldn't get the language off the page and into their mouths. They couldn't speak. None of them knew of teaching methods beyond the rote learning that had been standard Afghan practice for centuries, so they stood before a packed class of puzzled students and tried to teach English by lecturing in Dari or Pashtu. They made their students memorize mispronounced English sentences. The kids learned by repetition to mouth mangled English just as generations of madrassa students had learned to recite Quranic verses in

Arabic. When my students—these eager, ill-equipped teachers—launched themselves into English conversation, I understood why English studies in the schools were conducted largely by the book, and a very old book at that. All but one of my students had graduated as an English major from the Faculty of Languages and Literature of an Afghan university, and a few of them were fairly accomplished grammarians, though their terminology was dated. Later, when they'd got a grip on the spoken word, they asked me to define the difference between a "determiner" and a "demonstrative" or to identify the specific type of adverbial phrase that is neither an adverb of time nor of quality. They had the theory of language without the language itself, and they asked each question expectantly, as if the answer, like a sudden infusion of barq, might release an unstoppable flow of illuminated speech.

I knew how they got this way. I'd arrived in Kabul hoping to multiply the effect of my teaching by teaching those who taught others. I started at the top of the chain, at the institutions of higher learning. Kabul has four: Kabul University, Education University, the Polytechnic, and the Medical Institute. I visited the first three, met with the chairman of each English department in turn, presented my credentials, and offered to conduct a class in conversation and new teaching methods for any interested members of his faculty. I explained that I was a volunteer; there would be no cost to the department. All they had to do was provide a room and set a time for the class. Each chairman was enthusiastic and grateful for the offer. Each one said his faculty could use the help. At Kabul University the chairman convened his professors—a solid row of stolid scholars, all men. The elders of the group, who had taken their degrees forty years earlier as scholarship students at Columbia University Teachers College, seemed pleased to reminisce (fluently) about their years in New York City. The middle-aged were silent. The young, who still wore their Taliban beards, were hostile; and I realized that their seniors' chit-chat about big times in the Big Apple must have seemed to them surreal.

They had serious objections. They said that a couple of men had come from England or some such place to help them with teaching methodology only a few weeks before. They had brought new textbooks that contained pictures of young men and women doing thoroughly un-Islamic things together. Things like sitting at a table in a restaurant, or walking down the street. There was a picture of a woman wearing some sort of strapless gown and singing into a microphone. There was an exercise that instructed students to bring photographs of their families to class and show them to their classmates. Photographs of their mothers and sisters! How could Afghans use such books? Who were these men from England, or some such place, to tell them how to teach? And who in the world was I? It was a good question. When I left the building one of them hurried after me with an ancient textbook in hand. Just one question please—it was the only help he needed, he said, pointing to a nearly illegible sentence on the well-worn page. How exactly would I diagram that sentence, and that adverb there, what kind of adverb was that?

A week or two later the chairmen of Education University and the Polytechnic summoned me to say that they had been unable to find any faculty members to participate in a class. It seemed they were all too busy with their other jobs as translators or drivers or messengers at the UN or the embassies or the INGOs. They were all moonlighting. And who could blame them? Given their pathetic salaries—maybe forty bucks a month—the choice between improving their English and peddling the little English they had for cash was a no-brainer. Much later, in 2005, I met another American ESL teacher who'd come to the Ministry of Higher Education as part of a big USAID-funded education program. As an official "consultant" employed by a for-profit contractor she was drawing almost a thousand dollars a day to teach the same kind of classes I'd offered for free three years before. "I couldn't get it together," I told her, "because the professors were all moonlighting." She said, "They still are." They didn't want her help either. But given her contract, her job description, and her salary, she couldn't take no for an answer. The solution was to find another donor—the World Bank this time—to pay salary "supplements" of two hundred dollars a month to the professors, topping off their basic pay in exchange for their dropping extra jobs and attending the English class instead. "Isn't that something like bribery?" I asked. "No," she said. "It's an incentive." And then to make me feel better about my failure, she added in a kindly way, "It usually takes a really big donor to make people do what's best for them."

SINCE THE UNIVERSITIES DIDN'T WANT ME, I TRIED THE NEXT LEVEL down. Caroline, my boss at Madar, had already come up with the idea of helping high school English teachers with their English, and a class was already underway. She'd got the blessing of the Ministry of Education and a tiny grant from an American foundation—money to buy textbooks and audiotapes and to help the students with their bus fares. She had chosen the teachers from many different high schools; and she'd taught them herself for a week or two before handing them over to one or another of her Madar volunteers. The trouble was that neither Caroline nor any of her volunteers knew anything about teaching English as a foreign language. They subjected the high school teachers to the same kind of unintelligible lectures and boring textbook drills the teachers handed down to their own students; and before long the teachers started dropping out of class.

The day I took over, I met a little group of men and women whose wan faces were blank with despair. They greeted me politely—"Hello, Sir"—and tried earnestly to respond to my simple questions about their names, their health, and their teaching careers. They had their names down pat, and "Fantankou" was fairly intelligible if you knew what the question had been. But the rest was painful. Within five minutes my task had become clear. My job, as I saw it, was to close the textbook, turn a blind eye to adverbs, and get these fifteen teachers talking. For the next three months, this was to be my personal response to 9/11 and my tiny contribution to the recovery of Afghanistan. Tiny, but not easy, given that the native Dari comes equipped with far fewer vowel sounds than English. It's missing some of our consonants too, although it's got others of its own that leave native English speakers humbly gargling dust. Soon I introduce my students to tongue-twisting exercises: *The ship is tipping. The sheep is sleeping.* They confess they've never heard of anything like this before. They hesitate, embarrassed, and then one by one they begin to try. They concentrate intensely, wrinkling their faces and wrapping their tongues around unfamiliar phonemes, tentatively at first, then more surely and louder and faster until the whole once dignified group falls to laughing out loud. They are eager, brave, hilarious. And they get it, the difference between *sheep* and *ship*. They go home on the bus each day muttering to themselves, the women practicing behind their burqas *lickety split* and *clean jeans,* and their English begins to sound a little more each day like the real thing.

Our class meets in a school in the midst of a neighborhood of grim Russian-built apartment blocks. Once exclusively a high school, it is now used for primary and secondary (middle) school students as well. The different age groups are supposed to use the building in separate shifts, but at any hour the hallways seem filled with small noisy boys who run up and down screaming and fighting while little girls wrapped in big white chadors sit silently in the classrooms. Women teachers stand hopelessly in the corridors amid the swirl of shouting boys, as if there is nothing they can do. It is like a prep school for mujahidin—training up another generation of the kind of guys who wrecked the place during the civil wars.

The school reopened only recently, having been completely renovated by ISAF security troops, and already it is going downhill. Maintenance is not a strong point among Afghans because few Afghans have ever had much to maintain, and nowadays maintenance costs money. One day I go into a lavatory and find the brand-new Western-style toilets overflowing. The floor is strewn with turds and puddles of urine. I try to complain to the principal but we're stuck on opposite sides of the language barrier, so I drag him upstairs and open the lavatory door to give him a look and a whiff. Instantly he is apologetic. He hurries me back downstairs to his office and proudly offers me a key to another restroom reserved for faculty. How do I tell him he has missed the point? After class I have a talk with Palwasha, one of my best students, who happens to teach in this school. She must tell the principal, I say, that he should get the restroom cleaned. It is a hazard to the health of the children. "Do not worry, please," she says. "We do not let children to use school toilet. School toilet is dirty." Later, after I see some boys squatting in the schoolyard, I find out that the lavatory has not been cleaned, but the door has been locked. It is an Afghan solution. I learn to look the other way.

Our classroom is a tiny office on the ground floor. It wears a shiny coat of light blue ISAF paint, but the floor is torn up and the window broken. There is no furniture, but the men of the class cleverly steal a couple of tables and some benches from a classroom down the hall. The next day the room is empty again, but the men soon find what we need. Six days a week for three months the men start the day by hunting up furniture that the women students then dust with cloths they've brought from home for that purpose. I buy a whiteboard and a bunch of colored markers; and to save them from disappearing with the furniture, I carry them back and forth from home to school every day. The men take turns waiting for me at the gate to carry the big whiteboard into the classroom. We put it on the windowsill where every student can see it, and where it also blocks the big breezy hole in the window. Then the women peel back their burqas and take seats on the left side of the tables. The men seat themselves on the right. The building is unheated, and our north-facing room is always colder than the sun-warmed world outside. So we dress warmly. For me that means thermal long underwear and a turtleneck, heavy winter trousers, one or two very long wool sweaters, a down vest, and a long insulated coat. On the coldest days I leave my woolen gloves on and have to uncap the colored markers with my teeth. The last man in shuts the classroom door against the noisy boys. The students lay out their notebooks and their stubby pencils. These are the morning rituals. Then we are ready once more to begin.

We start from scratch. Everyone has a little English, but there are great, unpredictable holes in their knowledge, like the shell holes shot through schoolroom walls that explain why learning in Kabul has been a sometimes thing. There seem to be gaps in their minds as well: recesses that memory cannot, or will not, reach. Attention is brief and easily lost; a loud noise in the street makes them jump. Anxiety distracts them, and weariness often overwhelms. It's a wonder to me that they can learn anything, and an act of courage even to try. But day by day we slowly fill in the gaps. Later, when I learn a little about their lives, I wonder that they survive at all, and that they still want to teach. It is an optimistic profession, implying a future, but they prepared for it during a terrible past. Palwasha, who heads the English department in this school, is a very beautiful woman: tall, slim, graceful, and outwardly, improbably serene. She began her studies at Kabul University under the Soviet occupation. Then the mujahidin brought their brother war to the capital, lobbing shells and rockets at each other and the city that lay between them. No area of Kabul was harder hit than the Hazara neighborhoods that lie around the grounds of the university. Palwasha's classes moved to the Polytechnic Institute, almost out of range, and for another

year or two while the shelling went on she continued intermittently to study. At last she received her degree and took a job as
an English teacher in a Kabul high school. She loved the work,
but she had scarcely begun her career before the Taliban put an
end to it. She spent five years inside her family's apartment. She has
been back at her teaching job for only three months. "Teacher, I
am sorry," she says. "English. A beautiful language. In five years
I lose it."

Now in a few months I'm to bring it back and make it speakable.
Leaving young children and old mothers at home, my students
travel to school every day on packed public buses. For some of
them the trip takes almost two hours. They're all infected with an
old-fashioned idealism. They're too young to remember what
"peace" might look like, but they want to do something to help
their country attain it. Teaching, for them, is a high calling, and
because the pay is very small—at the time about thirty dollars a
month—an altruistic one. They lavish on me the respect they have
for the profession we share. They pause in the doorway, requesting permission to enter the classroom, before launching into pro-
fuse formal greetings. When class ends, they remain seated while
I pack up my things, thank them for attending, and leave the
room. Then they rise and file out behind me (men first) to bid me
goodbye as I stand in the hall, key in hand, waiting to lock the
classroom door in hopes of deterring the furniture thieves. It's no
good my telling my students that they're free to leave. To pass
through the door before one's teacher is shameful, and an Afghan
will do almost anything to avoid shame. Besides, my students
have come to like me and my unorthodox teaching. They see that
what seemed too hard for them last week is easier now. They hear
themselves and their classmates actually utter English. They speak,
and miraculously they understand one another. They dare to
make jokes. And they are profoundly, embarrassingly grateful.
By the end of the course they feel about me as I feel about the

electricity that finally, one night, comes on in my building and makes possible my first hot shower in Afghanistan.

All my students have terrible stories. A few fled to Peshawar and spent years in refugee camps there. (They speak the best English.) Many stayed in Kabul, the women locked up in their houses. Almost all of them lost fathers and brothers to the Soviets or the mujahidin or the Taliban. They lost mothers and sisters and aunts and grandfathers and children to illness and hunger and military assault. Women and girls were raped and murdered. Men and boys were taken as soldiers or "dancing boys," and never came back. The family of only one of my students survived intact. They lost just their house, in a rocket attack, two hours after they had fled. Some of the women risked their lives to teach clandestine classes at home—classes that often included boys as well as girls, for many boys had lost their place in school when women teachers disappeared. (That's why the young boys in this school are so wild, say the men in my class. They missed out on the proper school and the long stick that would have taught them respect.) The children always arrived at home school one or two at a time, and they were careful to drift out in the same way. One of my students says she never feared a Taliban raid because the neighborhood Taliban leader had secretly placed his own children in her school. But another tells me the story of a whole class of girls who once heedlessly left her home school together and ran into a Taliban patrol. The Taliban leaped from their vehicle, grabbed the little girls, hit them with sticks, twisted their arms, held them by their ankles upside down, shook them, and shouted at them to give up the name of their teacher. The little girls fought like trapped cats. They scratched and bit and broke free and ran away into a maze of rubble. They stayed in their homes for a week or more, and then one by one they went back to the home school. Their teacher, my student, says: "Girls learn fast to speak not."

It seems to be a lesson they don't forget, for at first the women in my class were still as stones. None of them would ask a question or volunteer an answer. If I called on a woman, she looked at me with pleading eyes and remained silent. Then the men would speak up, all at the same time. If I'd left it up to my students, the men would have done all the talking while the women sat quietly day after day, listening in. But I noticed that before and after class the women seemed to have plenty to say softly to one another. So we started with a lot of what language teachers call "pair work"—each student quietly working with a partner, and then I moved the partners farther apart so that each one had to speak up to be heard. The very act of speaking seemed to restore confidence, and hope. Silence slipped away in the din of eager discourse that drowned out even the noisy boys in the corridor. Sometimes the boys burst through the classroom door to see what was going on. Until one of the men rose to hustle them out, they gaped at the happily gabbing women.

At least the women could work together. In whispers at first, and then more boldly, they helped each other through every task. I shuffled the pairs every day, and each new female couple became a partnership right away. But not the men. They sat stubbornly on their side of the room, each one staring fixedly at his own book. I took away some books so that each pair of men had only one book between them. Then the partners sat side by side, each man clutching one edge of the book, both men staring at it. That was their idea of working together. But as for speaking to one another, asking and answering questions, engaging in some kind of dialogue, collaborating in the execution of a common task, they could not even begin. And what was the point? As teachers, they enforced silence in their classrooms so that they themselves could lecture. They believed that their job was not to encourage student conversation but to prevent it. The notion that students could help one another to learn was unfamiliar and therefore suspect. But the problem went far beyond pedagogy.

Privately one man after another explained to me that he didn't know the others. They weren't related. They hadn't gone to the same schools. They didn't teach in the same school. They knew nothing about one another's families—where they came from, who their fathers were. How could they be expected to work together? There were only seven men in the class, yet they formed seven separate factions, like the mujahidin. It wasn't that they didn't want to learn. They were all, separately, eager students. But cooperation was harder even than English. In the end, faced by this Afghan problem, I applied an Afghan solution that violated all my principles of supportive teaching. I shamed them publicly. The women were smarter, I said. Much better students. Look how beautifully they talked together. Anyone could do the same, really, unless of course he was completely stupid. The men looked stunned. They were hurt and angry—and ashamed. Then, like the women at first, they began to whisper together and little by little to talk. But they never did get the hang of helping each other. They tried to escape partnership by addressing all their remarks to me, and when that didn't work they turned their pair work into brutal competition. The women just smiled indulgently, the way the teachers in the corridor gazed benignly at the noisy boys. Palwasha said, "Teacher, they are men."

As for men and women working together, that would have been "bad." They could talk to each other across the table, but they couldn't sit on the same side. They couldn't share a textbook. They couldn't share a desk. Some days, when we were short of seating, all seven men crowded together on a single bench, while one or two women occupied another. Often I put posters or photos on the walls all around the room and gave the students some conversational task that involved circulating to look at them, but the men wouldn't venture into the women's side of the room even at the cost of missing out on half the lesson. Somehow, despite these cultural obstacles, we grew to be something like a family, so that at the end of the course the students could arrange a celebratory meal together. The women laid cloths over the tables and produced platters of *mantu* and *pilau* they had cooked at home. The men brought soft drinks and bread and cookies. Some students brought their sons and daughters because they wanted their children to see them graduate. All of them dressed up for the occasion and stood proudly to receive a Certificate of Achievement with their name printed in the biggest font I could find on the computer. But they still couldn't stand together in a single class photo. I had to photograph the sexes separately, they said; so I ignored the tradition of male privilege and took the photo of the women first. I see them now: eight women standing shoulder to shoulder in the sunny schoolyard. Their long skirts and coats and chadors are dark—black and gray and brown—against the dull yellow wall of the school. No blue. No burqas.

Men and women can't live this way without developing some psychic glitches. For one thing, my students of both genders have very strict definitions of what "men" and "women" are, and what they should be. The "should be" is an immiscible mix of pseudo-Islam and sexy Bollywood movies. The reality is something else. Because they've seen so few examples of the other sex at close range, they draw general conclusions from a very small sample. Based on what they've seen in their own families, the single men are eager to marry "good" women, and the single women don't want to marry at all. Half the women in the class are unmarried, and many have unmarried sisters. At first I suspect they are single because so many men died in the wars; but women died by the thousands too in bombardments and in childbirth, so that the population is more balanced than you might expect. (The American air raids alone killed at least four thousand Kabuli civilians, without regard to age or gender.)[9] Then I learn that the single women are scared to death of men. One of my best students, Nilab, who is thirty-two, lives at home with her parents and three unmarried sisters, all schoolteachers. Her father was a stonemason, but he is now too old to work. Nilab tells me in private one day that her father beat her mother nearly every day for sending their daughters to school, but her mother sent the girls anyway and took the punishment. Nilab and her sisters all graduated from university, became teachers, and ran a home school during the Taliban time. Most of their brothers disappeared during the wars, so now the household is supported entirely by the sisters' teaching salaries. At some point, when he became "too old," her father stopped the beatings; and now, Nilab says, he is proud that his daughters have good, respectable jobs. But when asked to write a paragraph about her future plans, Nilab says this: "I will not marry. I do not like the men. Men are very bad. Afghan men are very bad and dangerous."

The two most beautiful young women in the class are married, both sold into marriage as adolescent girls by parents who must have needed to make some money in wartime. One marriage is happy, and the other not. Fariba tells me that she wept all night before her wedding because she was so sad to leave her family and so fearful of meeting her husband. When she saw him for the first time at the wedding, she wept again because he was very homely; but then she turned to prayer. She prayed, even during the ceremony, that her homely husband would prove to be kind; and her prayer was answered. I ask the students to write a paragraph about "luck," and Fariba writes: "My husband is very kind and good man. He let me to teach school. He let me to visit my mother home. My friend husband is not kind man. I am woman is very good luck." She shows me photographs of her son and daughter and points out that both children are very beautiful. Another prayer answered.

Palwasha, on the other hand, is married to a handsome older man. She shows me her wedding photos. Although in the pictures she is just a girl, she wears the elaborate upswept hairdo and dramatic makeup of modern Afghan brides. She is stunningly beautiful in the green gown worn early in the proceedings—before the *nikkah* conference at which the men of the families negotiate the price—and later, in the white bridal gown. Out of respect for their parents, Afghan brides are not supposed to look happy about getting married and leaving home; and in her photographs, Palwasha displays the proper expression of sorrow and resigned compliance. But she wears the same look today. Her seeming serenity is sadness at heart. Later I learn the reason: she is childless. That is her bad luck, she says. But there is more. Her husband's parents are displeased with her because she cannot conceive a child. They urge her husband to take a second wife. Later still, after I arrange for her to see a visiting European doctor, I learn that the problem lies with the husband, and that both Palwasha and her husband know it. "Erectile dysfunction," the doctor says—not an incurable condition, but an unmentionable one in Afghanistan. So Palwasha must bear the shame and anguish of her childlessness, consoled only that her husband must resist family pressure to take another wife whose similar inability to conceive might give the game away.

Faruq writes about bad luck too: "I am not find good girl marry to me. I look out good girl. My mother look out. My sisters look out. My mother and my sisters not find." Faruq is more than ready and eager to marry, and he seems to me a good catch. A graduate of a provincial university, he's been in Kabul for several years, teaching high school and moonlighting as a messenger for an INGO. He is very ambitious and almost single-handedly persuades me to supplement the class with an additional early-morning conversation hour that he never fails to attend. He has initiative and ingenuity too. He takes it upon himself to devise a heater for our classroom; and although we have to scrap the contraption when a table catches fire, it's a good effort. He is hardworking, well organized, unfailingly polite and courteous, and he makes no secret of his search. In fact, he raises the topic nearly every day for our conversational consideration. He tries to enlist the women in the class to "look out" on his behalf. Several of them might be good prospects themselves, but Faruq does not want a wife from among his peers. He wants a girl of about thirteen, maybe fifteen at the oldest, and preferably one who has not gone "too far" in school, by which he means not beyond class six, the outer limit of primary school. I suggest that a more educated girl closer to his own age might be a better companion, and since he enjoys talking so much, a better conversationalist; but discourse is not what he desires from a wife. Still, the whole class pitches in to the search. The following year, I learn that he is still vetting prospects and has proposed himself to several families without success. He has even offered himself to my friend Lema, who is older and better educated. It is a measure of his desperation. Then, two years later, comes the good news: Faruq has found the perfect bride in a very young, uneducated girl. I try with some of his old classmates to find him, to bring gifts and meet his wife, but he has disappeared into wedded bliss.

But why was Faruq's search the focus of our English class? Why did every writing topic prompt compositions about husbands and wives? How had ESL become an Afghan soap opera? The subject seemed to squat like a giant wedding cake on the classroom table. We couldn't avoid it. I thought we were obsessed with relations between the sexes because they are forbidden. Anybody of the opposite sex who isn't a member of your immediate family is a strange bird, exotic as an ostrich. But I came to think there was more to it. To find a wife or a husband was to find a home, to find safety and security, and a future. It didn't always work out that way, we all knew. Two women in our class were widows. One man had lost a wife. And Palwasha's childlessness revealed the fallibility of the future. But to search was to hope. And in Kabul, at that time, hope was all there was to hang on to.

No one encouraged Faruq more than Nasir. He'd been a soldier in Najibullah's army, not because he believed in communism but because it was the best job he could find in Kabul near the end of the Soviet occupation. He fought with the army until he was captured by mujahidin. They treated him very well, he said, and they persuaded him that he was on the wrong side. So then he fought for the mujahidin. Next he was captured by another faction of mujahidin who treated him badly and forced him to fight for them. At last he got tired of fighting—he had never really taken to it—and made his way over the border to Pakistan. There, somehow, near Peshawar, he located his older sister who had married and moved away years earlier. He stayed with her and worked for her husband, learning to repair bicycles, until the Taliban overwhelmed the mujahidin and came to power in Afghanistan. In the first flush of law and order Nasir made his way back to Kabul, not because he believed in fundamentalism but because it seemed safe to go home. He had been away six years. He found his mother and father, who had thought him dead, but the girl he had hoped to marry had married someone else. So Nasir, like Faruq, searched anew for a girl until he found one—"the best one," he told Faruq—and soon he had two children. He started a little business, repairing bicycles. And then because he likes children so much he got a second job teaching in the elementary school. He had no training for this job, no education, but he took to the work, and his pupils took to him. He wasn't a high school teacher at all; he'd lied to get into the English class because he wanted to learn. How many lies had life compelled him to tell, I wondered, this gentle man who'd been a soldier in three armies, believing in none. He didn't like to dwell on the specifics of his life. He preferred the generalities of philosophy. He enjoyed poetry and aphorisms. One day when Faruq was going on about his unrelenting search for love, Nasir said: "*Life* is love." The last day of class, the day of the party, he brought his little boy along. The boy sat quietly, holding his father's hand, and when the graduation ceremony was over, he put Nasir's new certificate into his own schoolbag to carry it safely home.

THE FOLLOWING YEAR, WITH MADAR'S TINY GRANT WELL SPENT, IT was up to me to find the money to teach another class. So I sent an e-mail to my circle of friends, who recycled my request to wider

circles, and a remarkable amount of money poured into the office
of Madar. My second, bigger group of teachers came from different schools in a different part of the city. One year farther away
from the war, they seemed not quite so thin, not quite so tired, not
quite so deprived of electricity and satellite TV. The young men in
the class, who watched a lot of American action flicks on pirated
DVDs, were full of after-class questions about the exact meaning
and appropriate usage of such popular American expressions as
motherfucker, cocksucker, shithead, asshole, dumb ass, ball breaker.
The list seemed endless. And *Dick* as in Cheney—was that a noun
or an adjective? Was it a name or a description?

Perhaps Bollywood won them over, or maybe Kabul English
teachers mastered dirty discourse, because my third class, in the
winter of 2004–5, produced not a single question on the subject.
I saw other changes as well. I was getting senior teachers, who were
older and more experienced. Many remembered the good days
before the wars or during Najibullah's time—that little respite after
the Soviets left and before the mujahidin came to Kabul—when
both men and women dressed differently and seemed better
friends. The women looked back on interesting careers teaching
good students—much better, they said, than today's students
who, thanks to the Taliban, had never acquired the habits of discipline and concentration and hard work. The senior teachers
possessed all those old-fashioned habits, while their young colleagues still seemed scattered and easily distracted. The older men
and women could study together, even sit together on a single
bench when necessary and form a working pair, though some of
their younger colleagues were scandalized at the sight of a man
and a woman, unrelated, sharing a textbook. But the biggest
change in my students was this: they were demanding. At the first
class they laid out their terms. The young ones wanted more
money for bus fare; a dollar a day was all we could offer. They
wanted to know how much I was being paid, and by whom. They
didn't believe I was working for nothing. Why would anybody do

that? It was unimaginable. Was I working for the CIA? Perhaps
that was it. In that case, why couldn't I give them more money for
their bus fares?

The senior teachers, on the other hand, wanted to learn something new; if they didn't learn from the class, they weren't going
to attend. They were real teachers, after all, who thought about
things like curriculum and materials and methodology. First of
all, they said, they wanted new and better textbooks. Finding
such books is no problem, for the un-Islamic English texts the
Kabul University professors objected to are used in storefront
English courses all over the city. Bookstores have stacks of the
best British and American ESL books in cheap editions reprinted
in Pakistan, and the pirated audiotapes to go with them. Most
present a series of lessons focused on everyday situations like going
shopping or preparing a meal. I pick out the bits and pieces of ordinary Western life that may be intelligible and inoffensive to these
students and then improvise other materials and activities. Forget
the lesson about dating. (Once, after I explained what *blind date*
meant, a woman said, "Like my wedding.") Skip the one on sports
too, with its pictures of women Rollerblading and swimming, and
men playing golf. ("Why?") Try the lesson on special occasions we
celebrate. Housewarming proves to be a common custom; my students are surprised to learn that Americans also often bring gifts
to friends who've moved to a new home. They'd thought that
Afghans and Americans had nothing in common at all.

And here is a photo of a wedding—another celebratory occasion we share—where amazingly the American bride wears a long
white wedding dress apparently copied from the Afghan fashion.
(Western wedding gowns have been in style in Kabul since the
1920s when the bride of King Amanullah's eldest son set the
trend.) They want to know if we fire off our guns at the wedding
too, as Afghans do, and the answer disappoints them. Perhaps we
don't have so much in common after all. A photo of a handsome,
silver-haired white couple gazing lovingly into each other's eyes

brings the class up short and sets the women chattering. The caption says that the man and woman in the photo are celebrating their fiftieth wedding anniversary. (I remember too late that the whole life expectancy of an Afghan is forty-six years.) We practice pronouncing the word. "What means anniversary?" they want to know, and my explanation leaves them dumbstruck. "We celebrate wedding," one man says. "We are happy. But after wedding we are not celebrate." A woman says, "After wedding, we are not happy," and laughter ricochets around the room. But they are filled with curiosity. They want to know what the husband and wife do on the wedding anniversary. Do they have guests? Yes, some couples do, I say, but most often the husband and wife go out to a very nice restaurant and have a special dinner. (I do not mention the un-Islamic champagne.) They laugh, baffled by alien custom. A man and wife go to a restaurant? Alone? It is like golf. "Why?"

Later, after the new school year starts and my students go back to their own classrooms, I travel around Kabul to see what they've learned. Some of the shattered schools have been refurbished, and proud principals invite me to offices where tea is served on tables adorned with bouquets of plastic flowers. But more often I am ushered into a shabby classroom where empty light sockets drip from scaling ceilings over the heads of fifty or sixty students crammed together three by three on benches meant for two, and a teacher stands at the front of the room writing illegibly on a "blackboard" that is nothing more than a coat of black paint smeared crookedly on the wall. Sometimes the classroom is an old UNICEF tent in the schoolyard, and there is nothing to write on at all. I visit a boys' middle school in an outlying district, a rundown, badly damaged two-story building with a row of eight UNICEF tents in the yard. Behind the tents another rank of classrooms is under construction, paid for by Japanese aid. This school with a staff of 180 teachers operates in three shifts to serve more than 7,000 children. My student Aziz teaches four ninth-grade classes, with 65 boys in each. That's a total of 260 students he sees every day. I don't even ask how often he assigns them a writing task.

But the students are eager. Hands shoot up in response to every question. When called upon, a student stands and reads out the answer from the textbook, supplying the missing word needed to complete a sample sentence. As often as not, the answer is wrong, and wrong in a way that shows neither student nor teacher grasps the meaning of the sentence in question. The lesson is about those pesky adverbs again, adverbs of frequency this time. "He will buy two new stoves because it is <u>seldom</u> cold in the winter," says a student when the text offers a choice between *seldom* and *usually*. "Very good," says the teacher, my student Aziz, and moves on to the next sentence. Another student reads: "He likes to relax in the evening so he <u>seldom</u> watches TV." Aziz says, "Very good." It is true that watching Afghan TV, with its nightly reports of children kidnapped by black marketeers in body parts, is hardly relaxing, so perhaps the student's answer really is very good, but I don't think so. Maybe Aziz got this much from me, I think, always to be encouraging. But a right answer now and then would be helpful too. Still, looking around the room at the ambitious boys leaping to their feet, I think they'll learn despite their teacher's dodgy knowledge of adverbs and other elements of the English language. Somehow, because they know that English helps them get better jobs, and because their teacher praises them so much, they'll pick it up themselves.

The girls' classes I visit are better because the women teachers I observe happen to be better at their work. They know more English and come up more often with the right answers. But still they stand at the front of the room before the ranks of overcrowded benches and drill the students from well-worn textbooks that require the insertion of a single word in sentences the girls seem to find unintelligible. The students spit out syllables as if they tasted bad.

"Whatever happened to the new teaching methods we practiced in our class?" I ask the women teachers. "What about
pair work and group work and games and—please, remember—
conversation?" Only Sima had given her students little breaks
during the lesson when they could talk to each other to practice
what they'd learned. The girls had put their heads together and
chattered eagerly in English, but in whispers, as if they feared they
might be caught by the Taliban.

"Oh, Teacher," says Sima despairingly. "This is not allowed."

Momina backs her up. "My principal is also English teacher,"
she says. "He told me to stop these ways."

"We must give the lecture or the mothers and fathers make
problems for us," Sima says.

"Yes. We must study the book because the mothers and fathers
studied the book."

"Teacher, we like to do different. But this is not allowed."

FOR THREE YEARS I'D LOOKED FOR HELP FOR THESE TEACHERS.
They couldn't teach English better unless they improved their own
English. They couldn't abandon the old textbooks without having
new materials. They couldn't change their ways of teaching until
the number of teachers who wanted to change reached critical
mass. They needed help, and they asked for it, and I wanted to help
them. But I was a novice at "humanitarian aid." I didn't know how
to play the game. I thought that if I got a few more volunteer ESL
teachers to join me in Kabul, I could expand Madar's little program
to reach nearly every high school. In 2002, after my first class
ended, I dispatched an invitation by e-mail to ESL teachers I knew
in New York City. The first answer, by return e-mail, summed up
the general response: "Volunteer? In Afghanistan? Now? Are you
out of your mind?" I saw that I would have to offer what I later
learned to call an "incentive." So I wrote a brief proposal to
expand Madar's teaching program and a budget that included air

fares and monthly salaries and housing allowances for additional teachers, and I made the rounds of funding sources. Later an acquaintance at USAID told me I'd made the mistake of asking for too little money, only about twelve thousand dollars. "Multiply by ten or twenty," she said, "and somebody might at least take a look at it." But everywhere the answer to my overly modest proposal was some patronizing and dismissive variation of flat out *no*.

At the time I felt inept for failing to find help for Kabul's English teachers, and angry on their behalf. But reading an article by George Packer in *The New Yorker,* I learned that I was not the only flop. Another was Joe Biden, the Democratic senator from Delaware. In January 2002, as chairman of the Senate Foreign Relations Committee, he had visited Kabul in response to a request from Bush Two that he draft legislation to win the minds of young people in the Muslim world. Bush had cast 9/11 in the context of a religion-steeped culture war, perhaps to avoid discussing specific US policies that bin Laden said had prompted the al-Qaeda attacks. Biden had a different take on 9/11, though he too managed to avoid discussing US foreign policy. He located 9/11 in a kind of class war, arguing that the hateful ideology behind such attacks arises from poverty, human misery, and political repression. The way to counteract the ideology of hate, Biden thought, was to make a serious commitment to expanding around the world the material conditions that foster the values of liberal democracy, especially education. (After Biden failed him as a mind-winner, Bush hired a public relations firm to make a slick, sappy film about the happy lives of Muslims living in the US.) Biden drafted a proposal to build one thousand schools in Afghanistan at a cost of twenty thousand dollars each and staff them with all those teachers forced from their jobs by the Taliban. Packer reports that Biden (like me) thought he had a better chance of success by thinking small, though Biden's definition of small is not chicken feed. Biden said, "You could shove twenty million dollars anywhere in a two trillion budget, and this was something

specific. . . . It was something concrete we could show the Afghanis we're doing. . . . It was something other than the butt of a
gun."[10]

Behind Biden's proposal was what he described to Packer as "a
catalytic event." As he was about to leave a Kabul school, a
young girl stood up at her desk and said, "You cannot leave. You
cannot leave. . . . They will not deny me learning to read. I will
read, and I will be a doctor like my mother. I will. America must
stay." Biden told Packer that he understood what the girl was
telling him: "Don't fuck with me, Jack. You got me in here. You
said you were going to help me. You better not leave me now."[11]
But the Bush administration was already moving on to Iraq,
choosing the gun over the schoolhouse, and Biden's proposal for
education in Afghanistan went nowhere.

In 2005 I tried again with the help of Madar to get support for
my teachers. By that time the Ministry of Education had counted
more than seventy different education projects in the country,
from school construction to teacher training, and there were
many more run by people who hadn't bothered to let the ministry
know what they were up to. But there was still no program for
high-school English teachers. There were also more donors in
Kabul, more sources of funding. Or, as it turned out, more people
to turn me down with some canned variation of *no* couched in the
jargon of international aid. (I too was learning the lingo, getting
educated in Afghanistan.) This donor hadn't "prioritized" high
school education. That one hadn't made it a "focus." Another
said high school education lay beyond its "nexus of concern."
Another had another "vision."

The vision, as it turned out, was universal literacy. And the
vision—a powerful one that seemed to emanate from USAID—
seemed universal indeed. Who could doubt that it was a grand idea,
and long overdue? Who wouldn't want to see a whole nation
delivered from non-literacy to the pleasures and practical benefits
of the written word—a mother able to write a note to her child's

teacher, a father able to correspond with a son working abroad, a whole family able to read anything from the fine print on a box of medicine to the poetry of Rabi'a Balkhi. But was this the place to start? I still wanted to educate the educators, many of whom, being women, had been forced out of work for five or six years and traumatized besides. I still lobbied too for the almost educated, the female university students who needed refresher courses and moral support to complete their interrupted studies. But the education experts opted instead to educate those who had no education at all.

They called it the "democratic" thing to do. In a non-literate culture, they said, the previously educated and the almost educated are "elite classes" and should not be eligible for aid. The US Congress agrees, mandating foreign aid only for broad-based basic education. It probably is true that my thirty-dollars-a-month Kabul high-school teachers are better off than non-literate peasant women in the provinces—although I never could manage to think of them as an "elite class"—but what about the students these teachers would teach? Educate an educator, I thought, and the educator would do a better job of educating others right away—or in the language of the aid business, this "investment in human resources" would deliver an "immediate return." "That may be true," said my insider acquaintance at USAID, "but it's not sexy."

I hadn't factored sexy in. Sexy was how foreign aid in Afghanistan played out in American politics. Sexy was how Afghanistan looked on American television in a presidential election year. Sexy was the "vision" and the TV images of non-literate girls and women in remote villages in the mountains and deserts of Afghanistan throwing off their burqas and learning to write their names. (It seemed remarkable to me after years of high praise for Afghan "freedom fighters"—the guys Ronald Reagan called the "moral equivalents of America's founding fathers"—how little anyone cared anymore what became of Afghan men.)[12] Never mind that thousands of Afghans who had acquired literacy in compulsory education programs of the communist era quickly lost it again because there was nothing to read and no reason to write. One lesson I learned during my education in Afghanistan is that international aid "experts," especially American experts, have to answer to a higher political power. They can't afford to let historical experience obstruct the vision thing.

Besides, literacy and primary education are the aces the international-aid education experts have waiting up their sleeves. Many of the education experts have worked in Africa, where vision is often clouded by lowered expectations of Africans. Few (except Africans) expect African children to get past primary school, so primary school is what the experts have worked on for a very long time. (All that work has yielded mixed results, but that's another story.) The plans, the programs, the budgets—these are already worked out, along with "capacity building" and "trainings" for unskilled teachers, program evaluation criteria, and a long list of "indicators" that evidence success. Even the final reports are already in the hands of the experts, give or take a few alterations in the numbers. How sensible it must seem then to transfer these prefabricated literacy and primary-education programs to a new location.

You might think that if you wanted to help an impoverished, war-torn country, you'd ask the people who live there what their priorities are and what help they need. But that's usually not how international aid works. Instead, the donor countries or financial institutions decide what they want to give a poor or "developing" country, in line with their own interests, and then present the aid through projects designed and controlled by outside experts. Since the end of the Second World War, the donor countries' main concern has been economic "development." How to achieve economic growth is the subject of a debate monopolized in recent decades by free-market fundamentalists (or neoliberals), for whom growth is a function of investment and capital accumulation through the operation of markets unfettered by government regulations that seek to protect labor, resources, and the environment from exploitation.

In development aid, as in neoliberal economics, everything comes from the top down, at least in theory. In practice, of course, aid usually doesn't trickle or drip or even leak down much from the top. In fact, aid that was supposedly intended to help the world's poor has usually had the opposite effect. In most Third World aid-recipient countries the income gap between rich and poor has widened, just as it has in the United States. (Joseph Stiglitz, the Nobel Prize–winning economist, asks: "if this [has] not worked in the United States, why would it work in developing countries?")[13] The rich get richer, while the poor (especially poor women) lose access to land and resources and their traditional livelihoods. Scholars who think and write about the purposes and practice of aid concluded long ago that "economic growth . . . simply failed to filter down."[14] Stiglitz says flatly: "It is not true that 'a rising tide lifts all boats.'" Some boats, it seems, get smashed "to smithereens."[15]

That being the case, many argued for a more democratic approach to aid that would begin at the grass roots: ask common people in particular localities what they want, and then help them satisfy those basic needs. (Perhaps Congress thought it was taking that democratic approach when it authorized aid only for basic education.) Many tried to put such programs into effect, especially in the 1960s and 1970s, but they ran up against the interests of local bosses and repressive governments and powerful donors whose growth projects bore down on them from above. John Brohman, an authority on theories of Third World development, writes that "bottom-up, localized" aid strategies amounted to "swimming upstream against a strong current of economic and political power."[16] So top-down it is, even though everyone knows that "successful" development in any developing country is *likely to make life worse* for a large part of the population. Neoliberals count the deepening misery of the poor as a necessary price to be paid for "growth," rather like civilian collateral damage of American bombing: sad but unavoidable.[17]

Broadly speaking, the big international financial institutions, such as the World Bank and the Asian Development Bank, deliver aid to governments, while the aid program of the United States, USAID, prefers to funnel money through independent contractors and (secondarily) NGOs, bypassing the government of the recipient country, which cannot be relied upon to do what the US wants. European donors do it both ways. Next the donor hires a highly paid expert "consultant" to spend two or three weeks in the recipient country making a "needs assessment." The going rate for such consultants currently hired on USAID education projects in Afghanistan is somewhere around five hundred dollars a day plus transportation and accommodations plus per diem expenses and an additional percentage as "hardship" or "danger" pay. The rate for consultants on business projects funded by USAID may be twice as much. Since the consultant is employed by the donor, and future consultancies depend upon pleasing the donor, the good consultant invariably finds that the proposed recipient's assessed needs cry out for precisely the program the donor proposes. The next step is to find more consultants to deliver the goods.

Increasingly, at USAID, that means hiring a private for-profit contractor, for the United States has privatized foreign aid in much the same way it has privatized its proxy armies (like the contras or the mujahidin) and its own military operations. (By 2003 more than a third of the $87 billion then budgeted for war in Iraq was going to 10,000 private for-profit military contractors—that's one contractor for every ten members of the regular armed services.)[18] If you can harness the military to the capitalist bandwagon, why not hitch up the humanitarian impulse too? In 2001, Andrew Natsios, the head of USAID, spoke candidly about the self-serving nature of American aid. As "a key foreign policy instrument," he said, foreign aid "helps nations prepare for participation in the global trading system and become better markets for US exports."[19] Local Afghan markets, however, are so thoroughly dominated by drug-rich, politically connected oligarchs—the narco-mafia and friends—that some economists believe further economic growth may actually *decrease* chances for genuine national security and democratic change in Afghanistan.[20]

Nevertheless, because the underlying purpose of American aid is to make the world safe and open to American business, USAID now cuts business in from the start. It sends out requests for proposals to the short list of usual suspects and awards contracts to those bidders currently in favor. Sometimes it invites only one contractor to apply, the same efficient procedure that made Halliburton so notorious and so profitable in Iraq. In many fields, including education, it "preselects vendors" by accepting bids every five years or so on an IQC—that's an "Indefinite Quantities Contract." Contractors submit indefinite information about what they might be prepared to do in unspecified areas should some more definite contract materialize; the winners become designated contractors who are invited to apply when the real thing comes along. USAID generates the real thing in the form of an RFP, a Request for Proposals, issued to the "preselected vendors" and perhaps to others who then compete to do in another country the work assigned by Washington. This top-down imposition of what's to be done and what's not is now too routine to require justification. It's the way things are, and explains further why my little bottom-up proposal was dismissed out of hand: it wasn't just too cheap and "undemocratic," it was swimming upstream. As for the preselection process that puts certain suppliers on the inside track, USAID officials and leading contractors alike told me that it saves time, but nobody could explain why, if speed is so important and the process so efficient, education projects in Afghanistan were just getting off the ground about three years after the dispersal of the Taliban. "Nothing wrong with that," said a friend at USAID. "That's fast."

Time is relative, I suppose, and you could certainly argue that it's USAID's job to decide what's fast and what's not, who's in and who's out. But the criteria for selection are not exactly what you would call "transparent." Taking an example from the construction "sector," the case of the Kabul-Kandahar Highway is instructive. Under the headline, "Millions Wasted on Second-Rate Roads," Afghan journalist Mirwais Harooni reported in *Kabul Weekly* that even though other international companies had been ready to rebuild the highway for $250,000 per kilometer, the US-based Louis Berger Group got the job at $700,000 per kilometer—of which there are 389. Why? The standard American answer is that Americans do better work. (A USAID official told me that Afghan contractors are often excluded because "they don't know our methods of accounting.") But Louis Berger hired Turkish and Indian construction companies to build the road, at a final cost of about $1 million per mile; and anyone who travels it can see that it is already falling apart. Former Minister of Planning Ramazan Bashardost complained that when it came to building roads, the Taliban did a better job.[21] (On the USAID Web site the Kabul-Kandahar Highway is featured as a proud accomplishment—just one more example of the divide between American hype and Afghan reality.)

Maybe it's just coincidence that many of the big winners among the for-profit private contractors have vaguely grandiose names—like Bearing Point, Creative Associates International, and Social Impact, Inc.—after the example of the Defense Department's "Enduring Freedom," "Infinite Justice," and "Just Cause" operations. But by no stretch of language or imagination can they be called "humanitarian" organizations. If you ask, most will say they work in "development," a phase of nation-building intervention they regard as more sophisticated than immediate, life-saving humanitarian aid. Their country directors will confess modestly that their real business is "doing good," though of course their real business is doing business, which they do around the world. Bearing Point, for example, which specializes in "business systems integration," employs sixteen thousand people in thirty-nine countries. It used to be the consulting arm of the KPMG accounting business (currently under investigation for enabling clients to stiff the IRS through fraudulent tax shelters), but in the wake of the Enron scandal in 2002, it took a new name and most of the worldwide business of Enron's accountants, the disgraced firm of Arthur Andersen.[22] In 2003, just after it won two big contracts in Afghanistan and one in Iraq, Bearing Point, like Enron, wildly overstated its income, prompting a shareholder class action lawsuit for securities fraud. Who better to entrust with ninety-eight million taxpayer dollars to "improve economic governance" in the Afghan Finance Ministry and the Central Bank?[23]

Like Bearing Point, the "best" of the contractors are very profitable corporations, and like most, they pride themselves on their efficiency. "We have the systems in place to maximize achievement and deliver success," said one country director, without irony, when I asked what qualified his company for its multimillion dispensation of taxpayer cash. Having the same systems in place, no matter what the place, the contractors tend to look down on humanitarian NGOs as bumbling do-gooders who waste time and money trying to work out aid programs appropriate to individual countries. (Indeed, many of those stubborn Samaritans persist among the NGOs, still trying to work from the bottom-up, still talking about empowerment of the common people and grass-roots democracy.) The contractors, on the other hand, keep one eye on the donor and one eye on the bottom line, which doesn't leave much visionary capacity to apply to the local surroundings. To carry out the actual work on the ground they often hire the services of the same do-gooder NGOs whose principles they disparage. When that happens, the NGO may experience the sensation of being stood on its head as it too becomes part of the top-down package.[24]

I DIDN'T KNOW IT WHEN I WENT TO WORK TEACHING TEACHERS, but I had stumbled into the "multiplier effect" of "cascading." What that means is that you don't just import American men and machines to build a highway or an irrigation system; you teach Afghans some building skills that they in turn can teach others. That's called "applying the multiplier effect to your inputs" and "maximizing outputs" by "cascading," and it's a good idea even before you gussy it up in the jargon. One effort spills over into another like a series of waterfalls. USAID has built cascading into lots of contracts, so all the big-money education programs are mapped out in multiple tiers like California water projects. Take the literacy programs for example, of which there are two big ones funded at least in part by USAID. They're headed by international directors who supervise international consultants who train and supervise Afghan core trainers who train and supervise Afghan lead trainers who train and supervise Afghan field trainers who train and supervise Afghan teachers-in-training who teach literacy to non-literate Afghan girls and women and boys and men in several different places in the provinces. Each rank of trainers gets trained for several days, maybe even a week or two, before being turned loose to train the next rank down. Trainers visit their trainees frequently and gather them in periodically for another day or two of tune-up training. This pipeline of support, everyone agrees, is what keeps the content being passed along from evaporating into thin air. Knowledge flows along and out to the field, while the international consultant at the top tries to keep one bucketful ahead of the game. Or take TEP, the Teacher Education Program designed to upgrade the skills of elementary-school teachers in the government school system and funded by multiple donors, including USAID and the World Bank, and run in part by a private for-profit contractor. It has 20 core trainers training 150 master trainers who are supposed to train 2,500 teacher educators to train 125,000 teachers in 34 provinces.[25] So far they've trained only a few teacher educators in six provinces, but they're just getting started, and according to the best estimates there aren't that many teachers in the country anyway. The government schools alone still come up short by 40,000 teachers.

By 2005, all these ambitious and cumbersome literacy and primary-school teacher-training projects were falling behind even USAID's definition of "fast."

"How about cooperating?" I asked a panicked consultant, who worked for one of the contractors. Her program had barely left the launch pad. "Wouldn't it help to share materials?"

"We don't have time to cooperate. We're all too busy," she said, referring to other programs, run by other contractors. "And anyway, those guys are the competition."

"But aren't you all working toward the same goal?"

"One goal, many contractors," she said.

Soon the teacher-training programs began to use the offer of higher salaries to pick off one another's trainers. When I heard that one of the literacy projects was looking for experienced teachers to be trained, I recommended some of the high school teachers in my class. After being interviewed, they reported back that they'd lost out to others who'd already received training. I was certain they'd got it wrong. But no, the international consultant who was supposed to be training teacher-trainers was accepting only applicants who'd already been through a course offered by another aid project. "It's a lot faster," she explained, "to train a teacher-trainer who has already been trained." This is probably true. But the repetitive training of the same people swirling among projects can't be counted as a cascade. It's more like an eddy.

STILL, I WAS PLEASED TO SEE THESE PROFESSIONAL EDUCATION projects getting underway at last. The international consultants who headed them seemed an enthusiastic, experienced, and dedicated lot. And all the cascading made sense to me, probably because it's what I'd done myself, before I had the terminology to make it saleable. Now I wanted to see how it worked. So I made plans to accompany some trainers out to "the field" to take a look at how the trainee-teachers were doing. Having been soberly warned in advance that my security could not be guaranteed if I ventured into the provinces, I was surprised to find that the "provinces" in question lay just up the road—close enough for the trainer to visit two or three classes in a single day and still get back to Kabul before the office closed at half past three.

There on the Shamali plains, which the US had pummeled to powder with subatomic bombs only a few years earlier, there behind the walls of surviving farm compounds where spotted cows stood placidly in the yard, women of all ages sat on the floor of a sunny parlor and grappled with the Dari alphabet. One after another women old and young rose to take a turn at a makeshift blackboard, tracing with great care some sinuous shape that when combined one day with others would spell a name they knew. They were already acquainted with the equivalent of M and S and could assemble whole words that meant *salaam* and *Islam*. One teacher was barely fifteen years old, but she'd studied through class six in Kabul before she married and moved to her husband's village home. Now she was getting seventy-five dollars a month—much more than a Kabul high school teacher—to teach her neighbors what she knew; and she took the job seriously. She put her teacher-training to work, hustling the women into little discussion groups, leading them in learning games. In the Dari language, each character of the alphabet alters its basic shape when it appears in a word, connected to another character that precedes or follows it. The teacher-trainees taught the difference by drawing mittens on the characters at the points where they might link up. Sometimes they asked groups of students to form a word, each girl or woman representing a letter; and the students arranged themselves in proper order to spell the requested word, clasped hands as the alphabet required, and stood in front of their classmates beaming. In every classroom—a bright farmhouse parlor, a village storefront, a loft over a barn—women and girls happily bent themselves to the tasks of literacy under the guidance of newly minted teachers like this teenage bride and the trainers who dropped by each week to lend encouragement and provide lesson plans. It was humbling to sit among them. I was enthralled. I too began to dream the dream of universal literacy.

When I asked women in the classes why they wanted to learn to read and write, many said they wanted to be able to read the Quran. They wanted to see if it actually said what the mullahs and their husbands told them it said, especially about women. One old woman said, "I want to see if there is anything in there for me." She didn't care how long it took. She was willing to spend three years, the length of time it commonly takes a non-literate adult to acquire literacy, or even longer if need be. But unfortunately this program was scheduled to end in just a few months, and it had been slow getting started in the first place. It was overly ambitious, too. The American expert in charge told me, "You can't write a decent curriculum in the time we had. It takes at least two years, and we barely had one. We had to throw something together, and we never really got to test it."

"So why did you do it?" I asked.

"It's what the contract called for. It's what USAID wanted."

"But you're the educator," I said. "Didn't you tell them it couldn't be done?"

He laughed. "Couldn't do that," he said. "They'd give the contract to somebody else."

He was a pleasant man, this education expert, who assured me that he was doing the best he could, short of surrendering the job. He told me how it had come his way. USAID had given the contract to a private for-profit contractor "in the health sector," which in turn had subcontracted the job of developing a curriculum to an international education program at the big university where he worked. The university in turn did a deal with one international NGO to train the teacher-trainers and with ten other local and international NGOs, including such well-respected ones as CARE and Save the Children, to do the work they call "implementation." I'd been making notes as he spoke, and there running down the page was a stair-step diagram, like a sketch of the fish ladder at Grand Coulee Dam, with arrows diving from one level to the next like salmon, in water, headed downstream.

"Cascading," I said.

"What?"

"The money. See." I displayed my diagram of this fishy business. "The funding cascades from one contractor to the next. I suppose everybody gets a percentage. So tell me. How much of the original funding actually gets spent on the ground here, say, on salaries for Afghan trainers and in the villages to rent the rooms where the classes take place?"

"Gosh," he said. "You know I'm not really sure. I'm guessing at maybe twenty percent. Maybe ten."

"And the other eighty or ninety percent?"

"Well, that goes to pay the American contractors and subcontractors for their services. And their overhead, of course, back at the home office in the States and here too. Here it goes for office space and housing—you know how high the rents are in Kabul, so Afghan landlords make out on that—and transportation costs, cars and drivers—that's money for Afghans again—and flights and R and R, materials that have to be imported, furniture, food, alcohol, stuff like that."

"So maybe seventy or eighty percent goes into American pockets?"

"Probably. Give or take a little. I don't have the figures," he said. "But of course you understand that's the only way to set things up to get the money out of Congress. They'd never authorize these big aid programs if they thought we were losing control of the money. My salary gets paid in dollars straight into my American bank account. It never even leaves the country." He paused to share a confidential smile. "You know what they say in Washington. 'Charity begins at home.'"

MAYBE I WOULDN'T HAVE MINDED SO MUCH IF THIS MAN HAD spoken of the Afghans he was being so handsomely paid to help as something more than statistics or indicators of success. Or if any of the other contractors I met had been a little less cocksure that their half-baked projects would be "better than nothing" for people they'd never met. Like those earnest women in Shamali or Ghazni or Paghman tracing with precious stubs of chalk the lineaments of language they thought might lead them to a better life. But what would happen to the women, I asked him, and the men too who worked just as hard in other classrooms not far away? What about them? The men could find jobs, he said. But for the women there was a plan. "That's how this whole program came about," he said. Some consultants doing a needs assessment had found a shortage in provincial Afghanistan of women sufficiently well educated to become midwives. And midwives are sorely needed since the maternal and infant death rates in Afghanistan are among the worst in the world. So USAID had funded the health contractor that funded the education subcontractor that funded the NGOs that ran the literacy training program for women who were expected to graduate into the training program for midwives for which USAID had funded the health contractor in the first place. If you can follow that, it sounds like it makes sense; and it sort of explains why an education contract was handed to a health contractor in the first place. Except there was a problem with timing. Because the literacy program got off to a slow start, the training program for midwives got under way long before the planned-for literacy graduates were ready to enter it. And the next training program for midwives was scheduled to begin many months after the prospective candidates had completed their preliminary literacy course, which in any case was too short to make them literate. The expert had only vague notions about how the women might find their way to the midwifery class; he mentioned that not all twenty women in a village literacy class would be needed as midwives anyway.

I heard a lot of stories like this one, of projects that hadn't quite been thought through. Some were well designed, but they got started late and terminated early when experts on one-year contracts went home, or shortsighted donors switched the funds to something else. Take the case of a multimillion dollar USAID project to put 170,000 teenaged students in seventeen provinces through primary school at double time. Among many NGOs the for-profit contractor hired to do the work in the villages was an Afghan women's organization that usually addressed problems of women and children. It was their good reputation and the promise that the students would finish with a sixth-grade education that convinced provincial Pashtun parents, very suspicious of American motives, to send their children to class. Things went well until the contractor announced that the funding would terminate a year early, with the students still in the fourth grade. An angry woman from the Afghan NGO asked me, "What's wrong with America? Why do they keep starting things they can't finish? They could make a million Afghans grateful—all these students and teachers and their families—but instead they make them angry." At least 100,000 of those angry Afghans, I figured, were undereducated teenaged boys. "They're angry at us, too," the woman went on. She was close to tears. "They trusted us, and now we're losing face. We were so honored to be asked to join a USAID project, and such a good one. Some people warned us we would be co-opted by the Americans. But it's worse. They are shaming us."

None of the contractors or consultants or experts will stick around long enough to see what happens to discredited local NGOs or terminated students. They'll never know where those who are still cascading wash up. The Scandinavian countries, whose aid programs enjoy the widest respect, often work over a long term at the community level with the goal of empowering local people. The Swedish Committee has been assisting Afghan villagers for more than twenty years, uninterrupted even by the Taliban. The United States, by contrast, works in the short term, aiming to produce quick results while keeping power in its own hands, and incidentally transferring public taxpayer money to private corporate pockets, particularly to those who kick it back as "campaign contributions."[26] Many aid workers around the world hoped that the end of the Cold War might free foreign aid from political agendas and make it available to those in need. But that didn't happen. And since 9/11, US aid has become a weapon in the administration's war on terror. (The chief beneficiary is Pakistan.)[27] Used as an instrument of partisan foreign policy, American aid is a fickle friend.

Few aid workers are as naïve as I was when I first went to Afghanistan to offer help, though many are very idealistic. Except for the retired military and corporate men, most are considerably younger than I am and not yet cynical. Humanitarian aid workers tend to be multilingual citizens of the world who see what a small place it really is and how it spills together. Increasingly, they come from all parts of the planet, well equipped with graduate degrees, many from American or European universities in fields like international education, international law, and "development." Many are doctors, nurses, mental-health specialists, engineers, hydrologists, agriculturalists, de-miners, computer programmers. Many want a career that makes a contribution to the world. Some come for the money, some for adventure, some because they can't get a job at home. Some come because they feel uncomfortable amid the riches of their home country, some because the desperation of this poor one seems more real. Some, like those who worked here in the Peace Corps before the wars, remember a peaceful Afghanistan and want to restore it. For one reason or another, they all want to lend a hand. Some do good work—that is, work that actually makes life a little better for some ordinary Afghans, by their own report. Some don't. But the for-profit contractors start and finish in a different place.

It's not that profit-making contractors necessarily fail to "do good," but what they do best is to fulfill the contract devised by the donor, by the World Bank or USAID or their counterparts from Britain or Japan or Germany. There's no reason for them to be accountable one to another as international NGOs like CARE and Oxfam and Mercy Corps have been over the years, looking out for one another with the sense of being engaged in a common enterprise. No reason even for them to be accountable to the public or to the "beneficiaries" they're supposed to "service." The best INGOs have individual identities. Each was founded for a purpose, often implicit in the name—like Save the Children or the International Rescue Committee or Médecins Sans Frontières— and people have some idea of the kind of work they do. Ordinary citizens in their home countries contribute to support their work. But no grannies send spare change to Bearing Point or the mysterious DynCorp, which happens to be one of the biggest private military contractors in the world. Contractors have no particular identity, no founding principles, no purpose apart from making money—and perhaps taking the rap for the administration when things go bad, as Halliburton has done from time to time in Iraq with no apparent diminution in its profits. Broadly speaking, it's in the interests of NGOs to be cooperative with one another and open about what they're up to, while contractors stand to stay in business by running a tight ship with the doors closed.

Maybe because they're so good at profit making, many American contractors tend to think they're a whole lot smarter and better than the people they're supposed to help. (If Afghans are smart, why aren't they rich?) Contractors are clever enough to know that it's not easy to assign a value to many of the projects they're asked to undertake. How much *should* it cost for an American accountant to train employees at an Afghan ministry in book-keeping? How much *should* it cost for American education consultants to train 125,000 primary-school teachers? Who knows? So contractors understandably tend to charge what the traffic will bear; and the more money they ask for their services, the more valuable their services seem to the donor to be. (Besides, donors often prefer to give a few big contracts, rather than a bunch of smaller ones.) Successful contractors also know how to value themselves. They believe they're entitled to live well. So when a hot contractor with, say, 98 million taxpayer dollars to spend, brings in one hundred consultants and advisers (all men), it might spend a half million a pop. It might put them up in ten or twelve posh houses, each renting at about ten thousand dollars a month, in the most dollar-drenched part of town. It might provide them with fine food and wine flown in from Europe or the US, and armed male bodyguards of the macho type, and young male ser-vants of the vaguely feminized sort, and an SUV and a male driver and a male translator for nearly everyone. Then it might tack on a little something extra to the six-figure base pay—say, something for "danger," something for being "out of location," something per diem, and an expense account. (I say "might" because all these matters are secret for "security reasons.") You can do the math: that's a big chunk of the budget spent on supporting inter-national (mostly American) men, free of encumbering families, in a style and a psychosocial fantasy few of them could enjoy at home.

The rationale for squandering tax money in this way is that it's supposed to "buy the best people," but a surprising number of consultants and advisers working for contractors like Bearing Point will joke openly about how little they know about the task at hand. Like the high-powered lawyer I met at a party whose con-tract called for him to advise a government ministry on tax law. "I don't know dick about tax law," he said with a laugh. "Commercial real estate is more my line. But the neat thing about working with these Afghanis is they don't know the difference." But maybe they do. Afghan officials tried to terminate the Bearing Point contract in 2004, noting that some of the consultants were "not necessary" and others were "not the strongest professionals." But USAID said Bearing Point was "performing well" and kept them on.[28]

THE EDUCATION CONTRACTORS IN KABUL SEEM TO BE A CUT ABOVE the strictly business crowd. After all, the consultants on the ground are teachers, concerned about children. And a lot of them are women, which doesn't necessarily make them better, but a little different. (They don't patronize brothels, for one thing.) Yet just like that nice man caught in the cascades, they've slipped into the system of for-profit contracting, answerable in the end to the donors and their political aims. The biggest US education contractor in Afghanistan, Creative Associates International, cemented relations with USAID and the Defense Department during the Reagan administration running "vocational training courses" for the contras. Since then it's handled more than four hundred contracts, and USAID has become the source of almost all its revenue, which runs as high as $50 million a year. In March 2003, Creative Associates got a $60 million contract to work on primary education in Afghanistan and another for Iraq that may be worth $157 million. (The numbers always are elusive.) These back-to-back windfalls triggered the Inspector General to investigate the Iraq deal and led Senator Joseph Lieberman to conclude that "there was essentially no competitive bidding at all." Those who'd been invited to enter competitive bids but declined were rewarded instead by Creative Associates with handsome subcontracts. Maybe this happened by chance, or maybe contractors really do look out for each other after all. Anyway, the dodgy Iraq contract left Creative Associates looking like the Halliburton of the education crowd. (Nonetheless, they got a second $56 million contract for Iraq less than a year later,[29] and they're rumored to be first in line for another $75 million deal in Afghanistan.)

One of their first big ventures in Afghanistan was to have millions of much-needed textbooks printed. Unfortunately, they sent the print order to Indonesia, to printers who knew neither Dari nor Pashtu; and when the books arrived in Kabul by plane, at splendid expense, they were unreadable. Some texts had been shuffled and bound together, like Religion and Biology, so that a chapter on the life of the Prophet might be followed by one on plants. I got the story from an official at the Ministry of Education who said the books were still in storage somewhere.[30]

To be fair, Creative Associates wasn't the first American education outfit to bungle the books. That distinction belongs to the Center for Afghanistan Studies at the University of Nebraska at Omaha, sometimes mistaken because of its initials, UNO, for part of the United Nations. When Creative Associates had to come up with ten million textbooks to meet the terms of its USAID contract, it apparently tried to pass off reprints of texts originally developed by UNO under another USAID contract issued in 1984. UNO had produced the books—some thirty million of them—and used them in schools it set up for Afghan refugees in Pakistan, where USAID continued to fund UNO's education programs until all American aid to Afghanistan ceased in 1994. Among the refugees were Afghans of all political persuasions, but the books had been devised by and for the Islamist parties. (Later, of course, it came out that the CIA was behind the whole scheme—part of its anti-Soviet covert aid to freedom fighters.) After USAID funding shut down, UNO went to work for US oilmen; it picked up a $1.8 million contract with UNOCAL to train workers to build the trans-Afghanistan pipeline, and it helped host the UNOCAL-sponsored visit of Taliban cabinet ministers to the US in 1997. But all the while, UNO kept its book publishing business going in Pakistan, so in January 2002, USAID found it "uniquely positioned" to print eight million books and train four thousand teachers for the start of the new post-Taliban school year in Afghanistan.[31]

By that time, some critics had noticed that the original UNO textbooks had a lot of pictures of guns and bullets, and some of the math problems, couched in terms of killing Soviets, seemed to promote violence. So, working in Pakistan, UNO removed the violent pictures and references—or so they said—and delivered millions of books on time. Then critics noticed that the textbooks still contained plenty of violence and lots of Quranic verses besides. USAID regulations forbid the use of tax dollars to advance religion, but aid officials and the Bush White House said religious references were required in a religious culture—even, apparently, the kind of religious references that inspired the Taliban. So these texts, cosponsored by an American university, Islamist extremists in exile, USAID, and the CIA, have been the standard textbooks in Afghanistan ever since, and they might have appeared in new editions if Creative Associates had sent a Dari/Pashtu reader along to Indonesia to supervise the printing.

Some people in Nebraska were not very happy about all this. In 2005, Paul Olson, an English professor at the University of Nebraska at Lincoln and a member of Nebraskans for Peace, somewhat belatedly pointed out to the University Board of Regents that the texts "promoted violence and jihad." This violated University regulations forbidding dissemination of educational materials that contravene recognized human rights. "We provided the violence-laden propaganda to the Taliban-era Afghan children," Olson said. "The 9/11 terrorists emerged from this context." Defending the university, Regents' Chairman Howard Hawks claimed (incorrectly) that the books had not been intended for schoolchildren but for "illiterate Afghan Mujahideen who were fighting Soviet forces." Anyway, Congress and the State Department (not to mention the CIA) had specified that Afghans should write the books, so UNO bore "no involvement or responsibility

for their content." As for the textbooks currently used in
Afghanistan, Hawks said they are "the work of President Hamid
Karzai's administration and nothing to do with UNO."[32]

The 2005 school year was just getting under way in Kabul, so
after reading about the confrontation in Omaha, I took Salma, my
colleague at Frauen die Helfen, on a shopping trip to the central
bazaar where dozens of booksellers sat behind pushcarts laden
with stacks of schoolbooks and trashy novels. For a couple of dollars we bought a full set of the old UNO primary-school textbooks
in Dari. They were thin, paper-bound volumes clearly labeled by
grade level and subject. Whether they'd ever been "revised" was
impossible to tell. We lugged them to the car, and during the drive
back to the office, I tried to engage Salma to read some of the
books for me and tell me what they said. Salma was a law student
at Kabul University, equipped with a mind as sharp as a razor, and
always ready to take on more work. But this time she refused.

"I know what they say. I don't want to read again."

"You've already read them?"

"Of course. I read in school. We all read in school. That's why
I and my classmates in university do not know anything."

"What do you mean, you don't know anything?"

"Number one: we do not know history of our country." She
was flipping through the stack of books. She pitched one into my
lap. *History and Geography, Fifth Class.* "It is history of Saudi
Arabia," she said. "And geography of Mecca. Nothing from
Afghanistan." She tossed another book at me. *Dari, Fourth Class.*
"Look. It starts with victory of Islamic Revolution. It is information from the Prophet and mujahidin and jihad against *kharaji*—
foreigners—and outside ideas. Nothing from Dari. Nothing from
history of our language. Our literature."

"Do you know who wrote the books?" I asked.

"Of course. Mujahidin. Gulbuddin. Mullahs in Pakistan. Such
men as that." She spat out the answers in anger. "They are made
in Pakistan but they are American books."

Since I couldn't read the books myself, I took them to an Afghan scholar, an older man who had been well educated before the Soviet invasion. After he read them, he was very distressed. "These books are for the madrassa," he said, "not the school." No matter the subject—Dari, Math, History, Religion—the books revolved around the life of the Prophet and his teachings. I asked if there was anything about Afghan history, and he turned to the fourth class history text. "This one tells a little about King Amanullah," he said. "It tells that he returned from Europe with Western ideas, against Islam, and all the people hated him and proclaimed jihad against him." And this Dari text says the communist revolution was "the darkest day in the history of Afghanistan." There didn't seem to be much Afghan history before or between those two events, separated by fifty years.

The scholar showed me a long passage that defined the ideal mujahid as a man who would give everything he had—his property, his knowledge, his thoughts, even his wife and children—to his God. He is an honest man, always obedient to Allah, always ready to defend the life and property of fellow Muslims, always working for the unity of Muslims everywhere throughout the world. Such a person could easily become a martyr for Islam. The scholar ran his finger across the page of a ten-year-old's textbook and translated quickly: "'If a man is fighting against the enemy of Islam, he is the person who makes happy his God. If a man gives his life for this purpose he will have a high position with the God. . . . As the martyr sees his high position with God he wishes to have another life to be a martyr again.'" He closed the book. "You see it is inspirational," he said. "That is why I say the books are for the madrassa." I thanked the scholar, gathered up my inspiring texts, and walked home, passing the neighborhood school just as a flock of little girls in black dresses and white chadors poured out of the yard. There were millions of children in school now, more than ever before in the obscure history of Afghanistan, as the Bush administration liked to brag. That much was true, though the percentage of girls was higher during the communist era. But they were reading the same old books.

It's not that no one had thought of writing new books. That was among the earliest aims of the Ministry of Education, where specialists from Columbia University Teachers College spent a couple of years helping to design a new school curriculum and draft new texts. The new books are meant to challenge Afghanistan's old rote learning routines. They include a lot of questions, activities, and topics for discussion, all designed to promote the sort of "active learning" that engages students and develops critical thinking skills. (Many Western educators contend that without critical thinking, democratic processes can't take hold.) By 2005, the new texts for grades one and four were at the printer, in Afghanistan; texts for grades two and five were ready to go. There was a rough draft of the text for grade three, but nothing yet for grade six. And nothing for the higher grades, though Columbia and the Ministry of Education had hoped to prepare new texts all the way to grade twelve. Lack of funding was holding things up. A Columbia professor explained: "It's very difficult to get funding, unless you're tied into the US government, into USAID." So for some time yet, until the Ministry of Education can find the money to get the new books out, eager Afghan children will hurry to school, carrying the old jihadi textbooks in their backpacks, like bombs.

CREATIVE ASSOCIATES AND OTHER FOR-PROFIT EDUCATION CON-tractors funded by USAID report only to the professional, well-paid USAID education experts who live and work in a maze of white shipping containers behind the concrete and razor-wired walls of the Café Compound at Fort Paranoia, the American Embassy. Many of them are friends who got their advanced degrees in international education at the same universities and tend to hire one another; contractors get consultancies at USAID, while former

USAID officials become consultants or advisers to contractors—a friendly business practice a little like the Afghan custom of hiring infinite cousins. Many of the best USAID education experts decline to visit the projects of the contractors they oversee in the field because to do so means to travel in the company of at least two US military troop carriers bristling with soldiers in full combat gear who terrify Afghan villagers all along the way. (One frustrated education officer complained to me over cappuccinos in an embassy café, "How can I visit a primary school with all those soldiers? I'm supposed to be helping kids, not traumatizing them.") So the USAID education officials sit in their little white boxes and read the reports (via e-mail) of contractors who enumerate the "indicators" of their certain success. It's mainly a numbers game: so many million books printed, so many hundred schools built, so many million children in school. I asked several contractors for copies of their reports; being a taxpayer I imagined I had a right to see how they were spending my money. But no, the contractors told me they're not allowed to show their reports to anybody except their assigned minder at USAID. "That's in the contract," one said. I don't know whether that's true or not because the contract isn't a matter of public record either.

But you can see how the final report to USAID becomes the end of the story. Contractors don't have to think about what happens next on the ground in Afghanistan because they're packing up to move on to Iraq or Iran or wherever the empire builders head next. And USAID is accountable to no other nation on earth—least of all Afghanistan. A Swiss friend of mine was hired away from an INGO, drawn by the promise of twelve hundred dollars a day, to insure the "sustainability" of one contractor's project. Sustainability is a "key concept" or "pillar" of development, suggesting that a good project is one the locals will carry on without you, long after you're gone. It's the first concern of Scandinavian NGOs, but it seems to occur to contractors only very late in the day. After an American contractor had spent six months "building capacity" to handle budgets in a hundred men (no women), they hired my Swiss friend to place these upgraded guys in jobs in the government ministries. That was what the "sustainability pillar" of the contract called for. My friend did the job, knowing full well that in a matter of weeks every one of the men he placed would have found a new job for himself among the staff or trainees of another training program run by another contractor. "I can put them in the government," he said, "but I can't make them stay there if the government can't pay them. It can't possibly pay the kind of salaries they get with the contractors. It's just not sustainable."

So, like the teacher-training trainees bought up to be trained again by other teacher-training programs, the accounting trainees go on to higher things. And my Swiss friend, having fulfilled the terms of his contract, however briefly, rises to another more highly paid short-term stint with another short-term contractor. There are more and more of these people, internationals and Afghans alike, caught up in the swirl of money, spiraling skyward like the dust devils that appear now at the end of winter in the sunbaked streets, whirling fiercely upward to vanish in the bleached wide-open sky.

THE AVERAGE AFGHAN SAYS THAT ALL THE FOREIGN AID HAS changed nothing. Afghans say this even in Kabul, where in fact a lot of things have changed quite a bit. A driver points to glitzy new tile-and-glass narco-villas going up on our street and says, "Poppy. Not for me."

"Poppy is not for you?"

"No." He laughs. "Poppy okay. Big house not for me. Big house for poppy man."

"Who is this poppy man?" I ask. The driver laughs and gives me a wicked smile.

"One thing I do for you. I not tell you."

He shares the common opinion that Afghanistan's new riches are home-grown. Afghanistan's opium, which accounts for 87 percent of the world's total, is said to be worth more than $30 billion a year globally, though most of the profit goes outside the country. Still, the 2004 poppy crop brought Afghans $2.8 billion. That's equal to about 60 percent of the country's legal gross domestic product, or more than half the total national income; and it's more than twice as much as the US gave in four years to Afghanistan reconstruction ($1.3 billion), most of which never got to the country anyway.[33] But it's not Afghan farmers who are getting rich. Profits go to politically connected smugglers, warlords, commanders, government officials—the usual suspects. Still, the poppy crop has lifted lots of farmers from abject poverty and enabled them to hang on to their land. When I visited a poor northern farm family I'd met a year earlier, I was pleased to see they'd acquired a generator, electric lights, a TV set, and a motorbike. The source of this good fortune was poppy, growing to within a foot of the doorstep. "Please don't tell the Americans," the young son said. "Now we can go to school." His gesture took in two younger brothers. "If the Americans take our poppy, we must go back to work for the carpet-makers." The farmer's wife had gone to work in the poppy fields of a big local landowner instead, earning five dollars a day. She was getting out of the house and making top dollar—circumstances that were being duplicated all across the country and dramatically changing the status of rural women. Husbands won't keep them at home when there's money like that to be made.[34] Higher up the ranks of the opium trade, in the centers of provincial government and in Kabul, profits become visible in the flamboyant narco-villas. Their gaudiness signals that the owners fear nothing. It also suggests to ordinary Afghans, like my driver, that they have more to gain from the opium trade than from all the international aid donors combined. Late in 2004, the director of the UN Office of Drugs and Crime announced, "The fear that

Afghanistan might degenerate into a narco-state is becoming a reality."[35]

Here is yet another embarrassing unintended consequence of the US proxy war against the Soviets. Before the mujahidin took on the Soviets in 1979, Afghanistan produced a very small amount of opium for regional markets; neither Afghanistan nor Pakistan produced any heroin at all. By the end of the jihad, the Afghanistan-Pakistan border area was the world's top producer of both opium and processed heroin, supplying 75 percent of opium worldwide. As scholar Alfred W. McCoy reports in *The Politics of Heroin*, it was mujahidin who ordered Afghan peasants to grow poppy to finance the jihad. It was Pakistani intelligence agents and drug lords like the all-around villain Gulbuddin who processed heroin. (Gulbuddin reportedly owned six refineries.) It was the Pakistani army that transported heroin to Karachi for shipment overseas. And it was the CIA that made it all possible by providing legal cover for these operations. The CIA applied to Afghanistan the lesson it had learned earlier in Laos and Burma: a covert war demands a covert source of money, and there is none better than the drug trade.[36] How to end the drug trade along with the covert war seems a problem in synchronicity the CIA didn't solve.

Free-market fundamentalists pushing growth for globalization adhere to the principles of nineteenth-century British economist David Ricardo. His theory of "comparative advantage" holds that every country will obtain more goods in the international marketplace by specializing in exporting the thing it can produce most efficiently. In Afghanistan the comparative advantage goes hands down to poppy. It grows anywhere—as evidenced by the fact that it now flourishes in every province. You put a little manure on the field, a little water at the start. You send the women out to weed and collect the resin. That's all. It has lovely flowers and practically reseeds itself. A lot of Afghans think it's unfair for Western countries to ban the one thing they're good at producing, especially since there seems to be an insatiable demand for the product in precisely those countries that have outlawed it. Afghans think it's hypocritical, too. Afghans are always asking, "Why don't you ban alcohol?" Both drugs and alcohol are *haram* (bad or forbidden) in Islam, but just as Afghanistan bent the drug rules to finance the jihad, it now bends the rules on alcohol to make allowances for international residents who seem unable to live without it. The anti-heroin crowd in the West doesn't bend, though. One American consultant hired to make a poppy assessment voiced off-the-record the opinion of many who've studied the drug trade in the US and abroad: "The only sensible way out is to legalize drugs. But nobody in the White House wants to hear that."

Instead what they've done for years is look the other way. The British, who are responsible for international anti-narcotic operations in Afghanistan, Bush Two, and Karzai mumbled something on occasion about reducing poppy production, but they didn't actually do much. Then, late in 2004, under pressure from moralistic Republicans, Bush suddenly pledged $780 million for an Afghan war on drugs—a jump from $73 million the year before. Karzai was sworn in at last as elected president—over-elected actually. (There were about a million more registered voters than citizens.) In his inaugural address, he made a brash promise to wipe out the drug trade within two years. The British pushed for funding "alternative livelihoods"—getting the farmers to grow a different crop. But why should farmers work harder to produce something worth much less? The Americans argued for an intensive campaign of poppy eradication, complete with defoliant sprays.

Then in December 2004, farmers in Nangarhar province along the Pakistan border complained that planes had come at night and sprayed tiny gray pellets on their fields and houses, and now their poppies were dying. Their livestock and their children were sick. Karzai was furious. His spokesman called it "a question of sovereignty, a question of being aware of what is going on in the country."[37] Britain and the US denied that they had anything to do with it. Ambassador Khalilzad said the US hadn't even contracted out

266 KABUL IN WINTER

the job. Hajji Din Muhammad, the governor of Nangarhar, didn't buy it. He said, "The Americans control the airspace of Afghanistan, and not even a bird can fly without them knowing."[38]

You'd think the Americans would go after the drug kingpins, not the crops, but the military hesitates because, as one unnamed American official told the *New York Times,* they are "the guys who helped us liberate this place in 2001," the guys the US still depends on to hunt for the Taliban and al-Qaeda and Osama bin Laden.[39] A US soldier in Kandahar told the British *Independent,* "We start taking out drug guys, and they will start taking out our guys."[40] Maybe that's why Lt. General David W. Barno, the top American commander in Afghanistan, issued an official assessment in December 2004, just about a week after the crop-spraying flap, that said: "Poppy cultivation and opium production will continue to increase in Afghanistan."[41] My driver and a lot of other ordinary Afghans think that's just fine.

FOREIGN AID, ON THE OTHER HAND, SEEMS TO ORDINARY AFGHANS to be something that only foreigners enjoy, living like kings in their big houses, driving around in their big SUVs. Afghans don't like the restaurants where foreigners spend the evenings drinking alcohol, smoking, carrying on, men and women together. They don't like the brothels—eighty of them by 2005—where foreign men and Afghan men too sometimes are seen in the yard with naked women.[42] They don't like it that half the city still lies in ruins, that many people still live in tents, that thousands can't find jobs, that children go hungry, that schools are overcrowded and hospitals dirty, that women in tattered burqas still beg in the streets and turn to prostitution, that children are kidnapped and sold into slavery or murdered for their kidneys or their eyes. Afghans see no difference between big-bucks contractors and dedicated long-term humanitarians. We're all foreigners. We all live behind the guns of faceless guards and speeding security

patrols. We all plead our good intentions And Afghans keep asking: Where is the aid you promised us?

Some answers appear in a fact-packed report issued in June
2005 by Action Aid, a widely respected NGO headquartered in
Johannesburg, South Africa. The report looks at development aid
given by all countries worldwide and says that only a small part of
it—maybe 40 percent—is real. The rest is a "phantom." That is,
it never shows up in recipient countries at all. Some of it doesn't
even exist except as an accounting item, as when countries count
debt relief in the aid column. A lot of it never leaves home—like that
nice education expert's salary that goes directly to his American
bank, an arrangement that's standard practice. Much of it is
thrown away on "overpriced and ineffective Technical Assistance,"
all those hotshot international experts. And big chunks are "tied"
to the donor, which means that the recipient is obliged to use
the money to buy products from the donor country, even when—
especially when—the same goods are available cheaper at home.

To no one's surprise, the US easily outstrips other nations at a
lot of these scams, making it second only to France as the world's
biggest purveyor of phantom aid. Forty-seven percent of American
development aid is lavished on overpriced technical assistance,
while the percentage of annual Scandinavian budgets spent on
technical assistance ranges from 12 (Norway) down to 4 (Sweden).
Luxembourg and Ireland do even better at 2 percent. As for tying
aid to the purchase of donor-made products, Sweden and Norway don't do it all. Neither do Ireland and the UK. But 70 percent
of American aid is contingent upon the recipient spending it on
American stuff. The upshot is that eighty-six cents of every dollar of
American aid is phantom aid. According to targets set years ago by
the UN and agreed to by almost every country in the world, all the
rich countries should give 0.7 percent of their national income in
annual aid to the poor ones. So far, only Luxembourg (with real aid
at 0.65 percent of its national income), the Scandinavian countries, and the Netherlands even come close. At the other end of

the scale, the US spends a paltry 0.02 percent of national income on real aid, which works out to a contribution of $8.00 from every citizen of "the wealthiest nation in the world." (By comparison Swedes kick in $193 per person, Norwegians $304, and the citizens of Luxembourg $357.)[43] It seems that Americans are being conned even more than Afghans. When Bush Two boasts of millions in aid to Afghanistan, Afghans want to see it. Americans assume it's there. My guess is that most Americans would be shocked to think we're "aiding" the world to the tune of only eight bucks apiece. We could do more for Afghanistan by passing a hat. When I sent out that e-mail asking friends for money for my teaching project in Kabul, nobody sent back just a measly eight bucks.

The problem is that the US says one thing and does another. It's like a deadbeat dad, pledging millions and then neglecting to write the check. Often the president makes a splashy public promise, and Congress declines to appropriate the money. Or he sends his wife to Kabul to announce a donation that has already been donated. The US is not the only donor nation that acts this way, but it's the richest; and it seems to be the one with the shortest attention span. This behavior leaves the Afghan government with conspicuous "shortfalls." In the National Development Budget for 2003, Afghanistan requested $250 million for education but received only about $77 million from international donors. That's just 31 percent, leaving a shortfall of about $172 million. Donors spent better than $49 million on education outside the government—on things like USAID's literacy projects—but that still left a gap of more than $123 million.[44] The education budget for 2004–2005 called for the Ministry of Education to spend about $388 million, of which only $117 million, or 30 percent, materialized.[45] The government never knows what money is coming in, or when. It doesn't even know what's already gone out. As the Human Rights Research and Advocacy Consortium reported from Kabul: "There is hardly any correct data available on what has been spent and where and on what in the education sector."[46] So the government just goes on piling up short-falls.

Planning slips from its grasp, just like money. The Ministry of Education plans new textbooks, for which there is no funding, while massive American funding goes to promote literacy outside the schools or to rebuild a dormitory for women at Kabul University. Of seventy-odd agencies and organizations doing education projects in the country in 2003, many overlapped or duplicated services. Many didn't bother to report to the government. Some were downright secretive. Even if the government had money, it would be next to impossible to cook up a plan in such an environment, let alone get "stakeholders" to follow it. In these circumstances, plans come to resemble recipes for pie in the sky. One calls for all students nationwide to begin learning English in the fourth grade—though currently, as I've told you, there are not enough competent English teachers even to staff the high schools of the capital. Another directs that all instruction at Kabul University be conducted in English, a language few students and fewer faculty members know. A comprehensive long-term plan outlines where the government wants the "education sector" to be in seven years time. But it's short on strategies to get there.

So government plans, like Bush administration reports about Afghanistan, drift like springtime balloons farther and farther from the facts on the ground. Many schools are built to a standard $174,000 blueprint (though the contractor, Louis Berger, is years behind schedule); that's too expensive for communities to maintain, too big to find enough teachers, and too "centralized" for girls from outlying villages to walk to. (Joe Biden's little $20,000 neighborhood schools would have been just fine.) I visited one government school built by Japanese aid, now used as an office by a Danish NGO, and another occupied only by a watchman who slept in one classroom, cooked in another, prayed in another, received guests in another, and reserved the largest as a garage for his bicycle.

Even the dazzling numbers of new schoolchildren tell a story of incomplete success. It's great that more than four million children are in school (setting aside the question of the quality of the schools), but that number includes only about half of eligible primary-school kids and less than a third of the girls. City children fare best. Kabul and Herat enroll about 85 percent of their children, but go a few miles out of town and enrollments drop to less than 50 percent. In some parts of the country dramatically lower enrollments, especially of girls, reflect old cultural divisions deepened by radical Islam. Some provinces still have more madrassas than high schools. Nearly half of all students enrolled in schools in Afghanistan live in Kabul Province, most of them in the capital, while only about 10 percent live in the eastern provinces and another 10 percent in the south. The seven provinces of the south—Pashtun and Taliban country—have the lowest enrollments of all: only 19 percent of children who live in Helmand Province go to school. In Zabul and Badghis Provinces only one girl in a hundred. Students also drop out in stunning numbers. It is estimated that three-quarters of girls in first grade today will drop out by fifth grade, together with more than half the boys.[47] Girls will go first, most of them at the end of first or second grade. By ninth grade there will be very few boys left in school, except in the big cities, and practically no girls at all.

This is the kind of sobering news you can find in the field, but not on American TV. Since I really don't like always to be the one who spots the cloud around the silver lining, I'll tell you a happier story. One morning I came into the kitchen at Frauen die Helfen and found a young friend in tears. I took her hands to comfort her, and she told me she was weeping for joy. Marina is Afghan by birth but a citizen of Germany, her family having fled there after the Soviet invasion. Now a graduate student in Germany, she returns to Kabul during university holidays to work as a translator for FDH. That very morning, she said, the watchman had called her to the gate where a young girl stood waiting for her. "Do you remember me?" the girl had asked.

Three years before, when her family was desperate for money, the girl had found a temporary job at FDH as a kitchen helper during a monthlong training course. Marina was the translator for the course, and as the only Dari speaker, she was the one who gave instructions to the housekeepers. She was kind to the young girl who, she could see, was terrified to be on her own and working for foreigners in a strange house. The end of the course meant the end of the job for the girl, and for Marina who went home to Germany. She hadn't seen the girl again until she appeared at the house that morning with copies of precious documents to show that she'd graduated from high school and from an English-language course. She'd just been accepted by a training program at an Afghan NGO where she would learn to be a primary-school teacher. Marina said to me, "I was happy for her, naturally, but I didn't know why she wanted to show me these things. And then she thanked me and thanked me, over and over again. She said, 'I wanted you to know because you told me to stay in school, and I did what you told me.'" Marina was weeping again and we hung onto each other in the cold kitchen, both of us tearful now and laughing until other colleagues came in and Marina told the story again and someone put the kettle on for tea.

There are lots of stories like that in Kabul, of little things that happen, often unknown or unremarked, between one person and another, little things that change a life and through it the lives of others. So I won't say that aid for education in Afghanistan is all smoke and mirrors—merely that things could be done better, and for better reasons. But still, when Afghans say, "Where is the aid you foreigners promised us?" it's a fair question.

KABULIS BEGAN TO ASK THIS QUESTION OF THE KARZAI GOVERN-ment too. They'd all turned out to vote for Karzai in 2004, but what had he done for them? Afghans by longstanding tradition expect a khan to be powerful, but Karzai, whose public stature had been so carefully inflated by the Americans seemed to be shrinking day by day, despite his handsome multiethnic clothes, to the size of an American puppet. Ambassador Khalilzad overshadowed him. Condoleezza Rice upstaged him. (It was she, not Karzai, who announced the date of parliamentary elections.) Bush humiliated him, sending him back empty-handed to Kabul when he'd gone to Washington to demand control of Afghan prisoners after some held at Bagram airbase were tortured and killed by American interrogators.[48] Afghans expect a khan to deliver—security, jobs, food, turban cloths, something. Otherwise, what good is he?

In Kabul people suffered through the long hard winter of 2004–2005, the third long winter since the flight of the Taliban, and this one the hardest; and they began to grumble. Minister of Planning Ramazan Bashardost gave them a target: the foreign NGOs. He had an eye on "so-called NGOs that operate for profit, like private companies," but private contractors and humanitarian NGOs were all the same to him. He wanted a law to regulate the operations of NGOs, especially the foreign ones, because they were ineffective and corrupt. "International NGOs get big amounts of money from their own nations," he said, "but [they] spend all the money on themselves, and we are unable to find out how much money they originally received in charitable funds." The director of CARE responded: "These ill-founded, unsubstantiated and generalized attacks, from a government minister, are creating a climate in which the government is seen to be legitimizing attacks on NGOs."[49] Within a month, President Karzai (or Mr. Khalilzad) had replaced the outspoken planning minister; but in the spring, as discontent grew, Karzai took up the minister's tune himself.

In April 2005, at a meeting in Kabul of representatives of forty donor countries—the Afghan Development Forum 2005— Karzai accused the NGOs of "squandering funds." Only a week earlier at least thirty people had been killed and many more injured when a dam burst at Ghazni, an old dam that had been rebuilt in the past year by a Danish NGO. The engineers responsible for the job had long since left the country.[50] The news photos of yet another preventable Afghan disaster seemed to illustrate Karzai's accusation. Now his government had drawn up a budget calling for the expenditure of $4.75 billion in the coming year, and it was counting on foreign donors to come up with 93 percent of the cash. He wanted them to put the money directly into his hands because his government, he said, was "the ultimate body accountable to the Afghan people." He said to the assembled donors, "The Afghan government . . . must be better informed about, and play its due role in steering the development process."[51] It was a plea for help in hanging on to his job, but many took it, like Minister Bashardost's earlier accusations, as "legitimizing attacks on NGOs." Within a month, an aid worker from CARE was kidnapped.

Clementina Cantoni, a 32-year-old Italian, had been in Kabul for three years, leading a CARE project to assist a thousand widows and their families. One evening in May, as she and her driver were about to pull away from a house in the city center where they had dropped off a friend, four masked gunmen dragged Clementina from the car. The next day, from an old snapshot on the front page of the newspaper, she smiled upon a city that had changed.[52] Afghan women were angry. Widows Clementina worked with bravely gathered outside the CARE office, holding up her picture and handmade signs demanding that the kidnappers set her free. International aid workers were scared. Agency heads issued new rules for internationals: no walking, no driving alone, no restaurants. Curfew was set at six o'clock. It was a week or more before we saw Clementina on television, wrapped in a chador, seated on the floor between two men who stood over her, masked in black, aiming Kalashnikovs at her temples. Incredibly, she looked serene, and not a bit afraid. The Afghan government and the Italians negotiated with the kidnappers, while internationals in Kabul waited behind locked gates. Winter had passed, but spring would be overcast by Clementina.

IT WASN'T THE FIRST TIME AID WORKERS HAD BEEN THREATENED in Afghanistan. In 2003 fourteen Afghan and international aid workers had been murdered, and violence was rising. In the first six months of 2004 alone, another thirty-seven were killed. Among them were five Médecins Sans Frontières staff in Badghis Province, causing the organization to cease work in Afghanistan.[53] The civilian murders were shocking because they took place in parts of the country thought to be relatively safe. And they were doubly troubling because many such aid organizations had worked in Afghanistan for decades, through the civil wars and the Taliban time, without fear of casualty. Many NGOs blamed the US–led coalition for obscuring the line between soldier and civilian, between military and humanitarian operations. In many provinces the US Army had set up special units of fifty to a hundred soldiers called Provincial Reconstruction Teams, or PRTs. Defense Secretary Donald Rumsfeld, often accused of sending "too few to do too much for too few," called the PRTs the "best thing that can be done to ultimately provide security" in Afghanistan.[54]

Security in most of Afghanistan was up for grabs for a lot of reasons, mostly having to do with US policies. First, at the Bonn conference that followed the toppling of the Taliban, the US insisted on restoring to Afghanistan most of the old mujahidin warlords the Taliban had defeated and driven from the country— that is, all those civil warriors whose destruction of the country had made the law-and-order Taliban look so good in the first place to war-weary Afghans. Then, trying to conserve American soldiers, whose lives might be lost in ground fighting, the US rearmed the resurrected warlords and paid them about $70 million to track down Osama bin Laden, a mission to which they seem to have been somewhat less than truly dedicated. Then, to keep the international security forces from interfering in the provincial manhunt, the US saw to it that ISAF was confined to policing Kabul. These measures having restored the provinces to a state of lawlessness resembling pre-Taliban armed anarchy, the US then started installing PRTs, ostensibly to extend "security" and the reach of the Karzai government from Kabul to the rest of the country. (Security was so unknown in the provinces that the first PRT—in Gardez in 2002—spent the first six months building itself a fort.)

But the PRTs had other missions as well. They were charged with gathering intelligence in the war on terror and, in full combat gear, winning Afghan hearts and minds, work for which they were singularly unsuited and even more dazzlingly expensive than the puffiest international contractor. Later, British troops, with greater peacekeeping experience, established a PRT in the north, and Germans did the same. In 2005 a new Mongolian PRT was rumored, but that may have been a joke. The essential problem, lack of security, remained and got worse. Red-designated "High Risk/Hostile Environment" areas spread across the UN security map like a pool of blood. Many argued, as did Paul O'Brien of CARE, that "by 'blurring the lines' between the military and humanitarians they [the PRTs] put civilian aid workers at risk and politicize, and even militarise, aid work."[55] NGOs doing relief and reconstruction projects in the provinces joined ordinary Afghan citizens, the Karzai government, and the UN in pleading for internationally administered security forces to be dispersed throughout the country.[56]

Reports of the deaths of civilian aid workers in the provinces reached Kabul, where heavily armed ISAF patrols maintained security in the streets, creating the island of relative safety in which the Afghan government, the UN, and most international agencies worked. There was the odd bombing or booby trap, aimed mostly at ISAF troops. Some soldiers lost their lives. In

May 2004 a couple of Western "tourists" in Afghan clothes were found bludgeoned to death in a Kabul cemetery. (People said: Tourists? They must have been spies.) In October 2004 a young American woman and an Afghan girl were killed in a suicide bomb blast on Chicken Street, where internationals shop for souvenirs.[57] Soon after, three UN election workers were kidnapped and held for nearly a month before the government was able to negotiate their release.[58] The fashion for razor wire and sandbags spread through residential districts. Afghan friends proposed to open an international guesthouse in a cellar and call it "The Bunker." They were only half joking. Then, toward the end of winter a British adviser to the Ministry of Reconstruction and Rural Development, driving alone in central Kabul, was shot to death.[59] A month later, an American man was beaten and kidnapped in broad daylight. He threw himself from the trunk of the speeding getaway car to escape.[60]

International security offices issued warnings that the criminal gang responsible for kidnapping the UN election workers was likely to kidnap somebody else. Some of the original kidnappers had been caught and sent to prison; police guessed that the rest of the gang wanted a hostage to exchange for their release. The gangsters weren't Taliban. They weren't al-Qaeda. They weren't political. They were criminals out to make money in the big bucks, lawless world of post-conflict Kabul. That's who took Clementina, and that changed everything. Or maybe that's when those of us who'd been in Kabul for a while noticed that everything had changed. Nadene Ghouri of the BBC, a friend of Clementina, recalled conditions in Kabul in 2002, the year that she and Clementina (and I) first arrived. She wrote in *Kabul Weekly:* "The optimism in the air was tangible. Afghans welcomed foreigners with open arms. . . . Now the mood is markedly different. Frustrated by the lack of development and the grinding poverty, more and more Afghans are replacing initial gratitude with cynicism and a slow-burning anger."[61]

Anti-international—anti-American—sentiment grew by the day. I too felt a swelling resentment every time I had to cross the street to avoid the swaggering, black-shirted guards, waving automatic weapons, outside the floodlit concrete-bunkered headquarters of DynCorp, the ominous American "security" contractor. One morning, in central Kabul, an armored personnel carrier cut off the car I was riding in, and my driver slammed on the brakes just in time. A soldier leaned from the top of the APC, trained his automatic weapon on my driver, and screamed curses at him, as if it had been his fault that they had nearly run us over. At the sound of his American accent, I lost my head. I jumped from the car and ran at the APC, shouting at the soldier, unloading my righteous DynCorp-inspired wrath. The soldier turned red in the face, the APC drove on, and I got back in the car. My driver was grinning and so, I noticed, were Afghan pedestrians around us in the street. A newspaper boy threw me a high-five. My driver said, "Please not become shot for me. They do like this all time."

One day, when Salma and I went to the Ministry of Foreign Affairs and passed through the routine security check of our bags, the guard said to her in Dari, "Why do you still work with foreigners? They think they know everything, but they don't." When Salma and I walked across the university campus, male students shouted at her in Dari: "Whore. Prostitute. What do you do with the kharaji?" When Salma and I sat in an anteroom at the Supreme Court, waiting to meet with a judge, the men sitting about—there are always men sitting about in government offices—discussed in Dari their discontent with Americans.

"Why don't they give us food like the Russians?" says one.

"They don't do anything for us," says another.

"They do something," says a third. "They shoot people around Bagram, and they bugger the boys, and they hang men from the ceiling and beat them to death."

"They put the Quran down the toilet, don't forget," says another. The men nod, looking at me.

"What do you think the old woman is doing here?" asks one. Another says, "She comes all the time. She is a spy." Salma clutches her scarf to her mouth and giggles, and that shuts them up. She says to me in English, "Men are foolish."

Most remarkable to me is the bloom of rose-colored nostalgia for the Soviet occupation. I hear Afghans say that Soviet soldiers didn't swagger about or push them around. Soviets didn't raid their houses or hold them in secret prisons or beat them to death. Soviets gave them good jobs. Soviets gave them tons of free food. Soviets provided medical care. The teachers in my class tell me the Soviets greatly improved the schools, and they put girls in school all over the country, and they invited many students and teachers to study in the Soviet Union. One says, "The Soviets took a whole bus full of teachers to their country." Another says, "Yes. It is true. It is a good idea. America can send a bus to take us to America." The whole of Kabul, probably the whole of Afghanistan, has been waiting and waiting for the American bus.

GLIMPSES OF IT COME AND GO. LAURA BUSH CAME TO AFGHANISTAN in March 2005 (for six hours) "to offer support for Afghan women in their struggle for greater rights," as the New York Times reported, and "to promise long-term commitment from the United States to education for women and children."[62] The Times reported that the trip was "more than a year in the planning," which may seem excessive for a militarized PR junket that touched down in Kabul scarcely long enough to terrify the populace, but the president's wife brought promises of help that made headlines in America. Mrs. Bush pledged that the United States would give additional grants of $17.7 million and $3.5 million for education in Afghanistan. But the $17.7 million had been announced before. Worse, it was not for Afghan education but for a new private, for-profit American University of Afghanistan that would compete with public universities and attract Afghanistan's elite by charging tuition—rumored to be at least five thousand dollars a year. (It is likely to be a men's university since the chances that Afghan families will send girls at those prices are exceedingly slim.) You might ask how a private university comes to be supported by public taxpayer dollars, but I haven't a clue. The project should be a non-starter, given Mrs. Bush's "commitment" to women's education and USAID's "democratic" principles— (remember my "elite" high school teachers ineligible for American aid?)—but the Army Corps of Engineers is already working on the site. Ashraf Ghani, former finance minister of Afghanistan and president of Kabul University appealed to Mrs. Bush to support instead his historic public institution. Speaking very pointedly for an Afghan, he said, "You cannot support private education and ignore public education." But she could and she did. The smaller $3.5 million announced by the president's wife wasn't for Afghan education either. It went to a new English-language International School of Afghanistan—which is to say, a prep school for the children of internationals in Kabul, of whom there were many by 2005, with new waves rolling in.[63]

A fleet of combat helicopters whisked Mrs. Bush away to dine with American troops at Bagram base, and she was gone. Not long after, I read a report of the Afghanistan Research and Evaluation Unit on the dismal progress made in the country. It was called: "Minimal Investments, Minimal Results" and it spoke of the failure to find even basic security in Afghanistan.[64] Afghans yearn for security. Disarmament, security, and peace are what they want.[65] But everybody knows the US did things backward— trying to set up a government, a constitution, elections, a parliament, all the trappings of "democracy" without ever establishing anything like peace. At cross-purposes too—trying to set up "stability" in the capital and carry out a manhunt in the countryside.[66] But this report blamed the whole "international community" for never having made "the necessary commitments and investments" in the first place to give Afghans a chance to build a peaceful country. Tony Blair promised in 2003 that the international community would "not walk away" from Afghanistan, but the report asked: "When will the international community really walk *into* Afghanistan?"[67] Another report, from the Berlin Conference on Afghanistan held in March 2004, had warned that "staying too close to minimal effort for too long will adversely affect expectations and commitments of the different segments of Afghan society."[68] That's what happened. Afghans got tired of waiting for the bus.

I BUY A TICKET TO NEW YORK. MY DAYS IN KABUL ARE COMING to an end. In the long, locked-down evenings I start to write this book. Already I know it will be gloomy. Its been that kind of winter in Kabul—the winter of the frozen dogs. The worst winter in fifty years, the radio said. A leaden sky lowered over the city like a lid clamped down on a basin, and snow spilled down almost every day. It piled up in the streets. Sometimes the sun appeared long enough to make the snow slushy, but evening turned the world to ice. As night deepened, the dogs that lived among the ruined houses up and down the mountainside began to bark. I crawled into bed and pulled the quilts up over my ears, but there was no sleeping, night after night. I began to know the voices: Mr. Four-Bark, who always said just that—"bark!"—four times before pausing to catch his breath and begin again. Chuppy, who gave a high thin "chup, chup, chup." One who sounded as if he were strangling, another with a basso "gruff, gruff," and another who sobbed. I could see them: tied up in frozen yards, huddled against walls, burrowing under the snow, running in the narrow streets and crying out from the cold, for what? For help that would not come from people who themselves were freezing inside their ruined houses, their makeshift shanties cobbled together from tattered UNHCR tents. Toward morning, when the cold was deepest, they fell silent, curled in exhausted sleep, their bones shaking under ruffled fur. And I too slept, knowing that the next night I'd lie awake again listening to them cry out. The winter hung on. One night Chuppy fell silent. Then the voice of the sobber vanished. Opening the curtain onto a fresh fall of snow one morning, I saw a boy on a roof across the way pitching off the carcass of a frozen dog.

But it was May now, well into spring. Flowers were in bloom and the drooping wild rose trees, like exotic floral umbrellas, were trailing fringes of pale blooms. Early mangoes were coming up from Pakistan. Big white wheels of paneer, the country cheese, wrapped in fresh green leaves, were for sale on pushcarts in every bazaar. On the Shamali plains some of the old vineyards were leafing out, not ruined after all, and the jouies were running after heavy rains. The Kabul River was rising in its bed to sweep away the trash of many dry years, carrying a million discarded plastic bags downriver. "A gift to Pakistan," Kabulis joked. Vendors appeared in the streets with bouquets of bright balloons. *Zemestan khalas shud*. Winter is finished. Why couldn't I believe in the promise of the new season?

The anguish of my young colleague Salma only deepened my dejection. All through the hard winter and the violent spring, all through the anti-American, anti-Bush, anti-Karzai demonstrations breaking out across the country and in Kabul on the university campus, all through the uneasy nights and days of Clementina's captivity, Salma had been waiting to board the American bus. She had a ticket. She'd been promised a full scholarship to study at a college in the US. Salma was very smart and remarkably resourceful. When the Taliban interrupted her education, she'd educated herself and a hundred others in her own home school. When the Taliban fell, she qualified for medical school, a field of study reserved for those who score highest on university admission tests. On the first day of class, the hem of her burqa caught in the door of the car that dropped her off; and as the car drove away, it flipped her backward onto the pavement.

By the time she recovered from the skull fracture, she'd acquired an interest in international politics and formed an ambition to be an ambassador for Afghanistan. She went back to the university to study law. That's what she was doing when she got the invitation from the American embassy to apply for an undergraduate scholarship to the United States.

Salma was worried about her English. She'd learned it mostly on her own, without much formal training. So unlike my high school teacher-students who knew grammar but couldn't speak, Salma could speak but probably wouldn't do very well on a formal grammar test. She got on well at FDH, where she worked half-time—full-time during school holidays—but she didn't do much written work in English. Her job was to do research and organize activities and lobby the government, all in the cause of women's rights. At these things she was brilliant, though when it came to writing reports in English, she needed quite a bit of help. The officers in the cultural affairs division at the embassy told her not to worry. She was just the sort of female student they were looking for, a bold, articulate future leader of her country. She'd already participated (in English) in international conferences in Germany and Norway, and she had another conference coming up in Kenya. Besides, the cultural affairs officers told her, the first stop for all students would be an intensive months-long English-language program in Washington, D.C., to prepare them to enter college in September 2004. Salma was in. She need only wait for her departure.

Summer came and went, and September too. Then the students were told they'd be leaving before the year was through. But they didn't. Then the embassy officials told Salma that the undergraduate scholarship program hadn't worked out. The nameless contractor to whom they'd given the job of placing the students hadn't found colleges willing to host them. So the students' applications were being "folded into" the Fulbright Program for international scholars. This was better, they told her, because a Fulbright was the best you could get. Salma told me, "They're very nice." But she worried more about her English. She hadn't applied for "the best you could get," and surely now the standards would be over her head. The officials reassured her—and me, when I began to accompany her to embassy appointments to see what I could do to speed things along. Shouldn't she take an English course now? she asked them. No, not to worry, they said. And anyway, there wouldn't be time. She'd be leaving any day now. Law professors at the university asked Salma to join a team of four top law students for an international student competition in Washington, D.C., but Salma said somebody else should get a chance to go to America. She already had a seat on the American bus. Another woman went in her place.

Time went by. Salma reported that many of the students in her group had received letters saying they were no longer eligible for the scholarships because they were too close to graduation. They'd applied in their second year and gone all the way through university while they waited to leave. Salma herself had only one more semester to go. Should she delay her last semester? Should she go ahead and finish school? We'd had trouble all year at FDH trying to plan a work schedule that took account of Salma's imminent departure. Now Salma was having trouble planning her life. Into this muddle came the men. Salma was pretty and charming, and at twenty-three long past marriageable age. The mothers and sisters of suitors began to call on Salma's mother. Her father decreed that she must finish her education before talk of marriage could begin. But one suitor courted her by cell phone. Another began to appear, as if by magic, here and there around the city, wherever Salma had appointments. Another who wanted Salma as his second wife threatened to kidnap her to force her father's consent. Salma knew that her father could not keep them away forever. If she went to America to study, he would keep this little window of freedom open until she returned; but if she didn't go, the window would close and with it her ambitions for the future. She grew nervous and tearful. She couldn't sleep. She fell into confusion, lured by romance and repelled by the limitations it barely concealed. She said, "I must leave for America soon."

It was me the embassy official called, not Salma, to say that she'd be staying home. She and almost all the other students. Months before, they had taken the TOEFL exam, the standard international English proficiency test. Now the scores were back, and they weren't good. Only one student had passed. But what about the intensive English-language program in America? That hadn't worked out. What about all those promises that low English scores wouldn't count against them? Two answers this time: First, the person who made them had exceeded his authority, and second, no such promises had ever been made. The official was a young man, earnest and voluble, probably not very far along in his diplomatic training.

"She's got nothing in writing," he said. "We never gave them anything in writing."

"But surely you know that Afghans do business on good faith," I said. He'd been in Afghanistan only a few weeks.

"Well, we don't operate that way," he said.

"So I see. But you must know that in a few years time these students will be leading the country. Are you sure it's smart to smash their faith in America?"

He laughed at what he took to be exaggeration. I saw, not for the first time, that he knew nothing about the Afghans who surrounded Fort Paranoia. "That's a bit dramatic," he said. "We have to maintain standards."

"What standards would that be?"

"Academic standards. Fulbright has very high academic standards."

Later, after I returned to the States, I learned that the Fulbright Program wasn't really the Fulbright Program at all but merely a watered-down version called the Afghan Fulbright Exchange Program that USAID had tried feebly to revive (after a break of twenty-four years) by contracting it out to the University of

Nebraska at Omaha Center for Afghanistan Studies. But at the time I didn't have that information, and I was too angry to speak. So the cultural affairs officer, on a roll now, went on. "American standards," he said. "I'll tell you, we had one woman student— she qualified all right—but we had to pull her off the plane." I don't know if he meant it literally. "At the last minute we found out she was pregnant. She was planning to have the kid in the States. Thought she could get it a free ride to citizenship. Can you believe it? Talk about nerve."

"And you think this was some kind of underhanded plot? Having a baby?"

"You'd better believe it. That's what they're like. That's the first thing I learned here: they'll take advantage of us every time. After all we've done for them. You'd think they'd be grateful, but they're not."

THAT EVENING I FOUND MYSELF AGAIN IN A GARDEN BEHIND THE walls of an old Kabuli home. The house had been converted to pricey apartments for internationals, and the garden was to be the setting for a fashion show inaugurating a new Afghan design center. Zolaykha Sherzad, who headed the project, was the daughter of a prominent royalist family exiled by the communists. She'd grown up in Switzerland, trained as an architect there and in Japan, and practiced in New York City where she also studied fashion design. She taught in New York as well, at prominent art schools. In 2000 she established the School of Hope, a not-for-profit project that paired schools in Kabul with schools in the West, including two in New York City, so that children could learn about one another's lives and create a "communal bridge" on the way to peace. Her whole life, after the initial shock of exile, had been about education—always studying, learning, teaching. She said the Swiss schoolteachers who took a terrified refugee child in hand had been the ones who showed her how to have a life at all.[69]

After America bombed Afghanistan, Zolaykah went back to
Kabul to help. She found Afghan widows who could sew and
worked with them to develop fashions that could be sold in the
West. She taught them about design, and they taught her about
classic Afghan fabrics, and how they might be used. To start the
work, they got seed money from CARE, from the program
for one thousand widows headed by Clementina Cantoni. This
evening's fashion show had been planned long before Clementina's
kidnapping, and it was dedicated to her. Two weeks later
Clementina would be released unharmed, but that night she was
on everyone's mind.

Zolaykha stood at the edge of the terrace, smiling serenely, as
models stepped smartly down the stairs to make a circuit of the
lawn, displaying the new fashions to the assembled guests.
The models were international aid workers—German, British,
French, Italian, Swedish, Spanish, Dutch, Canadian. They were
Zolaykha's friends, and many of them mine as well. I knew both
their desire to help and the pleasure they took in learning from
Afghans. The eclectic clothes they modeled spoke of the "communal bridge" they and Zolaykha wanted to build. But to me the
bridge seemed to run uphill, from the Afghan widows serving at
the buffet to the international audience, now putting down dollars for exquisite garments sure to attract glances in Paris or
Milan. My faith in the possibility of bridges had been shaken by
my conversation with the embassy official who so diligently protected American privilege from Afghan aspiration.

To one side of the garden sat a group of Afghan musicians,
accompanying the parade with hand drums and strings. In their
midst stood a man draped in a splendid chapan, a singer famous
among Afghans. The master of ceremonies had announced that
the musicians would play later, indoors, in the salon, and the
singer would favor us with a performance. A stir of pleasure roused
the gathering. But soon, circulating to greet friends among the
crowd, I heard a couple of American men complaining loudly.

"What an asshole!" one said of the singer.

"They're all like that," said the other. "Arrogant bastards. I don't know who they think they are."

It seems they'd asked the man to give them a song. They had to leave soon, they'd told him, so they wanted him to sing now, here. He had looked at them for a moment and turned them down.

"But what did he say to you?" I asked.

I was thinking of all the reasons he might have given. He might have said that his songs are works of art to be attended to, not spent as background to cocktail conversation. He might have said that his voice is an instrument to be protected from the dusty air and the rising chill of evening. He might have said that the perfection of the music would lie in its performance within the walls of the resonant salon. But he had said none of these things. He was an Afghan, with an Afghan's dignity. He was not used to explaining himself. Or perhaps he saw little purpose in presenting his point of view to these foreigners. For reasons of his own, the singer had stated simply the practice of his own culture. He stood there under the darkening trees, regarding the insistent Americans before him, already rushing on to the next party, and what he said was "Afghans do not sing in the garden."

NOTES

I. IN THE STREETS

1. Chris Johnson and Jolyon Leslie, *Afghanistan: The Mirage of Peace* (London: Zed Books, 2004), p. 11.

2. Powell "worried" that much of the bombing of Afghanistan was "bombing for bombing's sake, unconnected to a military objective." Bob Woodward, *Bush at War* (New York: Simon & Schuster, 2002), pp. 175, 275. The bombing may constitute a war crime, done as it was without regard to consequences for the civilian population or the international legal principle of proportionality—"that a reasonable proportionality exist between the damage caused and the military gain sought." See Mahmood Mamdani, *Good Muslim, Bad Muslim: America, the Cold War, and the Roots of Terror* (New York: Doubleday, 2004), p. 183.

3. Roland and Sabrina Michaud, *Afghanistan: The Land that Was* (New York: Harry N. Abrams, n.d.), p. 246. The photograph appears on pp. 84–85.

4. Nancy Hatch Dupree, *An Historical Guide to Afghanistan* (Kabul: Afghan Tourist Organization, 1970), p. 27.

5. Nancy Hatch Dupree, p. 37.

6. Dominic Medley and Jude Barrand, *Kabul: The Bradt Mini Guide* (Chalfont St. Peter, UK: Bradt Travel Guides, 2003), p. 136.

7. Ahmed Rashid, *Taliban: Militant Islam, Oil and Fundamentalism in Central Asia* (New Haven: Yale University Press, 2001), p. 207.

8. John K. Cooley, *Unholy Wars: Afghanistan, America and International Terrorism*, 3rd ed. (London: Pluto Press, 2002), pp. xiii–xiv.

9. Karen Armstrong uses this phrase in *The Battle for God* (New York: Alfred A. Knopf, 2000), p. 239.

10. Sayyid Qutb, "'The America I Have Seen': In the Scale of Human

Values (1951)" in *America in an Arab Mirror: Images of America in Arabic Travel Literature, An Anthology (1895–1995),* ed. Kamal Abdel-Malek (New York: St. Martin's Press, 2000), pp. 9–28. More recent visitors voice the same criticisms. Witness Egyptian novelist Sonallah Ibrahim, who taught Arabic literature at Berkeley in 1998: "I despised the total individualism, the control of multinationals, the manipulation of the media over the ordinary person, the values of life, just living to eat, drink, fuck, have a car, and that's all. . . . There are no moral values, no broadminded attitudes toward life in general or a sense of what is happening in the world, no sense of the role America is playing in trying to control the resources of the world." Ibrahim was irked by "the genuine stupidity of the normal American citizen. He is ignorant. He doesn't know what his own country is doing in the world." David Remnick, "Letter from Cairo: Going Nowhere," *The New Yorker,* July 12 and 19, 2004, p. 80.

11. Hamid Algar suggests that the Egyptian Ministry of Education sent Qutb to the United States in an effort to modify his increasingly Islamist social criticism at home, but his thoroughly "negative" experience had the opposite effect, turning him conclusively to Islam. See his introduction to Sayyid Qutb, *Social Justice in Islam,* translated by John B. Hardie, translation revised and introduced by Hamid Algar (Oneonta, N.Y.: Islamic Publications International, 2000), p. 2.

12. Armstrong, *The Battle for God,* p. 238. See also Sayyid Abul A'la Mawdudi, *Let Us Be Muslims,* ed. Khurram Murad (London: Islamic Foundation, 1985). Mawdudi was the first to reject reformist hope of effecting some compromise between Islam and Western modernity. To counter the Muslim League of Pakistan's founder, the secular Mohammed Ali Jinnah, Mawdudi founded the Jamaat-i Islami (Islamic Society) of Pakistan that later aided Afghanistan's radical Islamist parties in exile. For Mawdudi's early life and later political activity in Pakistan, see Tariq Ali, *The Clash of Fundamentalisms: Crusades, Jihads and Modernity* (London: Verso, 2002), pp. 170–78, and Cooley, pp. 35–38.

13. Sayyid Qutb, *Milestones* (New Delhi: Millat Book Centre, n.d.), p. 61.

14. For discussion of the thought of Mawdudi and Qutb, see Mamdani, pp. 45–62; and Armstrong, *The Battle for God,* pp. 236–44, 291–94, and *Islam: A Short History* (New York: Modern Library, 2002), pp. 168–70. Armstrong notes that Qutb's emphasis on violent jihad distorts both the Quran which "adamantly opposed force and coercion in religious matters" and the life of the Prophet, *Islam,* pp. 169–70; *The Battle for God,* p. 243.

15. Telephone interview, August 1, 2002. The professor spoke off the record, requesting anonymity.

16. Not to be confused with the Pakistani Jamaat-i Islami founded by Abul A'la Mawdudi. Mawdudi equated Western modernity with *jahiliyya*

(barbarity), an allusion to the pre-Islamic ignorance battled by the Prophet himself. Sayyid Qutb, on the other hand, drew a distinction between the jahiliyya of Westernization and what he called "modernity," which offered technology that might be useful to Islamic societies. In embracing modernism, the Afghan Jamiat-i Islami aligns itself more closely with the teachings of Qutb.

17. Barnett R. Rubin, *The Fragmentation of Afghanistan: State Formation and Collapse in the International System,* 2nd ed. (New Haven: Yale University Press, 2002), p. 83. Kabulis commonly refer to Gulbuddin Hekmatyar by his first name, as if he is a particularly intimate enemy. I follow their example.

18. Gulbuddin is a member of the Ghilzai Pashtuns of eastern Afghanistan, rivals to the dominant Durrani Pashtuns of the south, who include the Karzai family and the leaders of the Taliban.

19. Rubin, pp. 83–84. A second Hizb-i Islami party was headed by Younis Khalis, an older Islamic scholar who had run a madrassa and was well respected among Pashtuns. Mullah Omar, later the leader of the Taliban, was a member. The two parties are usually distinguished by the name of the leader. Unless otherwise indicated, all references to Hizb-i Islami in this book are to Hizb-i Islami-Hekmatyar.

20. Robert D. Kaplan says Pakistani General Zia ul-Haq favored Hekmatyar because having "almost no grassroots support and no military base" in Afghanistan, Hekmatyar was "wholly dependent on Zia's protection and financial largesse (courtesy of American taxpayers)" and thus could be controlled. "Hekmatyar . . . was the classic artificial creation of an outside power." *Soldiers of God: With the Mujahidin in Afghanistan* (Boston: Houghton Mifflin, 1990), p 69. In May 1979, months before the Soviets invaded Afghanistan, the ISI introduced Heymatyar to the CIA's Islamabad station chief, who agreed to arm a Hekmatyar-led guerilla group, "a creature of the Pakistani military." For a full account, see Alfred W. McCoy, *The Politics of Heroin: CIA Complicity in the Global Drug Trade, Afghanistan, Southeast Asia, Central America, Colombia,* 2nd ed. (Chicago: Chicago Review Press, 2003), p. 475. Cooley describes the "exceedingly radical" Hekmatyar as a "CIA creation." Cooley, p. 141. Yet Texas Congressman Charlie Wilson, instrumental in securing taxpayer dollars for the mujahidin, backed Gulbuddin because he mistook him for a popular leader. See Mary Anne Weaver, *Pakistan: In the Shadow of Jihad and Afghanistan* (New York: Farrar, Straus and Giroux, 2002), pp. 79–80.

21. Over the years, the ISI diverted US money to other causes, such as its conflict with India over Kashmir. See Cooley, p. 203.

22. Rubin, p. 252.

23. Kaplan, p. 168, quoting Abdul Haq of Hizb-i Islami-Khalis.

24. For details, see McCoy, pp. 484–85.

25. Steve Coll, *Ghost Wars: The Secret History of the CIA, Afghanistan, and bin Laden, from the Soviet Invasion to September 10, 2001* (New York: Penguin Press, 2004), p. 186.

26. Some in the State Department argued for a political resolution promoting a broad-based moderate government that would exclude both the communists and the Islamist extremists of the Peshawar parties, but they were trumped by CIA schemes to carry on the covert war. See Coll, pp. 207–11.

27. Coll, p. 212. Bin Laden may have been acting on behalf of Saudi intelligence or on his own.

28. Rubin, p. 264.

29. Rubin, pp. 271–72; Johnson and Leslie, p. 5.

30. Amin Saikal, "The Rabbani Government, 1992–1996," in *Fundamentalism Reborn? Afghanistan and the Taliban,* ed. William Maley (New York: New York University Press, 1998), p. 33.

31. Rubin, pp. 272–73.

32. Johnson and Leslie, p. 6, citing ICRC News 44, November 6, 1996.

33. Larry P. Goodson, *Afghanistan's Endless War: State Failure, Regional Politics, and the Rise of the Taliban* (Seattle: University of Washington Press, 2001), p. 75.

34. Rashid, *Taliban,* p. 17.

35. Rashid, *Taliban,* p. 22.

36. There are many different accounts of the role of Pakistan in the episode at Spin Baldak. See, for example, Anthony Davis, "How the Taliban Became a Military Force," in Maley, pp. 45–46; Ahmed Rashid, "Pakistan and the Taliban," in Maley, p. 81.

37. Rashid, *Taliban,* pp. 27–28, 32.

38. "Pakistan's proxy army," Goodson, pp. 110, 114. Cooley writes that "the Taliban were, indeed, a Pakistani creation." p. 121. That both the ISI and the government of Benazir Bhutto worked decisively to destroy the Rabbani government and bring the Taliban to power is very widely recognized although still officially denied. See, for example, Saikal in Maley, p. 39; Davis in Maley, pp. 54–55, 69–71; Anwar-ul-Haq Ahady, "Saudi Arabia, Iran and the Conflict in Afghanistan," in Maley, pp. 126–27.

39. Coll, pp. 332–33. Accounts of the fall of Kabul vary in the details, but it seems clear that the decisive factor in the Taliban victory was the military planning and support of Pakistan and bin Laden. See also Rashid, *Taliban,* pp. 41–54.

40. Médecins Sans Frontières (Doctors Without Borders) withdrew from Afghanistan in 2004 after five of its personnel in the field were murdered.

41. There are two main sections of Pashtun tribes: the Abdali—now called Durrani—Pashtuns who chose Ahmed Shah Durrani as shah, and the

rival Ghilzai Pashtuns. Durranis claim descent from the eldest son of Qais, a companion of the Prophet, while Ghilzais trace their ancestry to Qais's second son. See Rashid, *Taliban*, p. 10.

42. In 1973 Daoud called on Pakistan's Pathans (Pashtuns) to secede. Pakistani President Zulfikar Ali Bhutto countered by inviting antisecular Afghan Pashtuns to defect. He organized the five thousand who responded into a guerilla force—mujahidin—to harass Daoud's regime, a full six years before the Soviets invaded Afghanistan. See Weaver, p. 60.

43. Martin Ewans, *Afghanistan: A Short History of Its People and Politics* (New York: HarperCollins, 2002), p. 7.

44. Louis Dupree, *Afghanistan* (Princeton, N.J.: Princeton University Press, 1973), p. xvii.

45. Letter of George Eden, Earl of Auckland, then Governor General of India, and the Simla Manifesto, quoted in Ewans, pp. 61–62.

46. Lord Hartington, quoted in Ewans, p. 97.

47. Jonathan Randal, *Osama: The Making of a Terrorist* (New York: Alfred A. Knopf, 2004), p. 78.

48. For a firsthand account of the retreat through the Salang Pass, see Artyom Borovik, *The Hidden War: A Russian Journalist's Account of the Soviet War in Afghanistan* (New York: Atlantic Monthly Press, 1990).

49. Kaplan, p. 19. Kaplan thought the "straightforward" Afghans easy to befriend because they were free of "the fears and prejudices toward the West" that "burdened" Muslims from countries colonized by Western powers.

50. George Crile, *Charlie Wilson's War: The Extraordinary Story of the Largest Covert Operation in History* (New York: Atlantic Monthly Press, 2003), pp. 470–75. Wilson's persistent problems with drugs, alcohol, and women are documented throughout the book. A member of the House Appropriations Committee, Wilson had secured millions in aid for Nicaraguan dictator Anastasio Somoza before becoming involved in the Afghan cause. Crile, pp. 34–39; Cooley, p. 89; Coll, pp. 91–92. Among the special interest groups who gave Wilson more PAC money than almost anyone else in Congress, "no group was more beholden to him than the defense contractors." Crile, p. 249. Reportedly, he was "always ready to promote the interests of the Texas defense contractors who supported him." Cooley, p. 89.

51. Coll, p. 100.

52. Rashid, *Taliban*, pp. 130, 128.

53. Coll, pp. 92–93, 97–98. Casey organized support for many other terrorist and prototerrorist movements, including Renamo in Mozambique, Unita in Angola, and the contras in Nicaragua, that fought regimes he considered pro-Soviet. See Mamdani, p. 87.

54. Coll, p. 168. Coll reports that although Shevardnadze made the request to Secretary of State George Shultz, "no high-level Reagan adminis-

tration officials ever gave much thought to the issue." For fear of being thought soft on communism, Shultz also kept to himself "for weeks" the Soviet decision to leave Afghanistan.

55. Ewans, pp. 280–81. Cooley writes that the CIA and the US military "would train a huge foreign mercenary army; one of the largest ever seen in American military history. Virtually all would be Muslims." Cooley, p. 14.

56. Cooley, pp. 69–72. Begun in 1980, the secret training was conducted at bases such as Fort Bragg and Harvey Point in North Carolina and Fort A. P. Hill, Camp Pickett, and the CIA's Camp Peary in Virginia; it continued into 1989, by which time the Arab-Afghan fighters were already moving on from Afghanistan to new target countries. The CIA also managed recruitment in the United States, often under the cover of legitimate Islamic charities and mosques or fronts like the Al-Kifah Afghan Refugee Center in Brooklyn, so successful at recruiting and fund-raising that it became known as the al-Jihad center. Among notable CIA collaborators there were Sheikh Omar Abdel Rahman (old Peshawar pal of Gulbuddin Hekmatyar and Osama bin Laden), the blind Egyptian prayer leader who was later convicted in New York of several conspiracies including the 1993 bombing of the World Trade Center, and Sheikh Abdullah Azzam, the Palestinian founder of Hamas, mentor to Osama bin Laden in Jedda and Peshawar, and founder in Peshawar of the Office of Services, his own recruiting and support network that became, after his assassination in 1989, bin Laden's al-Qaeda. See Cooley, pp. 27–30, 214–17; Coll, p. 204; Mamdani, pp. 126–28; on Sheikh Omar Abdel Rahman's Pakistan friendships, see Weaver, pp. 79–80, 201.

57. Kaplan, p. 19.

58. Coll, p. 182.

59. Mamdani, p. 139, citing, among others, the investigations of reporters for the *Los Angeles Times*. Mamdani makes the important point that the CIA's *"privatization* of information about how to produce and spread violence" is proving far more damaging than its distribution of arms and money. Pakistani President Benazir Bhutto complained to *New Yorker* correspondent Mary Ann Weaver: "The U.S. government armed these groups, trained them, gave them organizational skills; huge, huge amounts of money were spent, and both the money and the Islamic zeal spilled over here. Then the Americans retreated to Washington, and look at the mess they left." She intended to break "the stranglehold of the Islamic clerics." Weaver, p. 203. Now Bhutto is in exile, and the Islamic clerics are still in Pakistan.

60. Rashid, *Taliban*, p. 25.

61. The most notorious incident, known as the Ashfar Massacre, took place on February 11, 1993, when the forces of Rabbani's (and Massoud's) Jamiat-i Islami and Abdur Rasul Sayyaf's Ittihad-i Islami undertook a twenty-four-hour spree of rape, murder, arson, and child abduction in the

Shi'a Hazara district of Ashfar in West Kabul. President Rabbani later called the massacre "a mistake." International Crisis Group, *Afghanistan: Women and Reconstruction,* ICG Asia Report No. 48, Kabul/Brussels, March 14, 2003, p. 7. See also Peter Marsden, *The Taliban: War, Religion and the New Order in Afghanistan* (London: Zed Books, 1998), p. 39.

62. Kaplan, pp. 35–36, 49. In the introduction to a later edition, Kaplan says that Afghanistan appealed to him as an escape from the modern world, a place "unadulterated by cheap Western polyesters"; but polyester is precisely what women's tent-like burqas are made of. *Soldiers of God: With Islamic Warriors in Afghanistan and Pakistan* (New York: Vintage, 2001), p. xvi.

63. Scott Carrier, "Over There: Afghanistan After the Fall," *Harper's Magazine,* April 2002, p. 68; Borovik, p. 112.

64. Jason Elliot, *An Unexpected Light: Travels in Afghanistan* (London: Picador, 1999), p. 145.

65. Rubin, pp. 230–31.

66. Alexander Cockburn and Jeffrey St. Clair, *Whiteout: The CIA, Drugs and the Press* (London: Verso, 1998), p. 263; Crile, p. 463. Goodson reports that Pakistan received more than $7.2 billion during the decade of the 1980s, pp. 152–53. Only Israel and Egypt received more foreign aid.

67. Weaver, p. 99.

68. On the secret diverson, Lawrence Lifschultz, "Pakistan Was Iran-Contra's Secret Back Door," *Sunday Times of India,* November 24, 1991, cited in Rubin, p. 198, n. 7. Lifschultz reports the back door closed in November 1986. Bob Woodward reports that at one time money for both covert programs passed through the same Swiss bank account. *Veil: The Secret Wars of the CIA, 1981–1987* (New York: Simon and Schuster, 1987), p. 502.

69. Some say the suggestion to arm the mujahidin with Stingers came to the CIA from Osama bin Laden, on advice from his friends in Saudi intelligence. Peter Dale Scott, *Drugs, Oil, and War: The United States in Afghanistan, Colombia, and Indochina* (Lanham, Md.: Rowman & Littlefield, 2003), p. 32. By the end of the war, at least 500 Stingers had gone missing. Pakistan kept some. Gulbuddin's men reportedly made $1 million from selling about 16 to Iran's Revolutionary Guards. Others showed up in militant hands in the Persian Gulf and the Philippines and brought down planes in Tajikistan and Georgia. Within a few years the Russians were manufacturing passable copies. See Cooley, pp. 144–46; Weaver, pp. 77, 97–98.

70. Rubin, pp. 181–82.

71. Rubin, on "sidelining extremists," p. 251; on US and Saudi aid and Iraqi weapons, pp. 182–83; on the Red Crescent, p. 197; on the tally of assistance, p. 179.

72. Coll, p. 228. Coll does not name the official he interviewed.

73. McCoy, p. 478. Weaver reports that forty-two mujahidin commanders

led by Abdul Haq refused to try to seize Jalalabad. Haq opposed the "ISI's increasing determination to hijack the jihad." Weaver, p. 83.

74. Coll, pp. 264–65.

75. Ahmed Rashid writes, "it became apparent to me that the strategy over pipelines had become the driving force behind Washington's interest in the Taliban." Rashid, *Taliban,* p. 163. See also Mamdani, pp. 159–61.

76. Johnson and Leslie, p. 89. Khalilzad expressed this view in a 1996 editorial for the *Washington Post.* A political scientist, he is a disciple (like Paul Wolfowitz and Richard Perle) of University of Chicago professor Albert Wohlstetter, the Cold War theorist who famously became the model for Dr. Strangelove. Jon Lee Anderson reports that Khalilzad is regarded in certain quarters "as a Strangelovian figure" himself, "a dark eminence of American imperial power," a reputation he gained partly through involvement with the Taliban, Unocal, and the Defense Planning Guidance of 1992, the document that defined hard-line neoconservative doctrine, including preemptive war. See "American Viceroy: Zalmay Khalilzad's Mission," *The New Yorker,* December 19, 2005, pp. 54–65.

77. In April 2005, officials announced that construction of a gas pipeline was scheduled to start by the end of the year. On the same day, perhaps by coincidence, President Karzai and Secretary of Defense Rumsfeld met in Kabul to discuss the possibility of establishing permanent American military bases on Afghan soil. Al-Qaeda also chose that day to announce its vow to continue the jihad against US-led forces in Afghanistan. "Gas Pipeline Likely to Start by End of 2005," "Afghanistan Seeks Long-Term Security Relationship with US," "Al Qaeda Vows Jihad against US-led Forces," *Daily Outlook Afghanistan,* April 14, 2005 (25 Hamal 1384), p. 1. By summer 2005, American oil interests were fighting off an unfriendly Chinese government bid to take over Unocal. At House Armed Services Committee hearings, James Woolsey, President Clinton's director of the CIA, urged Congress to block the sale because keeping Unocal in American hands is "a national security issue." China withdrew its high bid and Chevron snapped up Unocal. Steve Lohr, "Unocal Bid Denounced at Hearing," *New York Times,* July 14, 2005, p. C1.

78. Coll, on bin Laden's manifesto, p. 380; on the embassy bombings, pp. 403–4; on the Taliban capture of Mazar-i Sharif, p. 429.

79. Coll, p. 429.

80. Journalist Christina Lamb quotes a widely shared Afghan opinion: "The Pakistanis are the real terrorists. . . . They were worse than the Russians because the Russians came here as men, as enemies, whereas the Pakistanis pretended to be our friends but sent all their fundamentalists here. They have the training camps, the finances, why isn't the West bombing them instead of us?" *The Sewing Circles of Herat: A Personal Voyage through Afghanistan* (New York: HarperCollins, 2002), p. 304.

81. Rashid, *Taliban*, pp. 120–21. Early in the covert war in Afghanistan, Washington decided as a matter of policy to "sacrifice the drug war to fight the cold war." McCoy, p. 480. For the full story of the CIA and the international drug trade, see McCoy.

82. Coll, on Musharraf's advice, p. 481. General Musharraf seized power in a military coup in October 1999. On the missile attacks, pp. 409–12; on Saudi financing, p. 512; on the games of Pakistan's ISI, p. 506. Cooley quotes an unnamed former US official: "The ISI never intended to go after bin Laden. We got completely snookered." Cooley, p. 206.

83. Richard A. Clarke, *Against All Enemies: Inside America's War on Terror* (New York: Free Press, 2004), p. 209.

84. Coll, p. 518; Clarke, pp. 209–10.

85. Coll, on pressure on Massoud to get bin Laden, p. 458, p. 489; on Massoud's view of American policy, pp. 468–69; on al-Qaeda, p. 471; on the 9/11 plot, p. 485.

86. Coll, on Abdul Ahad Karzai, pp. 459–60; on Massoud's place in history, p. 569.

87. Coll, on Rice, p. 539; on Bush administration imperviousness to warnings, pp. 541–43; on adoption of national security plan, pp. 560–61. On the national security plan, see also Woodward, *Bush at War,* pp. 34–36; for details see Clarke, pp. 227–47.

88. Rubin, p. 5. After the Vietnam war, the US waged covert proxy wars in Angola, Mozambique, Congo, Nicaragua, and Afghanistan, to name the principal battlegrounds, and conducted covert support operations in Cambodia and Ethiopia before openly invading Iraq once and adopting a policy of preemptive war (the Bush Doctrine) to invade Iraq a second time. For a full discussion on the politics of proxy wars, muffled in military parlance as "low intensity conflicts," see Mamdani.

89. On bin Laden as protégé, Chalmers Johnson, *Blowback: The Costs and Consequences of American Empire* (New York: Metropolitan Books, 2000), p. 10.

90. French sociologist Olivier Roy describes Afghan society as a "constant disequilibrium," a phrase that describes buzkashi as well. *Islam and Resistance in Afghanistan,* 2nd ed. (Cambridge, UK: Cambridge University Press, 1990), p. 23. Roy asserts that "there has never been such a thing as an Afghan nation" although "there is certainly an Afghan state whose history can be traced," p. 12.

91. G. Whitney Azoy, *Buzkashi: Game and Power in Afghanistan,* 2nd ed. (Prospect Heights, Ill.: Waveland Press, 2003), p. x.

92. The joke suggests the deeper issues of identity essential to Afghan politics. The mustachioed Khalqis were Pashtuns, mostly of working class or rural origins. The shorn Parchamis were non-Pashtun Dari-speakers, generally from urban elites. President Najibullah is often described as a "typical Parchami."

93. Vice President Hafizullah Amin wrote of Taraki: "Our great leader hit upon the truth that due to the fact that in developing nations the working class has not yet developed as a political force, there is another force which can overturn the feudal and oppressive government, and in Afghanistan that force was the army. He also gave a firm order that working-class ideology should be spread through the army. . . ." *Kabul Times,* April 19, 1979, quoted in Roy, p. 85.

94. Lamb, p. 130.

95. Pul-i Charkhi prison was built by Daoud, who first used it to house political enemies. As to massacres, an estimated 1,170 unarmed citizens in a village in Kunar Province were killed in one day. See Rubin, p. 115. Roy reports village massacres at Samangan, Farah, and Darrah-yi Souf as well. Roy, p. 97. The execution one night of seventy male members of the moderate Mujaddidi family has been widely reported.

96. Karl E. Meyer, *The Dust of Empire: The Race for Mastery in the Asian Heartland* (New York: Public Affairs Books, 2003), p. 127.

97. On the number of dead and missing, see Rubin, p. 115; Roy, p. 95; Kaplan, p. 115.

98. Ewans, p. 202. According to Coll, the Soviet KGB originally attempted to discredit Amin by planting false rumors that he was a CIA agent, but in a classic case of blowback, they later came to believe their own disinformation and acted upon it. Coll, p. 47.

99. Brzezinski first revealed his scheme in 1998 in an interview with *Le Nouvel Observateur,* January 15 and 21, 1998, and it is now routinely reported as fact. See for example, Mark Danner, "Taking Stock of the Forever War," *New York Times Magazine,* September 11, 2005, p. 49. See also Cooley, pp. 10–11; Mamdani, pp. 123–24; The text of the most significant part of the interview is reprinted in Scott, p. 35, n. 17. See note 101 below.

100. Azoy, p. 118.

101. For Brzezinski's scheme, see note 99 above. Coll, however, reports that Brzezinski's memos at the time of the Soviet invasion show no sign of satisfaction that the Soviets had taken some sort of bait. Coll, p. 581, n. 17. There is no question about the action he advised President Carter to take at the time, although he may later have exaggerated both his prescience and his importance.

102. Woodward, *Veil,* p. 79.

103. This spin about "regime change" is false. The goal at the outset, insofar as the administration had one, was merely to force the Taliban to hand over bin Laden and other al-Qaeda "thugs." See Woodward, *Bush at War,* pp. 124, 63.

104. On the number of personnel, Woodward, *Bush at War,* p. 314. On their withdrawal, Barton Gellman and Dafna Linzer, "Afghanistan, Iraq: Two Wars Collide," *Washington Post,* October 22, 2004.

II. IN THE PRISONS

1. "Afghan Recovery Report," No. 44, Institute for War and Peace Reporting, January 17, 2003.

2. "Afghanistan: Country Gender Report, August 2004," a draft report of the World Bank, Kabul, 2004, p. 64.

3. Quran 2:282. Some scholars note other passages that equate the testimony of both genders, such as Quran 24:6–9. But patriarchal cultures commonly derive the "rule" of Islam from selective reading.

4. Article 22 (2) Constitution of the Islamic Republic of Afghanistan, January 4, 2004.

5. Reference withheld to protect the privacy of the author of the report.

6. On Sayyaf's "enormous influence" on the court, see Chris Johnson and Jolyon Leslie, *Afghanistan: The Mirage of Peace* (London and New York: Zed Books, 2004), p. 163.

7. Interview, spokesman for the Afghan Independent Human Rights Commission, who requested that his name be withheld. March 30, 2005.

8. Johnson and Leslie, pp. 164–65.

9. Mohammad Hashim Kamali, "Islam, Pernicious Custom, and Women's Rights in Afghanistan," proceedings of the National Conference on Women's Rights, Law and Justice in Afghanistan, May 26–27, 2003, Kabul: International Human Rights Law Group, 2003, pp. 46–47.

10. Kamali, p. 53.

11. Article 3, Constitution of the Islamic Republic of Afghanistan, January 4, 2004.

12. "The Role of the Judiciary in Safeguarding Women's Rights: [proceedings of] A Conference of the Supreme Court of the Islamic Republic of Afghanistan, February 22–24, 2005," Kabul: medica mondiale, May 2005, p. 26.

13. "The Customary Laws of Afghanistan," Kabul: International Legal Foundation, September 2004, pp. 10, 13–14.

14. Penal Code of the Islamic Republic of Afghanistan, Articles 428 and 429.

15. "Bad Painful Sedative: Final Report," Kabul: Women and Children Legal Research Foundation, 2004, p. 8.

16. "Bad Painful Sedative: Final Report," p. 18.

17. "The Role of the Judiciary in Safeguarding Women's Rights," p. 26.

18. Amy Waldman, "The 15 Women Awaiting Justice in Kabul Prison," *New York Times,* March 16, 2003, sec. 4, p. 1.

19. Reference withheld to protect the privacy of the author of the report.

20. Reference withheld to protect the privacy of the author of the report.

21. Quran 33:59 and 33:53. Sura 33:59, the verse commonly said to "prescribe veiling," is open to wildly different translations and interpretations. It is

often translated to suggest that the Prophet's wives and daughters and "believing women" should "cast their outer garments [i.e., burqas] over their bodies so that they should be known and not molested." But how is a woman in a burqa to be "known"? Another translation seems to offer more common sense, saying that the Prophet's wives and daughters and the "wives of the faithful" should "let their veils fall low. Thus will they more easily be known, and they will not be affronted." But does letting the veil "fall low" imply exposing the face or lowering the hemline? Is a woman to be "known" individually or generically, as a follower of the Prophet? The possibilities for dispute are endless.

22. Louis Dupree, *Afghanistan* (Princeton, N.J.: Princeton University Press, 1973), p. 531; George Macmunn, *Afghanistan: From Darius to Amanullah* (London: G. Bell, 1929), p. 296.

23. Jan Goodwin reports such cases in interviews with Islamic women in *Price of Honor: Muslim Women Lift the Veil of Silence on the Islamic World* (Boston: Little, Brown, 1994).

24. Asne Seierstad portrays a typical case of "consent" in *The Bookseller of Kabul,* trans. Ingrid Christophersen (Boston: Little, Brown, 2003), pp. 3–8 et passim. She writes "To say nothing means to give one's consent." And although all family members opposed the bookseller's plan to take a second wife, "no one dared speak out against him—he always got his own way." p. 7.

25. Donald N. Wilber, et al., *Afghanistan: Its People, Its Society, Its Culture* (New Haven, Conn.: HRAF Press, 1962), p. 136.

26. Ludwig W. Adamec, *Afghanistan's Foreign Affairs to the Mid-Twentieth Century: Relations with the USSR, Germany, and Britain* (Tucson, Ariz.: University of Arizona Press, 1974), p. 44.

27. Louis Dupree, pp. 438–39. The man generally credited with initiating modernizing and liberalizing tendencies in twentieth-century Afghanistan is the nationalist intellectual Mahmud Beg Tarzi. He advised Amir Habibullah, tutored the amir's sons Inyatullah and Amanullah (his successor), and married them to his own daughters. See also Ewans, pp. 111–12; Louis Dupree, pp. 453–57.

28. Leila Ahmed, *Women and Gender in Islam: Historical Roots of a Modern Debate* (New Haven, Conn.: Yale University Press, 1992), p. 129.

29. Adamec, p. 90.

30. Adamec, pp. 132–34.

31. Adamec, p. 137.

32. Adamec, p. 140.

33. Adamec, p. 183.

34. Dupree, pp. 530–33.

35. Wilber et al., p. 80.

36. Interview, Dr. Laila Arash, Kabul, May 2, 2005.

37. Personal communication, March 13, 2005.

38. Both Afghanistan and the United States signed CEDAW in 1980; Afghanistan ratified the convention in 2003, but the US has so far failed to do so.

39. Presidential candidate Wakil Mangal told interviewers: "Woman can obtain all her rights when she is educated, but without financial self-sufficiency she can't get out of man's control." "On the Issue of Afghan Women: Interviews with Presidential Candidates," Kabul: medica mondiale, October 2004, p. 18.

40. Interview, Kabul, April 26, 2004.

41. Interview, Kabul, April 7, 2004.

42. Marjo Stroud, unpublished research, February–March 2004.

43. Bernard-Henri Levy, "A Tale of Love and Death in Afghanistan," *New York Times,* April 17, 2004.

44. Shawna Wakefield, "Gender and Local Level Decision Making: Findings from a Case Study in Samangan," Kabul: Afghanistan Research and Evaluation Unit, March 2005, p. 3.

45. In 2003, celebrity American feminists including Jane Fonda, Oprah Winfrey, and Eve Ensler brought a RAWA member to Madison Square Garden to shed her burqa in a spotlighted display of women's solidarity. Zoya, with John Follain and Rita Cristofari, *Zoya's Story: An Afghan Woman's Struggle for Freedom* (New York: William Morrow, 2002), pp. 210–12. For a sympathetic account of RAWA, see Cheryl Benard, *Veiled Courage: Inside the Afghan Women's Resistance* (New York: Broadway Books, 2002).

46. Johnson and Leslie, p. 171.

47. Louis Dupree, p. 411.

48. *Qanoon, or The Law,* story by Nasir Yosuf Zai, dialogue by Saba Sahar, Kabul, 2005. All quotations are from the original screenplay in an English translation prepared by the filmmakers.

49. "Afghan justice ministry promises to build new prison for women with many facilities," Pajhwok Afghan News Service, March 6, 2005.

III. IN THE SCHOOLS

1. Nancy Hatch Dupree, "Education Patterns in the Context of an Emergency," *Refuge* 17, no. 4 (October 1998), pp. 18–19.

2. United Nations Development Programme, "Security with a Human Face: Challenges and Responsibilities," Afghanistan Summary National Human Development Report, 2004 (Islamabad: Army Press, 2004), p. 6.

3. Nancy Hatch Dupree, "Education Patterns," p. 18.

4. Nancy Hatch Dupree, "Education Patterns," p. 18; Donald N. Wilber et al., *Afghanistan* (New Haven, Conn.: HRAF Press, 1962), p. 84.

5. Wilber et al., pp. 84–85; Nancy Hatch Dupree, "Education Patterns," p. 19.

6. The US Engineering Team (U.S.E.T.) included Carnegie Institute of Technology, University of Cincinnati, Georgia Institute of Technology, Illinois Institute of Technology, Lehigh University, University of Notre Dame, Rice University, North Carolina State University, and Purdue University. See Louis Dupree, *Afghanistan* (Princeton, N.J.: Princeton University Press, 1973), p. 598.

7. Louis Dupree, pp. 516, 598–99.

8. Muhsen Nazari, "Afghanistan Ponders Privatization of Electricity," *Kabul Weekly*, May 11–17, 2005, p. 1.

9. Chris Johnson and Jolyon Leslie, *Afghanistan: The Mirage of Peace* (London: Zed Books, 2004), p. 11, citing *The Guardian*, August 8, 2002.

10. George Packer, "A Democratic World," *The New Yorker*, February 16 and 23, 2004, p. 100.

11. Packer, p. 100.

12. Reagan's description is cited in Mahmood Mamdani, *Good Muslim, Bad Muslim: America, the Cold War, and the Roots of Terror* (New York: Doubleday, 2004), p. 143.

13. Joseph E. Stiglitz, *Globalization and Its Discontents* (New York: Norton, 2003), p. 78.

14. John Brohman, *Popular Development: Rethinking the Theory and Practice of Development* (Oxford: Blackwell, 1996), p. 203.

15. Stiglitz, p. 78.

16. Brohman, p. 224.

17. For neoliberals, the pain of the poor is offset by the profits of the powerful in both the donor and the recipient country. One reason the poor get poorer in a rich donor nation like the US is that their jobs have been "outsourced" to countries where the poor settle for lower wages. Thus, through globalization, the poor in rich countries subsidize the rich in poor countries, so that the rich get richer and the poor get poorer *everywhere*. See James Goldsmith, "The Winners and the Losers," *The Case Against the Global Economy: And For A Turn Toward the Local*, ed. Jerry Mander and Edward Goldsmith (San Francisco: Sierra Club Books, 1996), p. 176.

18. Ian Traynor, "The Privatization of War, $30 Billion Goes to Private Military; Fears over 'Hired Guns' Policy," *The Guardian*, December 10, 2003, quoted in Mamdani, p. 259.

19. Johnson and Leslie, p. 101.

20. Sarah Lister and Adam Pain, "Trading in Power: The Politics of 'Free' Markets in Afghanistan," Kabul: Afghanistan Research and Evaluation Unit, June 2004, p. 8.

21. Mirwais Harooni, "Questions Surface on Roads Going Nowhere: Millions Wasted on Second-Rate Highways," *Kabul Weekly*, March 30, 2005, pp. 1, 4; David Rohde and Carlotta Gall, "Delays Hurting U.S. Rebuilding in Afghanistan," *New York Times*, November 7, 2005, p. 1.

Louis Berger received the largest USAID Afghanistan contract awarded in 2002 and 2003, worth $665 million. In part, it called for construction of 96 clinics and schools by September 2004; but more than a year later, only 11 buildings had been completed.

22. On KPMG, "Criminal Case Is Broadened Over Tax Shelters at KPMG," *New York Times,* October 18, 2005, pp. C1, C9.

23. Rohde and Gall report that the Bearing Point contract "eventually grew to be worth $98 million." "Windfalls of War," A Report of the Center for Public Integrity, October 30, 2003, lists the original contract amount as $64 million. See www.publicintegrity.org. Some off-the-record sources say the contract grew to $165 million.

24. Experienced aid workers Chris Johnson and Jolyon Leslie write: "What is notable in Afghanistan is how far both the multilateral agencies, and even many of the supposedly independent NGOs, have been pulled into the free market project." Johnson and Leslie, p. 101.

25. Off-the-record interview, Kabul, April 18, 2005. In official documents and my own interview notes I have three different sets of numbers for the TEP program. Targets commonly shift downward as donor demands come up against hard facts.

26. For lists of contractors, contracts, and their campaign contributions see "Windfalls of War."

27. US bilateral aid to Pakistan jumped from an average $40 million for the years 1998–2000 to $770 million in 2002. USAID Greenbook, cited in Romilly Greenhill and Patrick Watt, "Real Aid: An Agenda for Making Aid Work," Johannesburg, S.A.: Action Aid International, June 2005, p. 19.

28. Rohde and Gall.

29. On the history and contracts of Creative Associates International, Inc., see "Windfalls of War."

30. "Windfalls of War"; Interview, Ministry of Education official who requested that his name be withheld, Kabul, May 17, 2005. On its Web site, Creative Associates International claims: "The books were flown to Afghanistan and distributed before the start of the new school year."

31. "Windfalls of War," University of Nebraska at Omaha; Steve Coll, *Ghost Wars: The Secret History of the CIA, Afghanistan, and bin Laden, from the Soviet Invasion to September 10, 2001* (New York: Penguin Press, 2004), p. 364.

32. Scott Bauer, "Peace Group: UNO Textbooks Distributed in Afghanistan Contributed to Terrorism," AP, April 16, 2005.

33. Christian Parenti, "Afghan Poppies Bloom," *The Nation,* January 24, 2005, p. 22; see also Amy Waldman, "Afghan Route to Prosperity: Grow Poppies," *New York Times,* April 10, 2004; Carlotta Gall, "Afghan Poppy Growing Reaches Record Level, U.N. Says," *New York Times,* November 19, 2004.

34. Parenti reports women's wages up to seven dollars a day. p. 24.

35. Gall, "Afghan Poppy Growing Reaches Record Level, U.N. Says."

36. Alfred W. McCoy, *The Politics of Heroin: CIA Complicity in the Global Drug Trade, Afghanistan, Southeast Asia, Central America, Colombia,* rev. ed. (Chicago: Chicago Review Press, 2003), p. 470 et passim. For a cogent discussion in the context of current American campaigns, see Mamdani.

37. Carlotta Gall, "Afghan Poppy Farmers Say Mystery Spraying Killed Crops," *New York Times,* December 5, 2004.

38. Gall, "Afghan Poppy Farmers Say Mystery Spraying Killed Crops."

39. Waldman, "Afghan Route to Prosperity: Grow Poppies."

40. Quoted in Parenti, "Afghan Poppies Bloom," p. 25.

41. Eric Schmitt, "Drug Eradication: Afghans' Gains Face Big Threat in Drug Traffic," *New York Times,* December 11, 2004.

42. Mirwais Harooni, "Behind the Chinese Lantern, Guesthouses or Brothels?" *Kabul Weekly,* February 9, 2005, pp. 1, 4.

43. Greenhill and Watt, p. 31.

44. Anita Anastacio and Dawn Stallard, "Report Card: Progress on Compulsory Education, Grades 1–9." Kabul: Human Rights Research and Advocacy Consortium, March 2004, p. 7.

45. "Current Realities and Future Prospects for Afghanistan's Public Education System," draft report of an unidentified organization, Kabul, October 31, 2004, p. 12. The figures cited are for the Ministry of Education only. For the entire Education Sector, the projected expenditure was $432.45 million, of which only 32 percent was available.

46. Anastacio and Stallard, p. 6.

47. Anastacio and Stallard, pp. 1–2.

48. Amy Waldman, "In Afghanistan, U.S. Envoy Sits in Seat of Power," *New York Times,* April 17, 2004; "US Ambassador Afghan's Chief Executive?" *The Nation* (Pakistan), April 18, 2004; Thom Shankar, "Prison Abuse: US Army Inquiry Implicates 28 Soldiers in Deaths of 2 Afghan Detainees," *New York Times,* October 15, 2004; Tim Golden, "In U.S. Report, Brutal Details of 2 Afghan Inmates' Deaths," *New York Times,* May 20, 2005; Reuters, "Karzai Demands Custody of All Afghan Prisoners," *New York Times,* May 22, 2005; "Karzai Fails to Gain Control of Afghan Prisoners Held by U.S. Authorities," *Kabul Weekly,* May 25, 2005, p. 1.

49. Ramtanu Maitra, "The Party's Over for Afghan NGOs," *Asia Times,* April 21, 2005. Bashardost's complaints were popular with Kabulis who gave him the third highest number of votes in the 2005 parliamentary election.

50. Salem Mandokhil, "Number of Dead Still Unknown in Ghazni," *Kabul Weekly,* April 6, 2005, p. 1.

51. "Karzai Asks for More Control as Government Questions NGO's Accountability," *Kabul Weekly,* April 6, 2005, p. 1.

52. "Italian Aid Worker Abducted in Kabul," *Kabul Weekly,* May 18–25, p. 1.

53. Carlotta Gall, "Ambush Kills 5 Aid Workers; Taliban Claims Responsibility," *New York Times,* June 2, 2004.

54. Paul O'Brien, "PRTs—Guaranteeing or Undermining a Secure Future in Afghanistan?" *FMR,* September 2003, p. 38.

55. O'Brien, p. 38.

56. Not until December 2005 was it announced that NATO would expand the NATO-led International Security Assistance Force (ISAF), which operates in Afghanistan under a UN peacekeeping mandate. By June or July 2006, 6,000 additional NATO troops were scheduled to join 10,000 troops already operating in Kabul and certain regions of northern and western Afghanistan. The plan called for the US to reduce its troop strength by a comparable number and turn over most operations in the south to NATO, coincidentally at a time when Taliban forces in that region are reaching their greatest strength since the ouster of the Taliban government. See Carlotta Gall, "As NATO Forces Ease Role of G.I.'s in Afghanistan, the Taliban Steps Up Attacks," *New York Times,* December 11, 2005.

57. Mike Dougherty, "American Killed in Bombing Was Due Home Soon," *New York Times,* October 25, 2004.

58. Carlotta Gall, "3 Election Workers Are Abducted in Afghanistan," *New York Times,* October 28, 2004; Reuters, "Kidnappers Free Three UN Workers in Afghanistan," *New York Times,* November 23, 2004.

59. Reuters, "British Man Shot Dead in Afghan Capital," March 8, 2005.

60. "American Escapes Kidnap Attempt in the Capital," *Kabul Times,* April 12, 2005, p. 1.

61. Nadene Ghouri, "Clementina Cantoni: A Force for Good," *Kabul Weekly,* May 25, 2005, p. 2.

62. Carlotta Gall, "Laura Bush Carries Pet Causes to Afghans," *New York Times,* March 31, 2005.

63. Gall, "Laura Bush Carries Pet Causes to Afghans." The American International School, grades 1–11, opened in November 2005 with 160 pupils. Annual tuition: $5,000. Scholarships are said to be available to Afghan children with "strong existing English skills."

64. Michael Bhatia, Kevin Lanigan, and Philip Wilkinson, "Minimal Investments, Minimal Results: The Failure of Security Policy in Afghanistan," Kabul: Afghanistan Research and Evaluation Unit, June 2004.

65. See especially "A Call for Justice: A National Consultation on Past Human Rights Violations in Afghanistan," Kabul: Afghanistan Independent Human Rights Commission, n.d.

66. The "manhunt" later became controversial in itself. During the 2004 presidential campaign, Senator John Kerry argued that the US should be conducting a war against al-Qaeda and the Taliban. The Bush administration claimed to be doing so when in fact it began to divert forces from the Afghanistan "war" within a few months of attacking that country in preparation for attacking Iraq. General Tommy Franks reported as much to Senator Bob Graham in February 2002. See Bob Graham, "Bush at War: Eye on the Ball?" *New York Times,* October 24, 2004.

67. Bhatia et al., p. 1.

68. Quoted in Bhatia et al., p. 1.

69. Interview, Zolaykha Sherzad, Kabul, March 12, 2005. On the School of Hope, see www.sohope.org; Julie Salamon, "From a Crisis, Children Reach Across the World," *New York Times,* November 15, 2004.

ACKNOWLEDGMENTS

I didn't go to Afghanistan to write a book. Helping to deliver humanitarian aid was my intention and my occupation all along. But on visits home, I found people full of questions—like "Are things getting better?"—to which the answers were invariably too complicated for conversation. The British literary agent Mary Clemmey, an old friend, first encouraged me to respond to some of those questions in print; and during my third long winter in Kabul I began to make the record that appears here.

I'm grateful to many Afghans and internationals who enriched my life in Kabul and gave me the benefit of their greater experience. For reasons of privacy, I won't name them here; nor do I identify them in these pages where most organizations and people, except public figures, appear with fictitious names and identifying characteristics. Colleagues in New York also encouraged and supported my humanitarian work and shared information; thanks to Lynne Hayden-Findlay, Leslie Painter, and Bonnie Tsai; Manizha Naderi and Masuda Sultan of Women for Afghan Women; and Zama Coursen-Neff of Human Rights Watch.

I owe a lot—I think we all do—to the historians, authors, and journalists (cited in the endnotes) who are still unearthing details of official and secret US meddling in Afghanistan. Their work helped me make sense of what I witnessed there. So did the suggestions of three colleagues in Kabul who read early drafts of portions of the manuscript. But my conclusions are my own, and so is the responsibility for any errors in fact or interpretation.

The whole team at Metropolitan Books has earned my thanks many times over—especially Lindsay Ross, Raquel Jaramillo, Kelly Too, and my brilliant editor, Riva Hocherman. Thanks also to Betsy Reed, my editor at *The Nation,* where a small portion of the second section of this book appeared in different form. I owe a special debt to my old friend Irene Young, the photographer beloved by musicians and actors on both coasts, who did me the favor of smartening my images for the printed page. And to my agent, Ellen Geiger, of the Frances Goldin Literary Agency. And to the magnificent Eleanor Torrey West, who for many years so generously shared her wild Ossabaw Island, on the Georgia coast, with artists and writers, and gave this writer long ago a chance to enter an utterly foreign place and embrace it.

My work in Afghanistan (and this book) wouldn't have been possible without my support team at home who helped in various ways to make possible my long absences and forgave them: the late Meri Straz, Paula Fackelman Pierce and Ken Pierce, Barbara Boris, Andrea Lurie, Nancy Rosen, Alison Baker, Catherine Ruocco, and Murray Dauber. And my cronies, fine writers all, who made a lifeline of e-mail to see me through—Valerie Martin, Patricia Lewis, Charles Wachtel, and Joan Silber.

Finally, of course, my greatest debt is to Afghans who befriended me and trusted me with their concerns. To them I say *Manda nabashen. Zenda bashen.* May you not be tired. May you live long.

INDEX

Iraq: Gulf War of 1992, 54; 2003
    invasion and occupation of,
    83, 86, 87–90, 237, 241, 264
ISAF (International Security
    Assistance Force), 197, 230,
    273, 274
Islamic Jihad Council, 25
Islamists of Afghanistan, 79;
    moderate, 20–21, 56, 78;
    radical, *see* radical Islamists
Ismail Khan, 60, 84, 214; Herati
    shelter girls and, 163, 164,
    165
Italy, 116, 119

Jabal ul-Saraj, Afghanistan, 64
Jalal, Massouda, 114
Jalalabad, Afghanistan, 55, 84,
    100
Jamaat-i Islami, 56
Jamiat-i Islami, 21, 22, 24, 25
jihad, 19, 115
journalists, foreign, 48, 49,
    124–25; Kabul of 2003
    described by, 13; reputation
    of Afghan fighters and,
    46–47
Jouvenal, Peter, 45
Joya, Malalai, 189
Junbish-i Milli-yi Islami, 24, 25

Kabul: The Bradt Mini Guide, 12
Kabul Hotel, 31
Kabul River, 7–8, 9, 282
Kabul University, 20, 56, 78,
    150, 213–14, 221, 279;
    English department, 216–17

Kabul Weekly, 243, 276
Kabul-Kandahar Highway, 239
Kamali, Dr. Mohammad
    Hashim, 116–17
Kandahar, Afghanistan, 9, 26,
    28, 31, 42, 84
Kanishka, King, 10
Karmal, Babrak, 80
Karte Se Surgical Hospital,
    170–71
Karzai, Abdul Ahad, 60
Karzai, Hamid, 39, 57–58, 60,
    71, 155, 168, 214, 271;
    accusation against NGOs,
    272–73; Afghan drug trade
    and, 261; Bush Two admin-
    istration and, 42, 271–72;
    cabinet of, 85, 86, 115;
    pardoning of women prison-
    ers, 137, 139; private mili-
    tias of warlords and, 85;
    women's rights and, 126,
    154, 157
Kenya, bombing of US embassy
    in, 58
Khair Khana hospital, 171
Khalilzad, Zalmay, 57, 86, 265,
    271
Khalq (The People), 78, 79–80
KPMG, 244
Kushan empire, 9–10, 11

Law, The (Quanoon), 190–93
legal system, 107–24; body of
    laws, 111, 113, 118,
    120–21; the courts, 119,
    137; defense attorneys, 107–